D1615372

The
Durable Desperadoes

WILLIAM VIVIAN BUTLER

The
Durable Desperadoes

Preface by
ANTHONY LEJEUNE

MACMILLAN

B. 1

SBN 333 14217 9

First published 1973 by
MACMILLAN LONDON LIMITED
London and Basingstoke
Associated companies in New York Dublin
Melbourne Johannesburg and Madras

Printed in Great Britain by
NORTHUMBERLAND PRESS LIMITED
Gateshead

To
Mary
with all my love
Bill

SPECIAL NOTE

John Creasey's sad death took place while this book was in production. This gives me an additional opportunity to express my gratitude for all his help, and to emphasise that both the book and its preface were shown to him, and met with his warm approval.

Nothing that I have written about the Toff and the Baron is invalidated by their creator's death—not even the statement that, while so many similar heroes have fallen by the wayside, they still 'stroll nonchalantly on'. John Creasey has left so much posthumous material that new novels in both the Toff and the Baron series will continue to appear until at least 1975, and possibly 1977.

June 1973

W.V.B.

Contents

Acknowledgements and thanks

ACKNOWLEDGEMENTS and my warmest thanks are due to the following authors, publishers and copyright holders:

To Walker & Co., New York and Hodder & Stoughton Ltd for permission to quote from 'The Flash of Light' and 'The Red Silk Scarf', two stories from *The Confessions of Arsène Lupin* by Maurice Leblanc, translated by Joachim Neograschal.

To Syndication International Ltd for permission to quote from *Union Jack* and other old Amalgamated Press papers.

To Miss D. E. Collins and Cassell & Co. Ltd for permission to quote from 'The Flying Stars', a story from *The Innocence of Father Brown* by G. K. Chesterton.

To Miss Penelope Wallace for permission to quote from *The Four Just Men* and *The Brigand* by Edgar Wallace.

To the Estate of H. C. McNeile and Hodder & Stoughton Ltd for permission to quote from *Bulldog Drummond* and *The Black Gang* by Sapper (H. C. McNeile).

To Hamish Hamilton Ltd for permission to quote from *Edgar Wallace* by Margaret Lane.

To William Heinemann Ltd for permission to quote from *Angel Pavement* by J. B. Priestley.

To the Hutchinson Publishing Group Ltd for permission to quote from *Blackshirt, The Return of Black-*

shirt, Son of Blackshirt and *Lord Blackshirt*, all by Bruce Graeme.

To the Howard Baker Press Ltd and Syndication International Ltd for permission to quote from *The Barring Out at St Franks* by Edwy Searles Brooks.

To Miss Penelope Wallace and the Hutchinson Publishing Group Ltd for permission to quote from *The Mixer* by Edgar Wallace (John Long Ltd).

To Miss Denise Robins for permission to quote from *Triumph of the Rat* by Denise Robins, a novel based on the Ivor Novello silent film of the same name, subtitled by Roland Pertwee. (Acknowledgements to Mr Michael Pertwee.)

To the Hutchinson Publishing Group Ltd for permission to quote from *The Saint and Leslie Charteris* by W. O. G. Lofts and D. J. Adley (Hutchinson Library Services Ltd).

To Leslie Charteris and Ward, Lock Ltd for permission to quote from *X Esquire, The White Rider, Meet the Tiger* and *The Bandit*, all by Leslie Charteris.

To Leslie Charteris and Hodder & Stoughton Ltd for permission to quote from *The Holy Terror* (*The Saint vs. Scotland Yard*), *Getaway* (*The Saint's Getaway*), *The Misfortunes of Mr Teal* (*The Saint in London*), *The First Saint Omnibus, The Saint in Miami, The Saint Steps In, The Saint on Guard, The Second Saint Omnibus, Saint Errant, The Saint on TV* and *The Saint in Pursuit*, all by Leslie Charteris.

To the Hutchinson Publishing Group Ltd for permission to quote from *Seven Times Seven, The Death Miser, Introducing the Toff, Meet the Baron, Here Comes the Toff, The Baron Comes Back, The Toff Goes to Market* and *The Toff on Ice*, all by John Creasey.

To Lionel Brooks and the S. Walker Literary Agency for permission to quote from *Mr Mortimer Gets the Jitters, Miss Dynamite, Six Feet of Dynamite, The*

Conquest Touch and *Conquest in Command*, all by Berkeley Gray (Edwy Searles Brooks).

To Mrs Elizabeth Martyn for permission to quote from *Trent of the Lone Hand* by Wyndham Martyn.

To Associated Book Publishers Ltd for permission to quote from *The Ten Black Pearls* by Cecil Freeman Gregg (Methuen & Co. Ltd).

To the Hutchinson Publishing Group Ltd for permission to quote from *Concerning Blackshirt* and *The Amazing Mr Blackshirt* by Roderic Graeme, and *Enter the Picaroon* by John Cassells (John Long Ltd).

To Jonathan Cape Ltd for permission to quote from *Casino Royale* by Ian Fleming.

To Collins Ltd for permission to quote from *Curtains for Conquest?* by Berkeley Gray (Edwy Searles Brooks).

To Hodder & Stoughton Ltd for permission to quote from *The Baron Goes A-Buying, Vote for the Toff, The Baron and the Missing Old Masters* and *Stars for the Toff*, all by John Creasey.

Three books have been particularly important information sources to me throughout: *The Saint and Leslie Charteris* by W. O. G. Lofts and D. J. Adley (Hutchinson Library Services Ltd); *John Creasey In Print*, published by Hodder & Stoughton and John Creasey; and *The Nelson Lee Library: A Complete Guide and Bibliography of the writings of Edwy Searles Brooks* compiled by Robert E. Blythe, and obtainable from him at 47, Evelyn Avenue, Kingsbury, NW9 OJF.

I should also like to thank: John Creasey, for giving me a personal interview, answering further questions by post, and very kindly reading the typescript; Bruce Graeme, for most generously allowing me to quote extracts from the Blackshirt chapter of an autobiography he is now writing; Roderic Graeme, for a number of facts about the later Blackshirt; Penelope Wallace for introducing me to Edgar Wallace's *The Brigand*; Lionel

Brooks for giving me many sidelights on his father's career; Robert Blythe for patiently putting up with innumerable questions, and Derek Rowles, Manager, Juveniles Division, Syndication International Ltd, for advice on old Amalgamated Press papers. I have also received invaluable help from Mr Robin Denniston, Managing Director of Hodder & Stoughton; Mr Roger Palmer of Hodder & Stoughton; Miss Kathleen Nathan, Manager, Contracts and Rights Dept, Hutchinson Publishing Group; Mr and Mrs Innes Rose and certainly not least, the management and staff of the St Brides Public Library, who unfailingly dug up for me every book I required.

I should add, of course, that unless otherwise stated all the opinions expressed and assumptions made in this book are emphatically my own, and the responsibility of no one else at all.

One last point. I have made every effort to ensure that this study in the desperadoes is a comprehensive one, but this is an enormous *genre*, created by perhaps the most prolific group of authors in the entire history of fiction, and a lifetime's reading would hardly suffice to make anybody fully expert on it. (John Creasey and Edwy Searles Brooks between them have published over 70,000,000 words.) If in the course of this book I have omitted—or, worse, betrayed my total ignorance of—a favourite desperado of yours, please accept my regrets ... and the assurance that, in my personal shrine of heroes, there is always a candle burning labelled 'To an Unknown Saint'.

W.V.B.

Preface

by Anthony Lejeune

IT'S said that we are what we eat: and, if that's true of our bodies, it is certainly true, to a considerable extent, that our minds are what we read—particularly during our formative years. So what we read is important, whether or not the books are, or should be, considered significant as literature. Like Mr Butler, I grew up with the Durable Desperadoes—the Saint, the Toff, Blackshirt, Norman Conquest—and was therefore fascinated to join him, now, in looking more closely at their characters and the books in which they appeared. Arguably, there are psychological and sociological conclusions to be drawn, and Mr Butler does touch on such matters: but, thank heavens, lightly. The main point is that these books gave me (and, obviously, him) more pleasure than most things in life, and there is a double pleasure in looking at them again from a fresh point of view.

I remember very well the glorious pile of 19 Saint books, the complete series up to that date, mostly in the Hodder & Stoughton two-shilling yellow-jacket edition, which the family joined in giving to my father one year for Christmas. I read most of them before he did. And I remember my mother bringing me the latest Toff novel, to read in bed when I was ill; and I remember opening a new Bulldog Drummond on the train to Bexhill, where I was going to spend the summer holidays with my aunt; and discovering Norman Conquest, one Saturday afternoon, in the 'For Sale—ex-Library' shelves of the local Boots, which, at sixpence each, offered a marvellously

13

cheap and endlessly renewed supply of books for one's personal library.

I may have known, in some abstract sense, that these authors—Leslie Charteris, John Creasey, Sapper, Berkeley Gray—didn't write as well, or were certainly not considered by adults to write as well, as John Buchan and Rider Haggard, whose books I also loved. But, if I knew, I didn't care. At that age, one doesn't create hierarchies of merit, only of enjoyment, and one is capable of enjoying an extraordinarily diverse range of authors at the same time. In his delightful thriller, *The Journeying Boy*, Michael Innes strikes an immediately recognisable note of truth when he quotes young Humphrey Paxton's reading-list:

> Please send also these books: *Biggles Flies East, Biggles Flies West, Biggles Flies North, Biggles Fails to Return*, Bertrand Russell's *History of Western Phisolophy*, George Moore's *Daphnis and Chloe, Biggles and the Camel Squadron*, Bleinstein's *More and More Practical Sex*, Blunden's *Life of Shelley*, also *Atalanta in Calydon, Biggles in Borneo, Women in Love* and any *close* translation of *Caesar's Civil Wars*, Book III and *Phaedrus' Fables*.

And perhaps youth is wise. No author who gives pleasure to his readers can properly be dismissed as a bad writer. The authors we are considering here possessed certain qualities which conventionally 'better' authors frequently lack. Their stories had pace and gaiety and innocence.

Mr Butler quite rightly treats James Bond as the legitimate descendant of his Durable Desperadoes. Ian Fleming himself would gladly have acknowledged the link. He said more than once that his original intention had merely been to produce an updated version of Bulldog Drummond and similar pre-war thriller series. He is, I think, the only recent author who, when I discovered him (which was not until his third book, *Moon-raker*), gave me the same authentic excitement which I received, as a boy, from my first acquaintance with the Saint and Norman Conquest. The James Bond stories have plenty of pace, and (though the world has, unfortunately, caught up with them somewhat since they were published) a breathtaking atmosphere of outrageous invention, and that most mysterious quality of all—compulsive readability. They are more intelligently written than the others; but they do not have much gaiety or innocence.

Mr Butler is at pains to fix his authors in the social and historical context of their period. The disadvantage of looking at them from that point of view is that the field then becomes inconveniently wide. The handful of Durable Desperadoes can no longer be isolated from other contemporary thrillers or from their opposite numbers across the Atlantic.

John Buchan himself, in the dedication at the beginning of *The Thirty-Nine Steps*, says that what he has written is 'that elementary type of tale which Americans call the "dime novel", and which we know as the "shocker"'. Frank L. Packard's Jimmie Dale preceded Blackshirt, whom he uncannily resembles, by several years, and Louis Joseph Vance's Lone Wolf first prowled even earlier, in 1914. The Shadow and the Spider were at least as familiar to American boys of my generation (and, actually, to me) as the Saint and Norman Conquest were in Britain. The similarity, almost the interchangeability, of the gentlemen-desperadoes—and we must include Michael Arlen's Gay Falcon—was underlined by the fact that George Sanders and his brother, Tom Conway, played quite a selection of them on the screen.

Nor were the clubland adventurers and secret agents of such writers as Dornford Yates and Francis Beeding wholly unconnected. Connected by contrast and con-

15

temporaneity, rather than by resemblance, were the tough private eyes then growing up in the *Black Mask* school, and the consciously more sophisticated, less heroic, more tortuous spies and counter-spies being developed by Eric Ambler and by John Marquand. But these *genres* too were very characteristic of the period. As Alfred Hitchcock wrote in his Introduction to an American omnibus of early Eric Ambler novels:

> The villains are not only real people, they are actually the kind of people who have generated violence and evil in the Europe of our time. And the wise men—the clever ones who solve or help to solve the riddles in these stories—they are not the traditional old-school-tie officers of British Military Intelligence. In two of these novels they are Soviet agents operating in Italy and Austria just before the outbreak of the war; in the other two they are Turkish political police. Again, people you can believe in—above all, the kind of people who really were clever in the corrupt and stupid years of the past decade.

Mr Hitchcock's implied strictures are not wholly fair. Despite certain notorious débâcles, the old-school-tie officers of British Military Intelligence have served their country well.

Ian Fleming knew it, and took his place unashamedly in the Buchan–Beeding tradition, proclaiming that realism was not to be equated with seediness. Nobody could call him an unsophisticated writer, but his sophistication is of quite a different kind from Eric Ambler's. He was interested in how the world worked, in how things were made and done. Although not himself particularly fond of luxurious food and drink, for example (I never saw him drink anything except whisky, and his favourite lunch was *œufs en cocotte*), he took care in writing about them. Contrast this approach with a famous passage in

16

one of the Toff books—it may be mythical, for I've never been able to find it—where the Honourable Richard Rollison goes into the Savoy and says to the barman: 'Jules, bring me a bottle of the special Moussec you keep for me alone.' Even if that quotation is not authentic, the point is that it might well be. Ian Fleming really did add something, a touch of class one might say, which the earlier desperadoes lacked.

But 'class' in this context—indeed in most contexts—is a word of which nowadays one must beware. Ravening hordes of left-wing critics, maddened sociologists, Marxist fanatics and otherwise normal persons who have been brainwashed by these enemies of contentment are always ready to pounce. Ian Fleming, when he found that the smallest item of clothing or equipment mentioned in the Bond novels was receiving valuable publicity, liked, he said, to give a boost to good craftsmen, in a world where individual craftsmanship and quality had an increasing struggle to survive. This harmless—I should say laudable —notion was promptly called 'snobbery' by his opponents. And, since then, class-obsessed critics have widened their attack into an indictment of almost all the detective stories and thrillers written until the newest wave. The whole *genre*, they contend, is poisoned with vile middle-class values. The heroes, disgusting to relate, were invariably gentlemen, and, worse still, often club-men: the heroines, unless of exotic origin, were ladies— was there not even Lady Molly of Scotland Yard? The villains too were gentlemen (the butler, in fact, never did do it), but that apparently doesn't help. 'Snobbery with violence', sneered one class-conscious pontificator. My copy of the first Norman Conquest novel, *Mr Mortimer Gets the Jitters*, would confirm his darkest suspicions; since the paper jacket shows Norman, automatic pistol in hand, clad in full evening dress—for no obvious reason, except that it makes him look dashing.

In fact, of course, unfashionable though the idea may be in Royal Court circles, Aristotle had a point when he said that tragedy should be about kings. Similarly, there are good practical reasons why it is often convenient for the hero of a thriller, if he's not a professional detective, to be a gentleman and preferably a gentleman of leisure. Besides, thrillers are read for fun: and, whatever some unreadable modern novelists may suppose, luxurious surroundings are more agreeable to read about than sordid ones.

Mr Butler concedes more than I would to the pseudo-sociologists of the left, but, happily, shows no inclination to join them. He doesn't read thrillers to 'contradict and confute'. To him, a hero is a hero, not a symbol of the class struggle.

The classic encounter on this topic was between George Orwell and that great and good man Charles Hamilton, the creator of Billy Bunter, in which Mr Hamilton (who, when asked on his 80th birthday by an interviewer from *Time* magazine if he had never wanted to do anything better, replied firmly, 'There is nothing better') wiped the floor with Mr Orwell. To the charge that he was providing opium for the people by looking back to an idyllic Edwardian society which never really existed, he said he could assure Mr Orwell that 'the world went very well before 1914'.

The world didn't go quite so well before 1939, but— for the majority of people in Britain—it went a good deal better than it is now customary to suppose. People didn't read thrillers in the '20s and '30s because they needed an escape from the darkness of their lives. They read them for the same reason people read thrillers today —because they wanted to be told a story; and this is something which other sorts of novelist scarcely provide any more.

18

Television has, to some extent, taken over the function which the creators of Mr Butler's Durable Desperadoes used to fulfil. But a lot of television story-telling seems insipid by comparison. Did these books possess some quality, however tenuous, beyond mere narrative?

In *The Puritan Pleasures of the Detective Story* (which is the best recent study of detective fiction, as distinct from thrillers) Dr Erik Routley explains, very percipiently and sympathetically, the cosiness and comfort which a classical detective story can impart, and goes on to suggest that one reason for the decline of this *genre* is that its brand of comfort isn't strong enough to help when the world is crumbling beneath our feet and times are really black. Detective fiction needs a secure social framework which we no longer have.

The same objection, it might be thought, would apply *a fortiori* to its less intellectually distinguished cousin, the 'cheap' (I use the cant word inaccurately) thriller. But perhaps not. From one point of view, life is a comedy: from another, a tragedy. There is a third point of view. Life may be an adventure. Nobody would look to the Saint or Norman Conquest to provide any very profound insights into the human condition: but they may, nevertheless, in their simple fashion, provide a certain lifting of the spirits, a touch of daredevilry which strikes a chord in the hearts of ordinary people. This is the conclusion of Mr Butler's thesis.

Anyone [he says] who has ever fallen deeply under the spell of the desperadoes, especially in childhood, carries at the back of his mind a vague ideal of piratical nonchalance. He is forever suspicious of pomposity, subservience and solemnity, and quite powerfully fortified against despair. Even on his darkest days, he can never entirely silence a mischievous voice drawling that life is a mysterious adventure; that, for all we know, there may be a chuckle instead of a tear at the

19

heart of things; that there's always a way out of the cellar, even if the water's rising past one's neck.

But, when all's said and done, no justification is needed, either for Mr Butler or for his favourite authors. The pleasure they give is reason enough. The proper attitude was succinctly expressed by Cyril Mulliner in one of P. G. Wodehouse's stories:

'I can't go to bed without that book,' said Lady Bassett. 'I had just got to the bit where Inspector Mould is trapped in the underground den of the Faceless Fiend.'
'*Is* there a Faceless Fiend?' he cried.
'There are two Faceless Fiends,' said Lady Bassett.
'My gosh!' said Cyril. 'Let's hurry.'

ANTHONY LEJEUNE

Introduction

THIS book is a study in a particular thriller *genre* which was born in the second half of the nineteen twenties, flourished throughout the thirties and to some extent has been flourishing ever since: the *genre* of the Gentleman Outlaw.

The current revival of interest in between-the-wars thrillers has, I suspect, a rather stronger motive than nostalgia. It is to quite a large extent an outside interest, a fascination felt from a distance by a generation too young to have been in at any Carl Peterson kill.

Somehow they sense, this generation, that thrillers were more than just casual indulgences to their parents and grandparents, and surely they are right. All through this century, the thriller has played a considerable part in colouring the mood of each successive decade, and is over and over again that mood's most faithful mirror. Nothing will take you to the heart of turn-of-the-century England more swiftly than an evening on the prowl with Raffles and Bunny. (Overgrown schoolboys they may have been, but they had the whole thriller-reading public sneaking alongside them out of the dormitory of late Victorian rectitude.) Similarly, nothing will show you more clearly what the Edwardian era meant by 'style' than an encounter with Flambeau or Arsène Lupin. And Sapper's *Bulldog Drummond* should be required reading for anyone trying to understand the grim, shell-shocked, passionately anti-Bolshevik middle-class world of 1919.

The twenties, it is generally admitted, would not have been the twenties without Noël Coward or Evelyn Waugh; but for everyone who went to *Hay Fever* or read

Decline and Fall during that slightly demented decade, there were thousands who followed Edgar Wallace, Buchan, Oppenheim, Dornford Yates. And if, in entertainment terms, the nineteen thirties is remembered as the era of, say, Fred Astaire and Ginger Rogers, Gracie Fields, Clark Gable, Busby Berkeley musicals and the rest, it should not be forgotten that it was equally—and for an almost equal number of devotees—the era of the Saint, the Toff, the Baron, Norman Conquest, Nighthawk and the innumerable other thriller heroes of the time.

In the thirties, as a matter of fact, thanks to the circulating-library bookshelves which were as ubiquitous in every shopping area as frozen-food dispensers are today—and thanks, also, to a smallish but fantastically prolific group of writers who filled not only the library shelves with novels at the rate of at least 6-12 apiece per year, but the bookstall counters with thousands more words of thriller fiction in 4*d* monthlies or 2*d* weeklies—public interest in thriller heroes was at its peak.

Boys of all classes were up to their eyes in thrillers before they were ten. I was a twelve-year-old myself when the thirties ended, and I can remember spending whole long summer days as a nine-year-old hidden behind the pampas grass at the end of the garden reading *Detective Weekly*. (This 35,000-word twopenny, the successor to *Union Jack*, was published every Thursday, and featured Sexton Blake's battles against a resident panel of arch-villains headed, if I remember rightly, by Mademoiselle Yvonne, Count Ivor Carlac and Dr Huxton Rymer.) A couple of years or so later, I can remember arguing about the respective merits of the Saint and Norman Conquest at school with all the heat a modern eleven-year-old would generate in a dispute about Spurs or Chelsea.

The Saint ... Norman Conquest.

Yes, the thriller hero who chiefly attracted this vast

22

public—who fitted the nineteen thirties as closely as a number like 'I'm In A Dancing Mood' fitted Jack Buchanan—was almost always of the Gentleman Outlaw type. He was tall, dark and handsome—usually with his hair brushed straight back in a swashbuckling sweep. He dressed immaculately at all times, unless he happened to be the Saint, in which case he didn't have to: Simon Templar could make any suit look immaculate just by wearing it. At the beginning of a book (before the first corpse with a dagger in its back fell at anybody's feet) his conversation consisted almost wholly of flippancies, many of them, in retrospect, alarmingly infantile. 'Boots full of feet and all that sort of thing?' he was prone to inquiring, even of his nearest and dearest.

Flippant repartee was not the only *sine qua non* of the Gentleman Outlaw. Standard equipment included a faultless evening suit; a bizarre *soubriquet*, breathed in whispers throughout the awestruck Underworld (Conquest's, incidentally, was 1066); an automatic pistol and, in the case of the amateur cracksmen, a black mask of the finest crêpe, always worn when flitting around baronesses' bedrooms removing pearls, but usually discarded for such jobs as laughingly tipping arch-fiends into the Thames.

A very quaint phenomenon, the Gentleman Outlaw. One which might well be written off as a dated curiosity, as irrelevant as a Nelson Eddy–Jeanette Macdonald recording of 'Rose Marie', if it weren't for the fact that a number of the gentlemen in question possessed one additional characteristic, which marked them out from 90% of other thriller heroes, of theirs or any age.

Staying power.

Having once walked (strolled, eased, lounged, or otherwise insinuated their lithe, muscular frames) on to the literary stage, they stubbornly refused to quit.

Five at least of the Gentleman Outlaws flourishing in

23

the thirties—the Saint, the Toff, the Baron, Blackshirt and Norman Conquest—survived (with interesting modifications) not only through the War years, but clean on through the fifties into the distinctly anti-debonair sixties. Three of the five are still around today; and 'still around' is putting it mildly. As any corner newsagent who stocks paperbacks will confirm, few thriller heroes produced by the forties, fifties and sixties can equal the immediate selling-power of the Saint, the Toff and the Baron in the High Streets of Britain here in 1973. Such an astonishing survival record suggests that perhaps there was always something more in the *genre* than met the critic's eye; that there were hidden depths to its appeal, giving it the same perennial fascination that so much else has on that mysterious thirties scene.

This study begins with the question of how the desperadoes came to be born, and takes a look at their surprisingly complex ancestry. Part 2 sets out to consider how they were built up and sustained by the crazy, cottagey, ramshackle yet fabulously prolific nineteen thirties thriller industry, and how they, in their turn, helped to build up and sustain a public harassed by memories of the Depression and haunted by the looming threat of war. Part 3 examines how this small handful of Outlaws managed the initial feat of surviving their decade, and how each in his own fashion went to war. Part 4 attempts to show how each, again in his own fashion, changed to meet the changing *mores* of first the Austerity, then the H-Bomb, and finally the Permissive Age. It also tries to probe, albeit rather tentatively, some of the secrets of the almost mesmeric hold which these surviving Outlaws have had on generations of readers, through in each case upwards of thirty books and thirty years. The whole makes a many-sided, fast-moving and (I hope you will find) pretty engrossing story.

The story of the Durable Desperadoes.

Part One

BEFORE THE SAINT
(1899–1928)

CHAPTER ONE

In which Robin Hood drops his mantle, and Raffles doesn't quite pick it up

THE first and most durable of all the Desperadoes of England was a certain twelfth-century guerilla leader. He was alleged to have carried out a series of deadly sporadic raids on a Midlands city which had become a hotbed of corrupt officialdom. His real identity was a matter for the liveliest speculation, but he was known throughout the underworld (or perhaps one should say the undergrowth) by a pseudonym related to his sinister method of facial concealment: a robin-redbreast-coloured hood.

Legend has it that Redhood (as an early twentieth-century author would have called him) was in reality a gentleman and that he was of a lively, humorous disposition. He and his associates must certainly have been dab hands at repartee: you don't, after all, send echoes of your merrie laughter travelling down the centuries if you're slow in thinking up a comeback line. He was also, apparently, a passionate royalist although, for his time, a singularly discriminating one, some members of the royal family signally failing to command his respect. Again according to legend, he gathered round him a devoted band of followers who would rather have died than let him down. And he and they between them invented an exciting new sport, subsequently played by countless characters in fiction but not too many hoodlums in real life, called Robbing the Rich to Give to the Poor.

What the real Robin Hood was like (or if, in fact, he

27

ever existed at all) is anybody's guess, and no one needs much telling what sort of guesses the psychological historians would favour. Nothing but the extreme paucity of surviving twelfth-century documentation saves us from endless theses exposing Robin as a renegade, murderer, rapist, bastard son of Cœur de Lion, jilted lover-boy of the Sheriff of Nottingham, and God knows what else. But even the most caustic historian can't theorise where there is a total absence of data, and so the most attractive of all thriller legends somehow survives intact. It remains only to ask just why it has proved so attractive down so many centuries, and the answers are pretty clear.

When you come to think of it, Robin Hood is a hero with an emotional and political appeal that is nothing short of miraculous in its universality, even today. If you are politically right wing, Robin is for you: he was a supporter of the true monarchy against a venal pretender; he was a gentleman, even an aristocrat, to boot. Yet no matter how far your politics incline to the left Robin is still your man. He fought a corrupt administration on behalf of the oppressed classes, and all that 'steal-from-the-rich-to-give-to-the-poor' stuff suggests an egalitarian economic policy in line with the most Marxist dialectic. And if you despise politics altogether, and are an Alternative Society enthusiast, well, what was Robin but a drop-out, and what could his greenwood enterprise have been but an early form of commune (complete with its own brand of pop music, if the strong element of minstrelsy in the stories is true)?

Not that his astonishing ability to be all things to all men is the only, or even the deepest, reason for Robin's durability as a hero. The most important element, surely, is the fact that it is supremely easy to identify with him. It is hard to imagine anyone in England who has not, at some time, played at being Robin Hood, usually as quite a small child—and it is early childhood memories that go deepest, decorating, so to speak, the cave-walls of the subconscious for life.

Why has there run, right through English thriller-fiction almost from its inception, the recurrent theme of the gallant gentleman outlaw? Why has he almost always indulged in some form of mocking repartee? Why is he so often known by a pseudonym? Why is he so often surrounded by a loyal, laughter-loving gang? Why does he nearly always end up sparring with a single police opponent? Why do we feel, against all logic, that he ought to give away a lot of his loot?

The answer to all these questions must lie in the particular nature of the British thriller-reading public. And it cannot be insignificant that it is a public every member of which, at some moment in his life, however fleeting, has flitted, laughing, through an imaginary green-wood in a quest for high adventure—and at a level far deeper than reason can reach, feels that he knows what it was like to be Robin Hood.

This is not to say that the mantle of Robin Hood is tailor-made for every outlaw thriller hero. As a matter of fact, the first really successful gentleman-crook character in English crime fiction had so little Sherwood Forest chivalry in his make-up that he should have been ashamed even to order a smoking-jacket in Lincoln Green.

His name was A. J. Raffles. He was the creation of Conan Doyle's brother-in-law, E. W. Hornung. He first appeared in the middle-to-late 1890s. And his immense popularity right through the turn-of-the-century period takes more than a little explaining, unless one makes a supreme effort to view him through late Victorian eyes.

Imagine, then, for a moment, that you are a solid citizen of the middle 1890s. You are intensely proud of Queen and Empire. You unhesitatingly accept that a public school upbringing puts a fellow a great many cuts above the rest, and that within that privileged circle sportsmen (particularly cricketers) are a super-élite. But the importance of sport and sportsmanship weren't the only things that your school impressed on you. It was a forcing-house for the ideas of an excited Empire at the height of its power and glory, and it flooded your head with high romantic ideals. The result is that you have been impregnated since childhood with vague yearnings to cut a dash, to be a hero, to give your life for your country; and yet you live in an England which, for all its Imperial splendours abroad, is unspeakably placid at home. Your mid-Victorian father and early-Victorian grandfather may well have had a similar boredom problem, but if they did they contemptuously dismissed it on religious grounds. Life to them—officially, at any rate—had to be viewed as a sombre, weary sacrifice; an occasion for daily taking up one's cross. But this kind of thinking, here in the 1890s, is somewhat out of date. There is a new mood abroad now, which has been building up for years; and it is a distinctly disturbing mood to someone already loaded with obscure dissatisfaction. You can't quote the Bible, for instance, without running the risk of being called 'pi'—short for 'pious', and a pejorative adjective as devastating as the comparable word 'square' is to become in the nineteen sixties. People don't talk about going to Heaven or Hell when they die: they use phrases like 'the other side of the Styx'. Similarly, they tend to philosophise about Moving Fingers Having Writ rather than the Will of God. It is the thing to read Swinburne rather than Tennyson. In the houses of fashionably highbrow friends (the 'trendies' of the day) you find a proliferation of books with wild, whirly *art nouveau* designs on their covers, containing pages of wild, whirly metaphysical speculation devoted to the theme that goodness is primarily a question of good taste, and that it is distinctly bad taste to suggest otherwise.

30

You are, in fact, not so much a late Victorian as a denizen of the *fin de siècle* no-man's-land, uncomfortably perched astride two centuries. You probably regard bohemians, aesthetes, anarchists and such as wild and wicked: at the same time you are fascinated by them. You are fascinated, for that matter, by anything that is uninhibited and *bravura*, although your whole upbringing pulls you back from admitting the fact. You are especially fascinated by lawlessness: by what the era is very significantly beginning to call 'The *Romance* of Crime'. Almost certainly one of your favourite authors is Arthur Conan Doyle, and one of your favourite characters his singularly un-pompous detective, Sherlock Holmes, a man who himself has his wild moments (symbolised by that cocaine bottle) and an undisguised respect for sportsmanlike opponents on the opposite side of the law. (That blackmailing adventuress, Irene Adler, for example: to Holmes she was always *the* woman, and you have long felt rather that way about her yourself.)

You have paddled, then, in the forbidden waters of vicarious crime half way up to your toenails: you are ready to plunge a little further—up to your ankles, maybe. And then suddenly along comes E. W. Hornung and these Raffles stories, and the next thing you know you're in up to the neck, gleefully committing burglaries right, left and centre, having (you might say) the crimes of your life.

It's all perfectly all right, you see. A. J. Raffles may be a cracksman, but he's an ex-public schoolboy and internationally famous as a cricketer: qualified, then, on all counts to be a member of the super-élite. And there is not even any need to battle with your conscience: Bunny, the narrator of the stories, obligingly takes that chore clean off your shoulders. Bunny does enough worrying about the ethics of each exploit for at least ten other men, and even though he is inevitably drawn into tagging

31

along with Raffles, rather like the mesmerised rabbit which his name suggests, he never ceases to be half-disgusted with himself at the same time.

Floodgates were loosened within me, and the plain English of our adventure rushed over me as cold as ice. Raffles was a burglar. I had helped him to commit one burglary, therefore I was a burglar too. Yet I could stand and warm myself by his fire, and watch him empty his pockets, as though we had done nothing wonderful or wicked!

My blood froze. My heart sickened. My brain whirled. How I had liked this villain! How I had admired him! How my liking and admiration must turn to loathing and disgust! I waited for the change. I longed to feel it in my heart. But—I longed and I waited in vain!

('The Ides of March',
from 'The Amateur Cracksman')

There are critics who complain bitterly about Raffles. Colin Watson, in his recent book, *Snobbery With Violence* (Eyre & Spottiswoode, 1971) writes, for example: 'There can scarcely be excluded from any theory of why the narration of his exploits sold so well the presumption that it reached some part of the reader's mind that was ready to applaud the success of even a bully and a thug, provided he had the right credentials.' Mr Watson takes particular exception to one of the later Raffles stories called 'The Wrong House', in which Raffles and Bunny accidentally break into a private tutor's establishment, and find themselves in a desperate war with a number of very courageous schoolboys. Bunny half-strangles one of them before he can induce him to release Raffles' hand, which happens to be protruding through a carefully cut hole in the tutorial establishment's front door. Snorts Mr Watson: 'Raffles described as "sporting" an expedition which has involved the carrying of firearms, attempted robbery, the near-strangulation and chloroforming of a perfectly innocent schoolboy, and the felling of another with a vicious blow to the face. The readers, it may seem, thus are being invited to enjoy vicarious sadism on the assurance that such things are quite acceptable in circles of society able to appreciate the licence of sportsmanship.'

This criticism leaves entirely out of account the fact that it is Bunny who narrates the story, and that at one point—the near-strangulation incident itself—his self-disgust becomes almost Poe-like in its intensity.

> Oh, but it was villainous, my part especially ... I began by saying I was not proud of this deed, but its dastardly character has come home to me more than ever with the penance of writing it down. I see in myself, at least my then self, things that I never saw quite so clearly before. Yet let me be quite sure that I would not do the same again. I had no desire to throttle this innocent lad (nor did), but only to extricate Raffles from the most hopeless position he was ever in; and after all it was better than a blow from behind. On the whole, I will not alter a word, nor whine about the thing any more ...
>
> ('The Wrong House', from 'The Black Mask')

Poor old Bunny. A lot of charges can be laid at his door (he lays most of them there himself) but I do not think sadism is one of them. On the whole, it is his contribution which gives the Raffles stories their especial flavour (the constant sense of a heart beating furtively, as fearful of the wrath of Heaven as of a tap on the shoulder from the police) and makes the series a major achievement on Hornung's part. To show a whole generation a living embodiment of their frustrated romantic urges (illicit romantic urges, if you insist) is itself a considerable thing to do; but to show, at one and the same time, the *flaws* in that embodiment—to split oneself in two, to be Raffles *and* Bunny, functioning throughout as both your reader's temptation and his conscience, his demon and his guardian angel—this is something that must, in popular crime fiction at any rate, be very nearly unique.

It is quite true that Raffles is a very curious creation, and often behaves preposterously. But what Hornung is presenting, criticising, evaluating—one could almost say, struggling with—is not really a man at all, but a dream. Other creators of dream heroes have unhesitatingly made them supermen. Raffles (to adapt a delightful phrase used in Arthur Koestler's *The Roots of Coincidence* to describe the incomprehensible behaviour of electrons) is a superman only on Tuesdays, Thursdays and Saturdays. He bungles exploit after exploit, and it is nothing but the literal truth when he says to Bunny at the end of one of them: 'By Jove, we're jolly lucky to have come out of it at all!' On one occasion, Bunny is jolly *un*lucky. Raffles and he are caught on board a ship by a detective called Mackenzie, and are on the point of being arrested. Raffles's subsequent behaviour could only have got him classed as a cad and a bounder by any Victorian reader outside the *fin de siècle* era. He turns to a girl with whom he has been having an intense little shipboard romance.

Suddenly—an instant—and the thing was done—a thing I have never known whether to admire or detest. He caught her—he kissed her before us all—then flung her from him so that she almost fell. It was that action which foretold the next. The mate sprang after him, and I sprang after the mate.

Raffles was on the rail, but only just.

'Hold him, Bunny!' he cried. 'Hold him tight!'

And as I obeyed that last behest with all my might, without a thought of what I was doing, save that he

34

bade me do it, I saw his hands shoot up and his head bob down, and his lithe, spare body cut the sunset as cleanly and precisely as though he had plunged at his leisure from a diver's board!

('The Gift of the Emperor',
from 'The Amateur Cracksman')

A fascinating passage, that, for the student of thriller heroes—it shows that litheness and nonchalance by no means started in the era of the Saint—but it cannot be said that Raffles cuts a very good figure when he cuts that sunset. By that spectacular overboard leap (which wouldn't have come off if Bunny hadn't helped), he is cold-bloodedly leaving Bunny to face, alone, a voyage clapped in irons, followed by 'long imprisonment and everlasting disgrace'. Not that Bunny ever dreams of holding it against him. On their next meeting, years later, his very first reaction (once he realises that it *is* Raffles to whom he is speaking) is: 'Oh, my dear chap, to think of having you by the hand again!' and not a word of complaint does he utter thereafter.

Obviously, the Raffles–Bunny relationship derives, basically, from the Holmes–Watson one. But, apart from the fact that they were contemporaries, and talked in the same late Victorian style, there are remarkably few real similarities between Sherlock Holmes and Raffles. Raffles is from the very outset a completely new kind of hero, and a far from prepossessing one. The chilling side of him comes across on his first appearance on the printed page. In the first Raffles story, 'The Ides of March', Bunny finds himself in dire financial straits after a card game at Raffles's flat. Later that night, he returns to the flat to appeal to Raffles for help. When this help does not appear to be forthcoming, he whips a pistol from his overcoat pocket and points it at his own temple, resolved on instant suicide. He expects, at the very least, to see a look of horror cross Raffles's face. Instead, all he sees is 'wonder, admiration, and such a measure of pleased expectancy' that he pockets the gun with an oath, saying: 'You devil! I believe you wanted me to do it!'

In actual fact, Raffles had *not* wanted Bunny to do it. He starts and changes colour at the very suggestion, and is suddenly all over Bunny with offers of friendship and help. ('I never dreamed you had such stuff in you, Bunny! No, I'm hanged if I let you go now. And you'd better not try that game again, for you won't catch me stand and look on a second time ... There, let me have the gun!') But just for a moment, the Raffles mask had dropped, and we saw him for what he was: a bored sensationalist, a man whose inmost instinct was to regard any sort of flamboyant action, however violent, however tragic, however amoral, as a welcome relief from *ennui*; as, in fact, a jape. And I do not think there is any doubt that, when that mask dropped, thousands of *fin de siècle* readers glimpsed—to their fascinated horror—a mirror image of something in themselves.

There are, of course, many other sides to Raffles than this. Some people have called him a pasteboard, two-dimensional creation. In fact, his character has more facets than any of the diamonds he tries (often so unsuccessfully) to purloin. There is Raffles the cool, cricket-disparaging cricketer. ('Where's the satisfaction of taking a man's wicket when you want his spoons?') There is Raffles the implacably determined criminal. ('A stern chase and a long one, Bunny, but I think I'm well to windward this time.') There is Raffles the schoolboyish taunter. ('You've grown such a pious old rabbit in your old age.') There is Raffles the dignified observer of niceties. ('When we took old Lady Melrose's necklace, Bunny, we were not staying with the Melroses, if you recollect.') There is Raffles the passionate romantic about

36

the one real love of his life, a simple Italian maiden called Faustina. ('Only to look at her—only to look at her for the rest of my days—I could have lain low and remained dead even to you! And that's all I'm going to tell you about that, Bunny; cursed be he who tells more!') There is the vulnerable Raffles, the very opposite of a durable desperado, ageing twenty years when his Faustina is killed by a Mafia-type gang; even his hair turns white at a stroke. And finally—a side of him usually forgotten—there is Raffles the patriot, who celebrates Queen Victoria's diamond jubilee by sending Her Majesty a priceless gold cup which he has just stolen from the British Museum. He makes quite a stirring speech into the bargain. ('My dear Bunny, we have been reigned over for sixty years by infinitely the finest monarch the world has ever seen. The world is taking the present opportunity of signifying the fact for all it is worth. Every nation is laying of its best at her royal feet; every class in the community is doing its little best—except ours. All I have done is to remove a reproach from our fraternity ...')

Of all the many Raffles, it is, significantly, the under-lying patriot who is dominant at the end. When the Boer War starts, Raffles rushes to volunteer, Bunny going along without hesitation, only 'a sudden regret that he had not always appealed to that part of my nature to which he was appealing now'.

Raffles has to dye his hair and fake his identity before he is accepted by the Army. Dyeing for his country, he calls it. An odd, ironic little joke of Hornung's, that—at the beginning of the short story that actually ends with Raffles's death from a sniper's bullet.

The last words which Raffles speaks describe how much he has been enjoying life at the front.

'It's not only been the best time I've ever had, old Bunny, but I'm not half sure—'

37

Of what I can but guess; the sentence was not finished, nor ever can be in this world.

('The Knees of the Gods', from 'The Black Mask')

It is tempting to try and finish that last sentence for Raffles. It might, I suggest, have gone: 'It's not only the best time I've ever had, old Bunny, but I'm not half sure it hasn't been the best time that any of us have ever had.'

He would have been speaking for his public as well as his fellow-officers. That public behind whose vague, bored longings for sensation has always been those basic, school-implanted urges to cut a dash; to be a hero; to die for their country.

And by Jove, through A. J. Raffles, gentlemen, cad, bounder, romantic adventurer, super-patriot and finally supreme sacrifice maker, they'd jolly well done the lot.

CHAPTER TWO

In which Inspector Ganimard is helpless, but Sexton Blake has something up his sleeve

WITH the ending of the Boer War in 1902, the year of the coronation of Edward VII, placidity returned to the English scene; and pretty soon, for perhaps much the same reasons as before (the nation's educators hadn't changed their stirring patriotic tune), there was discernible amongst the reading public the same boredom with normality, the same hankering after the Romance of Crime. Only the public was now no longer in any sense Victorian, and they wanted something altogether less hesitant, less conscience-stricken, this time. In Edwardian fiction, all criminals, whether romantic adventurers or vilest villains, have an extraordinarily imperious manner.

An outstanding example is the celebrated French 'Gentleman Cambrioleur', Arsène Lupin, whose adventures (wafted across the Channel by the soft breezes of the Entente Cordiale) won a large British following from 1907 onwards. Lupin was the creation of the prolific Parisian journalist called Maurice Leblanc, a man so shy of publicity that for years there were rumours that his name (significantly translatable as 'The Blank') was a pseudonym for some other crime writer, perhaps Gaston Leroux. Ill-founded though they proved to be, it is not surprising that such notions got about. There hangs over many of the Lupin stories a feeling that some kind of joke is being played on somebody, but so amazing is the author's ingenuity, so incredible his sleight-of-hand, that

39

you don't really mind even if that somebody should turn out to be you.

If ever a hero was a superman every day of the week, it was Arsène Lupin. Untroubled by scruples, contemptuous of bungling, capable of astounding feats of burglary and detection alike, he is confident to the point of extreme arrogance, and made tolerable as a character by two factors only: a gloriously eccentric imagination, and the most fantastic sense of style.

When M. Lupin wants to arrange a meeting with his arch-enemy, Inspector Ganimard, it seems the most natural thing in the world that he should employ an old man to walk in front of the Inspector and drop tiny pieces of orange peel on the pavement, and that he should then employ a small boy to mark each place where the peel falls with a chalked cross. The Inspector is so intrigued by this curious exercise that he follows the crosses, and *zut alors!* suddenly he is where Arsène Lupin wished him to be for the meeting.

Lupin has a positive army of assistants. You could almost call him crime fiction's first Organisation Man hero. And he is so many light-years ahead of officialdom in intelligence that even when he is in prison he continues to function completely unimpeded, contacting his associates so effortlessly that he can't even open his breakfast egg without finding a message from one of them inside. (He had only allowed himself to be imprisoned, he explains to Ganimard, as a bit of a rest cure; and we unhesitatingly believe him.)

Almost any paragraph from a Lupin story will show the curious (and, incidentally, quite inimitable Maurice Leblanc Grand Manner. Here is a bit from the beginning of one of his earlier escapades, 'The Flash of Sunlight': [1]

[1] All the Lupin extracts in this chapter are from *The Confessions of Arsène Lupin*, translated by Joachim Neograschal (Hodder & Stoughton, 1969).

At that time, Lupin was already famous, but his most fearful battles lay ahead of him ... Never dreaming of appropriating the ancient hoard of the Kings of France or of burglarising Europe under the Kaiser's nose, he was satisfied with more modest coups and more reasonable perquisites. He expended himself in everyday efforts, turning to crime or doing good as the mood took him, in keeping with his nature and his thirst for change.

There's quite a lot of significance in that last, lordly throwaway line. While Arsène Lupin is not basically much more worthy than Raffles to wear the mantle of Robin Hood, he does put in guest appearances on the side of the angels, normally dispensing in the process such withering disdain that he is lucky not to end up with a harp wrapped round his neck. 'Good little puppy-wuppy. Stand up. Here's a little bone for you' is how he jeers at Inspector Ganimard when he feels the Inspector is insufficiently grateful for having been presented with a clue.

In 'The Red Silk Scarf', Lupin's most famous appearance in the detective role, he throws upon a table a number of objects—a torn piece of newspaper, a large crystal inkwell with a long piece of string tied to the lid, a tiny fragment of glass, a piece of cardboard reduced to a pulp and a length of scarlet silk with a tassel of the same colour. He then says loftily: 'Let me sum up the whole case in terms of what this evidence reveals. Last night, between nine and midnight, an unmarried woman of rather eccentric ways was stabbed several times and then choked to death by a gentleman who was well-dressed, wore a monocle, frequented racetrack society, and with whom the aforesaid lady had just eaten three meringues and an éclair in a café.'

It sounds almost like a line from a Monty Python skit on detective stories. Yet—as no less an authority than

Michael Gilbert points out, in his introduction to Hodder & Stoughton's recent reissue of *The Confessions of Arsène Lupin*—the deductions Lupin makes from the objects described are all perfectly valid. One has reluctantly to admit that the man, on occasion, really can out-Holmes Holmes.

Why should the admission be so reluctant? Probably because, in Lupin's case, praise always seems *un peu* superfluous. 'What a masterpiece of intelligence! What a reconstruction, Ganimard! What a superb intuition, what an exquisite hypothesis ... What truly brilliant guesswork!' he says at the end of the story, not merely foreshadowing Poirot but out-Poiroting him into the bargain.

That's the trouble with Lupin, in the end. He outclasses everybody so effortlessly that it is finally impossible not to regard him as a sort of boneless wonder. There are, actually, technical reasons for his baffling basic elusiveness. Unlike Holmes and Raffles, who were created largely for a magazine public, Lupin appeared from first to last in *newspapers*—the first of them a journal not inappropriately entitled *Je Sais Tout*. If you were a French newspaper-reader of pre-1914 Paris, you took your Lupin between sips of Pernod at café-tables on the boulevardes: you allowed him to entice your idle eye away from neighbouring columns about Blériot's channel-crossing or the assassination of the Archduke Charles. As a result, the stories give you the feeling that you are reading eye-witness reports of audacious *coups* rather than meeting a person. The sayings of Lupin are there for all to read. His deeds are known throughout the Kaiser's Europe—particularly, no doubt, in those vast areas of it which he has burglarised. But try to get through to Arsène Lupin the man—try to find out what made him sweat, what made him hope and dream—and you will suddenly find that you are as hopeless as

42

Inspector Ganimard at the job of pinning him down.

And that is quite an admission. Because of all the hapless Inspectors in fiction (we shall be meeting droves of them before this study is through) no one, I will swear, is quite so paralysingly powerless in the presence of the enemy as he.

Ganimard was furious. He pocketed the revolver and leaped upon Lupin.

'What now?' said Lupin, stopping him short with a kick in the leg.

They were almost touching. Their eyes dared one another like those of two adversaries about to come to blows.

But there was no battle. The recollections of past fights made the struggle futile. And Ganimard, remembering all his past defeats, his vain attacks, the lightning reactions of Lupin, refused to move ... Lupin had forces at his disposal that made individual effort pointless. What could he do? Nothing.

It wasn't only Inspector Ganimard who had trouble with this new, imperious breed of outlaws. The man who was afflicted by more of them than anyone else was the London private detective, Sexton Blake.

Blake dates from before Raffles—from before anybody, in fact, except his model, Sherlock Holmes. The first Blake story, 'The Missing Millionaire', by one Hal Meredith, appeared in a boys' paper called *The Half-penny Marvel* on 20 December 1893.[2] (The *Union Jack*, which rapidly became Sexton Blake's own paper, was launched some six months later.) Blake, on his first appearance, was a dullish character. He was described merely as 'refined and clean-shaven', and his first recorded

[2] According to *The Men Behind Boys' Fiction* by W. O. G. Lofts and D. J. Adley (Howard Baker Press) there have been 176 Blake authors between 1893 and the present.

43

observations indicate a depressingly mercenary turn of mind. ('So! My wealthy client has come at once, thanks to the influence of my friend Gervaise of Paris! I wonder what kind of mission he has in hand that is to bring me such high rewards!')

By the Edwardian era, though, the Sexton Blake team of writers had improved their hero's image considerably. He now voiced sentiments entirely in keeping with the *Union Jack*'s proud title. ('I would rather work for nothing for a naval man like yourself, one of the best protectors of our precious flag, than take banknotes from those who are careless of the honour of old Britain!') By this time, too, he had acquired rooms in Baker Street, his boy assistant Tinker, his famous bloodhound Pedro, his Malapropish landlady Mrs Bardell (who was proud to state that she had joined the Woman's League of Freedom, and become a humble decipher of Mrs Spankhard) and a score of colourful super-criminals who were to buzz round him like eternally DDT-proof wasps for the next thirty to forty years.

When, in researching for this book, I was fortunate in obtaining some *Union Jacks* of the pre-1914 era to study, I was astonished to find that Mademoiselle Yvonne, Count Ivor Carlac and Dr Huxton Rymer had been as prominent in those early days as they were in the *Detective Weeklies* of my own childhood.

I even found a bumper issue (in *Union Jacks*, 'bumper' usually meant that Blake would bump up against at least two of your favourite villains in the course of the story) which featured not only Mademoiselle Yvonne, not only Dr Huxton Rymer, but one Prince Wu Ling, Chief of the Brotherhood of the Yellow Beetle, as well.

There were, in the Sexton Blake stories, strict degrees of villainy. Mademoiselle Yvonne (a direct descendant of Conan Doyle's Irene Adler) is so chivalrous that she really ranks as half a heroine. At times in this particular

44

adventure, 'The Sacred Sphere', she is called upon to be a heroine and a half. She is shanghaied by the agents of Prince Wu Ling, and finds herself on board a ship with one of the most colourful crews ever assembled. The second mate, for example, a rough-looking, bearded seaman seated on a bench in the corner of her cabin, is busily writing in a notebook a treatise on 'The Emanations of Radium and the Curative Powers Thereof', which alone would have told any Sexton Blake fan that he was none other than the twisted ex-Harley Street surgeon, Dr Huxton Rymer himself.

Before long, Yvonne and the doctor are having a dialogue that must rate as one of the finest examples of High Imperial thriller-writing anywhere. Rymer tells Yvonne that he is on this ship to help her. ('For you, I would do anything if it would bring me your love in return!') His protestations, however, leave Yvonne singularly unimpressed. ('If a man's love is worth having, Dr Rymer, it does not promise to perform upon conditions. Even if I needed your help, I could hardly accept it on such terms—for I do not love you!')

Rymer becomes furious.

'By heaven, let me tell you that whether you love me or no, you will be my wife! I had a chance until Sexton Blake came on the scene. Why you should care for a man who has hounded you all over the globe, and even put you in prison, I cannot see. At all events, he is not here to help you now. Unless I intervene, you will go to China as sure as the sun rises, and once there, no one on earth can help you. If you prefer to be the wife of a Celestial rather than mine, that is a matter for your own taste. Only—and mark my words—either you marry me or go to your fate!'

Yvonne's reply is nothing short of magnificent.

'I regret that I must refuse to entertain any such

45

suggestion, Dr Rymer. Be quite sure that before anything forced me to become the wife of either you or a
Celestial, I would choose—and would wed—death!'

It is possible to object that all this was not exactly a
helpful contribution to the colour-bar problem, such as it
was in those days. But please note that when the chief
of these despicable Celestials actually appears in the
story, he is allowed to cut a figure of even greater dignity
than Yvonne. He is introduced, in fact, with a positive
explosion of rhetoric, suggesting that he was one of the
top circulation-building characters of the year.

Prince Wu Ling, Chief of the Brotherhood of the
Yellow Beetle, is (like Sax Rohmer's Fu Manchu, to
whom he bears a close resemblance[3]) the 'descendant of
a dynasty which could trace its philosophy back to the
time when the Anglo-Saxon race was unheard of'. To
him all the English are 'but as the flies of yesterday'. He
longs 'from the innermost depths of his princely nature
to feel the heel of the East on the West, to carve a path
of saffron through a field of white, to raise on high
Confucius, Buddha and Taoism across all the world!' He
lives for nothing else, and is all the more dangerous to
humanity because he is 'honest in that purpose and—by
his own lights—honourable in his methods'.

Rymer, Yvonne and the whole ship's company are
taken to the Prince's secret headquarters (not, after all,
in China, but for some obscure reason in Boston). Wu
Ling recognises Rymer on sight, and even recollects the
events of the previous occasion when they had starred
together, possibly in the last bumper issue.

'Silence! How dare you stand and lie to me? Do you

[3] It is a moot point which came first. Fu Manchu first appeared
in *book* form in 1913; Wu Ling was in *Union Jack* slightly
earlier.

46

forget the time when I dragged you out of an opium den, a weak, doddering imbecile, and put you on your feet? Bah! You child, to pit your wits against Wu Ling! Your punishment will be lifelong slavery in the ricefields of China, with the rawhide lash when you shirk. San Loo, take him away!'

Now Sexton Blake readers would no more have stood for Rymer being sent to lifelong slavery in China than they would have contemplated Yvonne becoming the bride of a Celestial. This adventure is obviously going to have to end with Blake taking on the somewhat illogical task of rescuing his arch-enemies from each other's clutches. How he does this makes a fascinating study in the protocol of pre-1914 villainy.

Once Blake has secured the release of Yvonne, she immediately asks him to do something for the doctor. Blake is 'suddenly cold'. ('It is strange to hear you pleading for Rymer.') Yvonne hastens to make it clear that she is motivated purely by magnanimity. ('Oh, please do not misunderstand me. He is a white man, and no matter what he has done, it would be awful to let him go to that living hell.')

Blake turns to Wu Ling and makes a request as formal as a petition to the Chinese embassy.

'Prince Wu Ling, I have come here tonight to make certain demands. You agreed to them. That being so, I can make no fresh demands. And yet, I would ask one more favour. Hand over to me Dr Huxton Rymer.'

This request is met by an implacable refusal, couched however in such fulsome terms that we almost forget Wu Ling is an incarnation of evil. Across the whole scene there spreads a positively golden glow of international goodwill.

'Though we are on opposite sides, and though your race and mine must one day clash together in a final struggle, I have for you the love of a brother, Sexton Blake. And always you know that if you join us, the East will receive you and place you second only to Wu Ling. But what you ask now I cannot grant.'

Blake's hands move 'deep into the sleeves of his costume'. (He happens to be disguised at the moment as a Chinese coolie.) They emerge with 'a chamois bag containing a round object', and he says, coldly:

'You are a representative of the Ming dynasty. It is unnecessary to tell you what it is that I hold in my hand.'

For a devotee of Buddhism, Taoism, Confucianism and the rest, Wu Ling becomes extraordinarily excited.

'How you come to possess the Sacred Sphere of the Son of Heaven, I will not ask. You ask me will I give you the man Rymer for it. I would give a thousand such dogs. I would give honour, life, wealth! I would give a kingdom!'

San Loo is peremptorily ordered to bring Rymer back, to receive a stern lecture from Blake.

'Rymer, you were condemned to slavery in the rice-fields of China. Knowing nothing of it, I would have done nothing to preserve you from it. Mademoiselle Yvonne, however, has seen fit to plead for you, and her plea has been granted. You belong to her, and what she says shall be done! Well, Mademoiselle— what is your wish?'

Yvonne, ever generous, merely issues a brief policy statement.

'You deserve little from me, Dr Rymer, and if we meet again on an equal footing I shall exact payment for every moment of suffering you have caused me. But Yvonne de Cartier strikes no one when they are helpless. My desire is that you go, and I hope I never see you again.'

Wu Ling, meanwhile, has remembered his Buddhism, Taoism or whatever. He is 'bent low over the desk, his arms almost flat on the desk-top'. There is a little golden god on the desk before him, beside the Sacred Sphere.
Blake is quite impressed.

'He is giving thanks to the idol, I think ... A strange man, even a great one, in his fashion.'

Yvonne remarks that it is lucky Blake had the Sacred Sphere, and the detective casually agrees.

'Oh, that ... Yes. I usually make a point of bringing back one or two unusual jade pieces when I go to China. This one I had intended, as a matter of fact, to give you as a Christmas present.'

The pre-1914 dream-picture of an Englishman effort-lessly but magnanimously lording it over all the world, including the blackest-hearted depths of the underworld, is complete. So is our glimpse of the unique Sexton Blake hero–villain relationship. It is not at all the black and white affair you would expect in a penny-a-week boys' paper, but such a mix-up of love, hate, chivalrous codes of honour and Imperial condescension that it would be better described as red, white and blue.

There is one very obvious reason for the ever-growing importance of the villains in Sexton Blake. All the authors had to share Blake and Tinker: but each author was allowed to regard his own particular villain, or villains, as more or less his own private property, upon which his fellow-authors were not encouraged to trespass. A Blake writer wouldn't have been human if he didn't acquire a greater fondness for his own creations than for the central communal ones. It says, in fact, a great deal for the discipline exercised at the Blake editorial centre, the Amalgamated Press's Fleetway House, that Blake wasn't completely upstaged by his adversaries. He remains dominant in all the stories, but only just. You can't help getting the feeling that if the writers really had their way, the Rymers, the Wu Lings and the Yvonnes would move in on Baker Street and take over.

No. Perhaps not the Rymers, the Wu Lings and the Yvonnes. They were copies of other characters,[4] just as Sexton Blake himself was basically a copy of Sherlock Holmes. What the Fleetway House school really needed was to evolve a style of hero who was peculiarly, unmistakably, their own. He would have to be a hero-villain, of course: they were on their home ground with villains, especially chivalrous ones. Perhaps a gentleman crook who was an outright Robin Hood ...

It took them, in the end, almost a generation to evolve this distinctive kind of hero. It wasn't, in fact, until the late nineteen twenties and early thirties, when writers of the calibre of Leslie Charteris and John Creasey temporarily swelled their ranks, that they finally made it. But Fleetway House's efforts are perennially worth watching. It was there, and nowhere else, that the Gentleman Outlaw *genre* of the nineteen thirties was finally born.

And if you number Raffles and Arsène Lupin amongst the ancestral shades present at that event, it is only fair to

---

[4] Wu Ling may have preceded Fu Manchu, but the fiction of the day abounded in sinister Celestials of his type.

remember that Sexton Blake & Co. had long been actually resident on the premises at the time.

Nothing is easier than to sentimentalise the Edwardian thriller scene; to present it all as jolly high jinks in a hazy golden glow. But there was a dark underside to the Edwardian thriller reader's fancies; a side which still has the power to startle and sometimes even to chill. Despite the high-toned rhetoric about codes of honour, an extraordinarily wide range of crimes had become vicariously enjoyable, from straightforward burglary to cold, premeditated murder.

From 1902 right up to 1914, an increasingly open admiration for the daringly lawless crops up all over crime fiction. Even G. K. Chesterton, perhaps the most moralistic crime novelist there has ever been, had to take a firm hand with himself over the Lupin-like cat-burglar, Flambeau, who figured in so many of the Father Brown stories. In one story, 'The Flying Stars', published in *The Innocence of Father Brown*, 1911, Flambeau escapes after a particularly daring jewel robbery, in the course of which he has invaded a Christmas party disguised as a harlequin, and treated the guests to what they imagined at the time was a hilarious harlequinade. Afterwards Father Brown, Chesterton's mild and saintly priest-detective, rushes into the garden, espies his enemy leaping from tree to tree like a monkey, and delivers a homily which comes perilously close to turning into a paean of praise. So does Chesterton's prose, which is never more purplish than when he is describing this thief whose very name is a synonym for flamboyance. In his harlequin get-up, up there in the treetops, Flambeau sparkles 'from head to heel, as if clad in ten million moons'. The real moon catches him at every moment and sets 'a new inch of him on fire' even as Father Brown harangues him.

'Well, Flambeau, you really look like a Flying Star,

51

but that always means a falling star at the last ... You were going to steal the stones quietly; news came by an accomplice that you were already suspected, and a capable police officer was coming to rout you up that very night. A common thief would have been thankful for the warning and fled; but you are a poet ... The worthy officer started from Putney police station to find you, and walked into the queerest trap ever set in this world. When the front door opened he walked straight on the stage of a Christmas pantomime, where he could be kicked, clubbed, stunned and drugged by the dancing harlequin, amid roars of laughter from all the most respectable people in Putney. Oh, you will never do anything better ...'

(*The Innocence of Father Brown*, Cassell)

It is only fair to add that Father Brown follows this with the most effective sermon of his life: a sermon which finally persuades Flambeau to abandon his career of crime. The romantic allure of that career, though, could hardly have been more frankly admitted, or, indeed, more powerfully presented than in the passage above; and no fuzz-baiting hippie from the 1970s could have contemplated with greater relish the acute, painful and abject humiliation of a perfectly unexceptionable arm of the law. Even, then, to Chesterton, arch-advocate of Christian orthodoxy, there was a side to which respectability seemed a burden and a bore.

But by far the most remarkable example of the Edwardian willingness—you could almost say eagerness—to compound vicarious felonies had come much earlier, in 1905, when a nationwide competition was staged to find a way of committing a murder (more specifically, of carrying out a political assassination) right under the noses of the police.

This really somewhat sinister competition—we call *ourselves* the Permissive Society, but it would, I suspect, cause quite an outcry if it were staged by, say, the *Sun* or the *News of the World* today—was promoted by a fiery *Daily Mail* journalist called Edgar Wallace.

There appeared on the bookstalls a smart yellow volume called *The Four Just Men*. I was lucky enough to pick one of the original copies up at a second-hand shop the other day, for the astonishingly low price of 5*p*. I fancy it would be worth at least a hundred times as much to a collector, for this was the book—written, published and extravagantly publicised by Edgar Wallace single-handed —which, in effect, launched Wallace on his whole thriller-writing career.

As a publication, it may have looked garish and sensational in its time. Today, the cover seems as sober as a political book club's tract. It carries, though, an unprecedented amount of wording for the cover of a cloth-bound book.

THE FOUR JUST MEN by Edgar Wallace
£500 REWARD
A Remarkable Offer is made in connection with this Novel. Apart from its interest as a most brilliant piece of storytelling, Mr Edgar Wallace has heightened its charm by leaving at the end one mystery unsolved. The Publishers invite the reader to solve this mystery and offer Prizes to the value of £500 (First Prize, £250) to the readers who will furnish on the form provided the explanation of Sir Philip Ramon's death.

Nothing, you would imagine, very sinister there. And the inside cover of my copy is even less disturbing. It states that Edward Grove, Tailor and Outfitter of 37, 38, 39, 40 and 41, Lower Marsh, Lambeth, is presenting this volume to all his customers as his Annual Christmas Gift, with Best Wishes for a Merry Christmas and a Prosperous New Year.

What Mr Grove is actually encouraging his customers

to do is spend Christmas playing the merry little game of putting themselves in the shoes of an anarchist assassin.

The Four Just Men, the book reveals, have decided that a certain Bill, the Aliens Political Offences Bill—'calculated to hand over to a vengeful Government men who now in England find asylum from the persecutions of despots and tyrants'—must not be passed through the Commons. Since 'opinion in England is divided over the merits of the Bill', the only way they can be certain of preventing its passage is by murdering the British Foreign Secretary, Sir Philip Ramon, a man who is admitted on all sides to be brave and honourable, but who unfortunately happens to be the Bill's chief advocate.

'It grieves us to warn you,' thunder the Four Just Men in a note to Sir Philip, 'that unless your Government withdraws this Bill, it will be necessary to remove you, and any other person who attempts to carry into law this unjust measure.'

And they do, in fact, 'remove'—by simple murder—quite a number of people before turning their attention to Sir Philip. So much for democracy. So much for freedom of opinion. So much for almost every basic Parliamentary right. No wonder it was a greatly toned-down version of *The Four Just Men* that Dick Powell and Richard Conté starred in, back in the early days of commercial television.

Their final warning to the unfortunate Sir Philip is painfully specific.

'We allow you until tomorrow evening to reconsider your position in the matter of the Aliens Extradition Bill. If by six o'clock, no announcement is made in the afternoon papers of your withdrawing this measure, we shall have no other course but to fulfil our promise. You will die at eight in the evening. We append for your enlightenment a concise table of the secret police

54

arrangements made for your safety tomorrow. Fare-well.'

There wasn't, in fact, all that much you could call secret about the police arrangements, as it turned out.

Within an hour there was witnessed in London a scene that has no parallel in the history of the Metro-polis. From every district there came a small army of policemen. They arrived by train, by tramway car, by motorbus, by every vehicle and method of traction that could be requisitioned or seized ...

Whitehall was soon packed from end to end; St James' Park was black with them. Automatically, Whitehall, Charles St, Birdcage Walk and the eastern end of the Mall was barred to all traffic by solid phalanxes of mounted constables. St George's Street was in the hands of the police, the roof of every house was occupied by a uniformed man, not a house or a room that overlooked in the slightest degree the Foreign Secretary's residence but was subjected to a vigorous search. It was as though martial law had been pro-claimed, and indeed two regiments of Guards were under arms the whole day ready for any emergency ...

Notwithstanding all this, exactly at the appointed hour there sounds, from the room where Sir Philip had insisted on waiting alone, 'a quick sharp cry of pain, a crash—and silence', and the Foreign Secretary is found sprawled over his writing-table.

The Commissioner stepped to the fallen man and raised him. One look at the face was sufficient.

'Dead!' he whispered hoarsely. He looked around—save for the police and the dead man the room was empty.

How had the Four Just Men done it? That was the

problem in which thriller-reading (and maybe tailor-patronising) Edwardian England gleefully involved itself, although the enthusiasm changed to anger as months and even years went by without the competition being wound up. (My own copy furnishes an interesting illustration of what a fantastic time-lag there must have been. On the title page the publication year of the book is given as 1905; yet Mr Edward Grove's customers are getting it as a gift for *Christmas, 1908*, still with the competition wide-open, still with the entry form—No. 22578 in this particular instance—intact at the rear.)

The solution, vouchsafed by Edgar Wallace only when he had finally succeeded in borrowing from Lord Rothermere the money to pay the prizes (even awarding them wasn't at all easy, because by this time a few correct entries had piled up) had all the simplicity and ingenuity of his showman's genius. The Four Just Men had intercepted the Foreign Secretary's telephone line, and since receivers were not made of bakelite in those days, and hence not insulated, they had been able to send an electric shock along the wire, mild but fatal to someone like Sir Philip, who suffered (as the story had established) from a heart condition.

It is not the cleverness of the solution, or the daring ingenuity of the competition concept, that makes *The Four Just Men* such a fascinating subject for the student of thriller heroes. It is the staggering fact that so many thousands of readers eagerly, and with never the slightest scruple, accepted Wallace's invitation to align themselves with his quartet of high-handed political murderers.

The 'honourable code' factor was present, of course; the Four Just Men were presumably saving the lives of hundreds of gallant émigrés. But their methods seem more appropriate to a Wu Ling or a Huxton Rymer than to a hero: it's almost as though we're glimpsing a Sexton Blake anti-world in which the villains *have* taken over.

56

Miss Margaret Lane, in her fascinating biography *Edgar Wallace* (Hamish Hamilton, 1964) quotes a Captain Kendall as saying that Dr Crippen was reading *The Four Just Men* during the fateful voyage across the Atlantic which ended in his arrest. It would be fascinating to know if the doctor got the answer right. It is not too surprising that the Just Men's murderous methods should have charmed and intrigued him, but the fact that they had the same effect on such large numbers of rather more ordinary people surely demonstrates what distinctly odd forces were astir in the *Zeitgeist* at the time.

The British thriller-reading public, in 1902 still sufficiently sensitive about vicarious crime to need the conscience-stricken Bunny to share its guilt and hold its hand, changed, then, both rapidly and radically during the next twelve years. Its subconscious impatience with respectability, authority and the *status quo* became so intense that suddenly it could open its heart, not merely to Europe-burglarising bandits and cop-bashing harlequins, but to an entire clutch of Gentleman Terrorists.

What could follow that—except (perhaps significantly) the First World War?

CHAPTER THREE

In which Hugh Drummond discusses goldfish, and Carl Peterson is icky-boo

W E come now to the arrival, in 1919, of the most unpopular, in current critical circles, of all British thriller heroes: Captain Hugh Drummond, the creation of 'Sapper' (Lieut. Col. H. C. McNeile).

In at least two books about thrillers—Richard Usborne's *Clubland Heroes* (Constable, 1952) and Colin Watson's *Snobbery with Violence*, Sapper takes a beating on the grounds of his fascist proclivities. (Mr Usborne remains, in spite of everything, a Sapper fan: I somehow doubt if Mr Watson is anything of the sort.)

Although Drummond was never a fascist or anything resembling one politically, I don't think it is possible to deny his authoritarian tendencies. Or his general detestation of 'Bolshies'. Or his dislike of foreigners, especially Jews. One suspects he would have been more readily moved to violent action in defence of the Aliens Extradition Act than against it.

Nor is it exactly easy to defend the particular Drummond brand of outlawry. His Ku-Klux-Klan-type organisation despatched his enemies (who have sometimes done nothing more offensive than run a left-wing newspaper) to an uninhabited island off the west coast of Mull, which can, without much stretch of the imagination, be described as a concentration camp, though of a rather unusual variety. One Inspector McIver visits the island at the end of *The Black Gang*.

He found it occupied by fifty or sixty rabid anarchists
—the gentlemen who had so mysteriously disappeared
—who were presided over by twenty large demobilised
soldiers commanded by an ex-sergeant-major of the
Guards. The sixty frenzied anarchists, he gathered, were
running a state on communist lines, as interpreted by
the ex-sergeant-major. And the interpretation moved
even McIver to tears of laughter. It appeared that once
every three hours they were all drawn up in a row, and
the sergeant-major, with a voice like a bull, would
bellow:

'Should the ruling classes have money?'

Then they answered in unison—'No.'

'Should anyone have money?' Again they answered
'No.'

'Should everyone work for the common good for
love?' 'Yes.'

Whereat he would roar: 'Well, in this 'ere island
there ain't no ruling classes, and there ain't no money,
and there's damn little love, so go and plant more
potatoes, you lop-eared sons of Beelzebub.'

At which point the parade broke up in disorder.

(*The Black Gang*, Hodder & Stoughton)

Such passages are hardly liable to endear either
Drummond or his creator to any reader with the remotest
revolutionary sympathies. But let's put both in strict
historical perspective, as simple justice, after all, demands.

The first two Drummond books—*Bulldog Drummond*
and *The Black Gang*—were written respectively in 1919
and 1921. They were written by an officer just home from
the front line, and written primarily—as he himself might
have put it—for others of his ilk. In the mind of Sapper
as he wrote, and of his devotees as they read, was the
fresh memory of four years of blood, mud, bits of friends'
bodies hanging on barbed wire, and all the rest of what
trench warfare meant. Behind those hellish—hellish but
also, in Sapper's case, magnetically compelling—

memories, there must have stretched an idealised recollection of the golden pre-war years—and, of course, they *had* been golden for members of the officer class. What, basically, had they all been fighting for? What but Old England, respectability and the *status quo*—ironically, the very things with which the Edwardians themselves had begun to exhibit such weariness twelve years before.

Now, these things seemed to be seriously menaced. In Russia, there was the Bolshevik revolution, by any standards brutal and merciless, filling the streets with bourgeois blood. It was an unknown phenomenon, and in a sick, weak, ravaged Europe, no one could say how far, how fast it might spread. To a man of the Sapper type, what could that prospect conjure up but visions of himself, his parents, his family and all his surviving friends being bayoneted by a raving rabble? They must have been pretty vivid visions, too: coming across bayoneted corpses had been an everyday event to him when he had been at the front, only a matter of months before Drummond was first created.

In this context, and in these circumstances—and considering that they were a fictional projection of their creator's very sharp personal fears—Drummond's treatment of his enemies on that island west of Mull begins to seem astonishingly good-humoured.

But then, half of Bulldog Drummond—the half at the opposite end of the pole from the masked, Ku-Klux-Klan 'flog-those-filthy-Huns-to-within-an-inch-of-their-lives' inquisitor—*is* astonishingly good-humoured. He stems, I suspect, straight from Sapper's nostalgia for England As She Used To Be, and has direct affinities, not with any other character in crime fiction, but with all the aristocratic burblers from the comedy side of pre-1914 literature. Take away his vast beefiness—and it is immediately disscernible that he has a lot in common with Jerome K.

60

Jerome's *Three Men in a Boat* and even Martin Clifford's *Tom Merry & Co. of St. Jim's*.

Here he is, gatecrashing his way into the Inner Sanctum of Sir Bryan Johnstone, Director of the Criminal Investigation Department of Scotland Yard—an old friend, incidentally, for whom he had fagged at school:

Hugh Drummond grinned all over his face, and lifting a hand like a leg of mutton, he smote Sir Bryan on the back, to the outraged amazement of Inspector McIver.

'You priceless old bean,' boomed Hugh affably. 'I gathered from the female bird punching the what-not outside that the great brain was heaving—but, my dear old lad, I have come to report a crime....'

'Has someone stolen a goldfish?' queried Sir Bryan, with mild sarcasm.

'Great Scott! I hope not,' cried Hugh in alarm. 'Phyllis gave me complete instructions about the brutes before she toddled off. I make a noise like an ant's egg, and drop them in the sink every morning. No, old lad of the village, it is something of vast import: a stain on the escutcheon of your force. Last night— let us whisper it in Gath—I dined and further supped not wisely but too well. In fact I deeply regret to admit I became a trifle blotto not to say tanked. Of course it wouldn't have happened if Phyllis had been propping up the jolly old homestead, don't you know, but she's away in the country with the nightingales and slugs and things ...'

(*The Black Gang*)

Drummond in this mood almost echoes P. G. Wodehouse's Bertie Wooster. And if you think I was unfairly exaggerating in mentioning Tom Merry & Co., listen to this early Council of War held by Drummond and three of his gang, Toby Sinclair, Peter Darrell and the monocled Algy Longworth:

'Has it struck you fellows,' remarked Hugh, at the conclusion of lunch, 'that seated around this table are four officers who fought with some distinction and much discomfort in the recent historic struggle?'

'How beautifully you put it, old flick,' said Darrell.

'Has it further struck you fellows,' continued Hugh, 'that last night we were done down, trampled on, had for mugs by a crowd of dirty blackguards composed largely of the dregs of the universe?'

'A veritable Solomon,' said Algy, gazing at him admiringly through his eyeglass. 'I told you this morning that I detested your friends.'

'Has it still further struck you,' went on Hugh, a trifle grimly, 'that we aren't standing for it? At any rate, I'm not. It's my palaver this, you fellows, and if you like ... well, there's no call on you to remain in the game, I mean—er—'

Hugh stammers on about there being no need 'for you fellows to get roped in and all that' until:

'Well—er—' mimicked Algy, 'there's a big element of risk—er—don't you know, and I mean—er—we're sort of pledged to bung you through the window, old man, if you talk such consolidated drivel.'

(*Bulldog Drummond*, Hodder & Stoughton)

If, by any chance, Drummond's 'consolidated drivel' makes you want to heave up, then I'm afraid you're in bad company. It once had almost literally that effect on Carl Peterson, who, with his beautiful consort Irma, was resident arch-fiend of the first four Drummond novels. Towards the end of *Bulldog Drummond*, the 'first round' of their fight to the death, Peterson and Drummond encounter each other on the deck of the boat express at Boulogne. Peterson is heavily disguised, but has a trick of drumming a ceaseless tattoo with his left hand which always gives him away. Presumably on this occasion he must have been drumming it on the deck-rail. At all events, Drummond recognises him instantly, and embarks on a few pleasantries which rapidly reduce Peterson to that standard state of arch-fiends: snarling fury.

'Some day,' snarled Peterson, 'I'll—'
'Stop.' Drummond held up a protesting hand. 'Not that, my Carl—anything but that.'
'Anything but what?' said the other savagely.
'I felt it in my bones,' answered Drummond, 'that you were once more on the point of mentioning my decease. I couldn't bear it, Carl: on this beautiful morning I should burst into tears. It would be the seventeenth time that that sad event has been alluded to by either you or our Henry,[1] and I'm reluctantly beginning to think that you'll have to hire an assassin, and take lessons from him.' He looked thoughtfully at the other, and an unholy joy began to dawn on his face. 'I see you have thrown away your cigar, Carl. May I offer you another? ... No? But why so brusque? Can it be—oh, no! surely not—can it be that my little pet is feeling icky-boo?'

A few minutes later, Drummond's friends find him 'leaning by himself against the rail, still laughing weakly'.

'I ask no more of life,' he remarked when he could speak. 'Anything else that may come will be an anti-climax.'
'What's happened?' asked Jerningham.
'It's happening,' said Drummond joyfully. 'It couldn't possibly be over yet. Peterson, our one and only Carl, has been overcome by the waves. And when he's feeling better, I'll take him a piece of crackling ...' Once again he gave way to unrestrained mirth, which finally

---

[1] Peterson's sidekick in this particular story, Henry Lakington —the man who dissolved bodies, clothes and all, in an acid bath, and was finally pushed into the bath himself.

subsided sufficiently to allow him to stagger below and feed.

This, then, was the sunny side of Bulldog Drummond. Just to balance it, here is a glimpse of the grim Hugh—in an account of his time in the trenches, before his crime adventures began.

And there would be nights in No Man's Land when his men would hear strange sounds, and knowing that Drummond was abroad in his wanderings, would peer eagerly over the parapet into the desolate torn-up waste in front. But they never saw anything, even when the green ghostly flares went hissing up into the darkness and the shadows danced fantastically. All was silent and still; the sudden shrill whisper was never repeated.

Perhaps a patrol coming back would report a German, lying huddled in a shellhole, with no trace of a wound, but only a broken neck; perhaps the patrol never found anything. But whatever the report, Hugh Drummond only grinned and saw to his men's breakfast. Which is why there are in England today quite a number of civilians who acknowledge only two leaders —the King and Hugh Drummond. And they would willingly die for either.

(*Bulldog Drummond*)

'The King and Hugh Drummond.' It sounds like a solemn toast at the end of a ceremonial occasion, or perhaps a bit from a speech out of Noël Coward's *Cavalcade* Try to replace Drummond's name in it with that of almost any of the characters mentioned earlier—try to say 'The King and A. J. Raffles', 'The King and Flambeau', 'The King and the Four Just Men'—and you will appreciate what a very big change had come over the outlaw hero since 1914.

He had been created by, and in answer to, the demands of first the *fin de siècle* and then the Edwardian public—

64

publics jaded by respectability and increasingly (if sub-consciously) needing the titillation of forbidden waters: a sprinkling, if no more than that, of what we should nowadays call anti-social thoughts and actions.

In the aftermath of the First World War, though, these demands were completely reversed. Four years of slaughter, plus the spectacle of the Bolshevik bloodbath and mass unrest at home, meant that thriller readers now wanted, above everything, a 'sound-chap' hero—if possible, one rousingly reminiscent of the safe, glorious, golden Old England they thought they used to know.

Bulldog Drummond, himself, as I have suggested, a creation of those self-same emotional pressures, came like a miraculous multiple answer to every aspect of his public's needs. He was an outlaw, but basked in Establishment approval: so much so that, even when his past activities were fully known, he was still *persona grata* in the Inner Sanctums of Whitehall. He was a worshipped leader of the type of men his readers most admired (straight-from-the-front Army officers in 1919 must have been much what ex-Battle-of-Britain pilots were in 1945). He was a formidable—indeed, a satisfyingly savage—enemy of the forces his readers most feared. He was a gentleman, a member of pretty good clubs and a sportsman.

And on top of all that he was a priceless old bean.

CHAPTER FOUR

In which Blackshirt becomes a gentleman, and hears a little too much from a lady

WHATEVER reservations one may have about Sapper's politics, class attitudes, chauvinism and so on, one thing it is impossible to deny: the extraordinarily strong influence his Bulldog Drummond had on the development of the British thriller between the wars.

It was an influence, curiously enough, that was long-term rather than short. The basic myth which Drummond enshrined—the myth of a huge, genial Englishman fighting his way out of trouble with his bare fists, and forever foxing his enemies by talking affable gibberish which they, being humourless foreigners, couldn't begin to appreciate—was to have an irresistible appeal to what might be called the 1930s wave of thriller writers. From around 1927, and right on through the 1930s, thrillers in the Sapper tradition became ten a penny (or, to be absolutely accurate, one for 3*d* a week) at every circulating library. Sometimes the Bulldog touch showed itself in the physical characteristics of the hero: hulking great characters with Charles Atlas torsos, hamlike fists and 'brains-were-never-my-strong-point-old-man' grins chased slimy neo-Petersons all over Europe. As often, the tendency showed itself in the dialogue. Gradually the Jocular Hero became virtually essential to any action thriller, with results that sometimes varied from the melancholy to the disastrous, since Sapper's line of amiable burbling, by no means always scintillating in itself, becomes instantly leaden in the hands of a humourless imitator.

These developments, though, are still the better part of a decade away. In the early twenties, Sapper was just one of the stars in a spectacular thriller scene glittering with magic names, many of which had been well established even before the war. This was the era of John Buchan, E. Phillips Oppenheim, Dornford Yates and above all Edgar Wallace. Many of these names, like Sapper's, were most frequently to be seen on the backs of Hodder & Stoughton Yellow Jackets—the ubiquitous hardback library that became far and away the most familiar series of all to the between-the-wars thriller fan.

Most of these writers were meeting, in one way or another, the general demand for 'sound-chap' heroes; for safe, and safely Establishment-orientated, fictional worlds. Were you unhappy about the state of the Empire, uneasy about Britain's place on the post-war scene? Then John Buchan was ready to whisper at your elbow that Things Were Not As Bad As They Seemed; strong, masterful men were secretly seeing to it that affairs were settled in the old country's favour, after all. But they were doing it in quiet Club smoking-rooms, or very likely on some Highland grouse moor, well out of sight of the common man, who was not equipped to grasp these things. Identify with a Buchan character—a Hannay or a Sir Edward Leithen—and for the space of a book you emphatically ceased to be a common man yourself. Buchan's heroes were always known and respected in the best Government circles from Montreal to Calcutta— everywhere, in fact, that the Game (as the Buchan school tended to call espionage) was played.

But perhaps your anxieties were personal rather than global. Perhaps what bothered you was the size of your overdraft; the sheer impossibility of making ends meet in a world where, as the twenties wore on, deflation was becoming increasingly rampant. In that case, E. Phillips Oppenheim was on hand to transport you to Monte Carlo, to turn you loose and let you lose yourself amongst the millionaire yacht set. Oppenheim did not always provide a 'sound-chap' hero as such; his Michael Sayers in *Michael's Evil Deeds* (1924) was a thoroughgoing swindler and *Aaron Rod, Diviner* (1920) was very little better; but financial juggling was one form of outlawry that did not deeply offend the 1918–25 public. Everybody's money seemed to be draining away like water down a plughole, and most people suspected that obscure international syndicates, directed of course from the decks of foreign millionaires' yachts, were at the back of it somewhere. The thought of an English sportsman sauntering around those decks, elegantly scoring off these millionaires by a bit of barely graspable fiscal roguery, was a not unwelcome distraction from the grocery bills.

On the other hand, perhaps you weren't quite so hard up as to need extreme opulence as a palliative. Perhaps your annoyances were social; a cousin who had married into the County and cut you off her Christmas-card list as a consequence, or something like that. In that case, a dose of Dornford Yates was the obvious prescription. Yates (real name, Major Mercer) considered himself, not unreasonably, to be a writer in the direct Anthony Hope tradition. When he wasn't writing the Berry books—humorous novels along the lines of Hope's *Dolly Dialogues*—he specialised in English landed-gentry adventurers who lived in houses with names like White Ladies, and whose Ruritanian exploits in remote Continental châteaux he described in positively Biblical prose. ('Night came upon us soon after eight o'clock, but a fine moon was westering, and two and a half hours later we entered Austria.') It is only right to add that he was an extraordinarily cunning storyteller, and could hold you spellbound for 100 pages with a largely technical description of how four men, hampered by a gang of criminals, succeed in getting a hoard of bullion out of a deep well.

68

(*Blind Corner*.) Snob appeal was by no means the whole secret of a writer with the craftsmanship to bring off a feat like that.

That it was *part* of Dornford Yates's secret, though, is undeniable, just as it is undeniable that all the above writers succeeded partly because they were supplying the economically beleaguered middle and upper classes with compensatory dream-worlds. There is far more fussing about gentility in Oppenheim, Sapper and Yates than there was in Chesterton, Leblanc or even Hornung, and the picture that emerges is one of an extraordinarily class-preoccupied thriller readership. But isn't this a distorted picture? Weren't there any readers who were a bit exasperated by all this society stuff, and who wanted, not to escape into high life, but just to get some relief from the exceptionally worrying daily grind?

The evidence suggests that there was, indeed, a great and growing army of such readers, and one thriller writer, Edgar Wallace, made (and incidentally lost) a whole series of fortunes catering for it.

We last met Wallace back in 1905, startling and titillating the bored Edwardians with his darkly rebellious *Four Just Men*. He became a very different writer with the approach of the War years, and achieved a major success with Sanders of the River, a Kiplingesque carrier of the White Man's Burden. From then right on until his death in 1932, Wallace turned himself into the greatest one-man thriller-factory the world had ever known. His books—177 in all, not counting numerous plays and such celebrated screenplays as *King Kong*—take us into a fabulous fantasy world, summed up by Margaret Lane in her biography (*Edgar Wallace*, Hamish Hamilton) as a world

of impossibly clever criminals who assume a hundred different disguises and slip like quicksilver through

69

the fingers of Scotland Yard; a world in which Things and Terrors alarmingly abound, gibbering in secret rooms and rattling their chains, performing terrible murders between-whiles at the bidding of a master-mind and driving off with cackles of fiendish laughter in high-powered cars.

Miss Lane adds:

There are comforting figures, of course, in this fantasy world, for the hero is always brave, humorous and resourceful, just the thing for the heroine, and there is a sprinkling of Cockney criminals whose hearts are frequently in the right place even if their fingers are slippery ...

It would be hard to call *that* a class-ridden or Establishment-orientated world.

Wallace's heroes are, in fact, a very mixed bunch indeed. Apart from Sanders and the Just Men, they include the Cockney tipster Educated Evans, and the mild, side-whiskered Mr J. G. Reeder of the Public Prosecutor's Office, a character who has moments (in *Terror Keep*, for example) when he becomes as authoritatively perceptive as Holmes himself. Wallace's experience as a crime reporter enabled him to create far more convincing policemen than most of his readers had met before. The most notable of them, perhaps, are O. Rater and the quarrelsome 'Sooper'. But the typical Wallace hero is a one-book-only character, usually a likeable young detective whose name you've forgotten ten minutes after the book is back at the library. So nondescript is he that you almost have the impression that you have been on the scene in his place, beating the 'impossibly clever criminal' yourself.

There, I suspect, we have the real clue to Edgar Wallace's success. He became the most popular of all the thriller writers of the 1920s because he supplied heroes with whom anybody, in any walk of life, could comfortably identify. It was an extraordinarily skilful performance, akin to a cautiously egalitarian landlord slyly removing the partition between the saloon and public bars at around 9.30 p.m., when his patrons were too merry to notice that they were mingling. Fans of the Sapper–Buchan–Yates thrillers took no exception to Wallace: they were conditioned to recognise a 'rattling good yarn' when they saw one. Moreover, wasn't Wallace the creator of Sanders of the River, almost the Soundest Chap of all? On the other hand, readers who disliked a strong class element found Wallace's mixed world refreshingly congenial.

Wallace's own attitude to class was ambivalent. In *The Northing Tramp*, his celebrated love-across-the-class-barriers classic, he rather weakly makes his tramp hero turn out to be the son of a lord at the end. In another novel, *The Lady of Ascot*, he allows a character to argue passionately that becoming a lady or a gentleman is just a matter of education—'education and surroundings'—but he does not question that it is intrinsically highly desirable to *be* a lady or a gentleman. Despite this, throughout Wallace's books, the working class are described with a warmth and a freedom from facetious condescension all too rarely to be found elsewhere.

The anarchic streak which had showed itself with such startling clarity in *The Four Just Men* is now under pretty firm control. Wallace was greatly fascinated by the *minutiae* of criminal activities, and sometimes these activities are described with a suspicious relish, almost approaching glee—but on the whole the nineteen-twenties Wallace was a well-behaved citizen, firmly labelling crime as evil and criminals as wicked. The Just Men themselves were reduced to three, and considerably tamed. ('The Three Just Men', comments the Assistant Commissioner in *Again the Three*, 'have become so respectable that now we give them police protection.')

71

Respectability, indeed, had come to prevail almost everywhere on the thriller scene. Chesterton, literally for Heaven's sake, had long ago turned Flambeau into a private detective. Sapper himself, after one book, disbanded the Black Gang, closed down that controversial establishment on the island west of Mull, and brought Drummond & Co. into such close cahoots with the police that from thenceforward they and the Yard were almost (as Algy Longworth might have put it) 'twin souls, old fruit'. The outlaw hero, in fact, was in considerable danger of being outlawed by a public which had become fantastically *preservationist*, as though every member of it, whatever his class, was struggling to preserve appearances, to preserve his job, to preserve his way of life, to preserve that *status quo* that seemed to become shakier every day. Mr Smeeth, the clerk in J. B. Priestley's *Angel Pavement*, always seems to me the archtype of nineteen twenties man:

> They could easily see him as a drab ageing fellow forever toiling away at figures of no importance, as a creature of the little foggy City street ... Nevertheless, he was not a grey drudge. He did not toil on hopelessly. On the contrary, his days at the office were filled with important and exciting events, all the more important and exciting because they were there in the light, for just behind them, all round them, was the darkness in which lurked the one great fear, the fear that one day he might take part no longer in these events, that he might lose his job ...
>
> (*Angel Pavement*, Heinemann)

The last thing the Mr Smeeths of this world require is a hero who will rock the boat. Unless, of course, it is made crystal clear that it is the yacht of some bloated foreign millionaire.

No circumstances, though, can repress the thriller public's basic love of daredevilry for very long. We have only to wait five short years after the end of World War I to find a major attempt being made to revive the gentleman cracksman hero in the person of Richard Verrell, alias Blackshirt. It is rather an odd attempt, though: a contradictory urge to remain law-abiding is present in the first set of Blackshirt stories throughout. Indeed, it interrupts them—literally—in the form of a rarely silent telephone, with very fascinating results.

Blackshirt was the first novel of a young literary agent, Bruce Graeme. In 1922, Graeme was in the office of the publisher, T. Fisher Unwin. (The same Mr Fisher Unwin who had once advised Somerset Maugham that 'writing was a very good walking-stick, but a very poor crutch' and subsequently demonstrated this truth by paying him a miniscule sum for *Liza of Lambeth*.) The Unwin editor, A. D. Marks, told Graeme that they were proposing to create a new line of novels to sell at three shillings and sixpence, and that at the moment they were looking for 'a really first-rate story' to launch the line. On a sudden impulse, Graeme asked if they would mind if he tried to write a book to fill the bill himself. 'Good Lord, no,' Marks said. 'We don't mind where it comes from, or who writes it, as long as it is what we are looking for.'

The following day Graeme started a book, about a man with an evil face, called 'Eyes of Hell'. He finished it, submitted it, and found himself being interviewed by a reader who told him, bluntly, that the 'Eyes' did not have it, but that nonetheless the manuscript showed merit. Would he care to try again?

A few months later, Graeme was relaxing in the garden late one evening, after a hard day's work. He writes: 'I was joined by my mother. As she came across the lawn, I did not hear her. Neither did I see her until she was practically upon me. Because she was still wearing black

73

only her face and hands were vaguely visible. At that moment it occurred to me how difficult it would be to see a man in the dark if he were wearing black clothes, black gloves and a hood of black material over his head to conceal every vestige of flesh. Yes, I thought, but what about his shirt? That would betray his presence, wouldn't it? But suppose his shirt were also black. Imagine a criminal—no, a gentleman cracksman after the style of my favourite character Raffles—dressed in black and working on his own. What could he not get up to, particularly if he were an athlete? Why shouldn't I write a story about—about—what should I call my character? Something short, easily remembered, like Raffles. The name of Verrell flashed into my thoughts. That was a good short name, and comparatively rare. And suppose he masked his criminal activities by writing books? An author? That was the answer. But what would the underworld call this unknown cracksman? Blackshirt. That was it. BLACKSHIRT. I would make a start on a story about Blackshirt the very next day ...'

He wrote a 10,000-word story, which was taken by the *New Magazine*, a Cassell publication; and the editor, Harold Winbury, liked it so much that he commissioned seven more. With the first two already in print, Graeme returned to Unwins. Within a week, A. D. Marks rang him to say that they had picked *Blackshirt* for the long-sought launch-novel for their 3/6 series.

It was a good choice. *Blackshirt* came out as a book in 1925, was reprinted within a few weeks, and continually reprinted from then onwards right up to 1939. Its total sales approximate 1,000,000, and a further 1,000,000 copies have been sold of the immediate sequel, *The Return of Blackshirt*.

In the light of the accusations of fascism made against Bulldog Drummond, it is, perhaps, important to stress that there was no connection whatsoever between Black-

74

shirt and the Mosleyites. Graeme evolved his hero in 1923, when Mosley was still an enthusiastic Labour M.P. Insofar as the name had any political implications at all, it was a jocular reference to the earliest followers of Mussolini. Il Duce had come to power a year before, in 1922, and was still thought of as a likeable Itie who stood for law and order. Blackshirt (or, to give him his real name, Richard Verrell) was to be the very opposite: the ultimate enemy of law and order, the thoroughgoing Gentleman Cracksman, the A. J. Raffles of the nineteen twenties.

In fact, as we shall see, he is so much of the nineteen twenties that he is really nothing like Raffles at all. The fascinating but alarming coldness of the original A. J.— who in his first few moments in print watches Bunny's suicide bid with 'pleased expectancy'—is completely absent. The first time we meet Richard Verrell, we are warmed rather than chilled:

> Sitting there in his chair, with the flickering reflection of the firelight playing on his features, his frank, open countenance betrayed no signs of his secret, which he kept hidden from the world. It was a pleasing characterisation, one chiefly of virile manhood, of integrity, of trust ...

It is true that his eyes make one blink a bit. They are suggestive less of virile manhood than of virulent manic depression.

> One minute they could be hilarious with merriment, the next mistily on the verge of tears. When angry they assumed a steel-like hardness; when gazing at a woman they were full of unspoken love and passion. Above all, they created an impression of honest uprightness. Perhaps they were lying eyes, for was he not a criminal, outside the pale of the law? Was he not—a thief? Yet

in a way they did not lie, for the soul of Verrell was as straight as his eyes gave him the credit.

This straightness of soul, Graeme goes on, is evidenced by the fact that Blackshirt 'played the game for the love of it and not for profit or gain.' In the morality stakes, then, he has already got Raffles and Lupin beaten at the post. Moreover, he is so scrupulous that he has never been known to carry a gun, and so sartorially sensitive that he not only wears an evening suit on all his escapades, complete with black hood, black silk gloves, black shoes, black socks and, of course, black shirt, but he also has a special pocket in his coat from which he can 'spring out' an opera hat, to be set rakishly on his head as, a 'gentleman of the world' again, he sets out for home. This jauntiness is deceptive: he is not always carefree, by any means. He is particularly prone to agonising reflections on his boyhood, which appears to have resembled Oliver Twist's.

In these reflective moods, he lives again 'the moment when he had been lost in a maze of streets, parted from parents of whom he had no memory'. He glimpses himself 'shrinking into the shadows sick with fear; a hairy hand gripping his shoulders till he shrieks with pain'. (He was adopted by two 'drunken, cringing sycophants' from the depths of the criminal underworld.) Through 'a hazy recollection of lessons and more lessons, of scaling walls, of slipping window-catches' he pictures himself growing taller and stronger, until the day arrives when his 'finely keyed intelligence' becomes aware that he is 'ignorant, uneducated and uncouth'. His foster-parents having been killed in a timely accident, he embarks on 'years of study, with interludes of thrills and more excitement' until at last 'the slum-bred grub' emerges into 'the polished, educated gentleman of the West End'. It almost looks as though a major desperado has arrived who originated from the lower orders, but the sentence ends with the carefully ambivalent: '... perhaps, for all he knew, the ultimate position to which he had been predestined by birth'.

We come now to the all-important telephone moment. It occurs half-way through the first episode, and turns the story from a fairly conventional yarn about a cracksman hero into something unique; not so much a study of super-cracksmanship as of supreme masculine gallantry. (Or abject male humiliation, if you decline to take a romantic view.)

Verrell has returned home from an exploit in which he has disguised himself as one Sir Allan Dunn, and helped himself to a string of pearls intended as a coming-of-age present for Sir Allen's daughter Bobbie. He takes hold of the pearls and plays with them lovingly, a 'tiny smile of contentment' chasing itself 'up and down his face and into his eyes'. He then embarks, typically, on one of his soul-searching reveries ('the one thing that marred his life was that he knew not who he was' etc.) but is interrupted by the raucous ringing of the telephone.

He lifts the receiver. A woman's voice with 'just the slightest tinge of a nasal intonation' says: 'Hullo. Is that Blackshirt speaking?'

His eyes stared at the instrument in horror, and the blood slowly receded from his face ... At last—after all these years—his identity was discovered—and by a woman!

He is so shaken that he replies with what must surely be the oddest bit of repartee in light literature.

'No, this is not Mr Backsheesh speaking.'
There was a ringing little laugh at the other end.
'Very clever! Mr Blackshirt, very clever! but you mistake me; I am not out for blackmail.'

The lady is not, however, exactly undemanding. Unless the pearls are back in Sir Allen Dunn's home by nine the following morning, 'Scotland Yard will hear from an anonymous source that Richard Verrell and Blackshirt are the same. Goodnight, Mr Blackshirt!'

Dazed, as well he might be, by such inexplicable omniscience, Blackshirt spends the rest of the episode dutifully returning the stolen pearls. The moment he is back in the flat, the phone rings again.

'Thank you, Blackshirt. It was sweet of you to put the pearls back as I suggested.'

'Suggested!' Blackshirt smiled wryly.

Note that he is not in the least angry. And—

When, later on, he laid his head on his pillow and gradually dozed into slumber, he tried hard to make himself dislike the unknown partner in his cherished secret, but in this he was unsuccessful.

It was only the sound of her voice of which he could think.

Some of his thoughts on that subject are worth recording. From that nasal intonation, he concludes that 'she might belong to the nation which undoubtedly owns the prettiest female speaking voices in the world—the United States of America'. He decides that 'it was a voice which he would have had his Ideal Woman possess'. He begins to regret 'the intervening distance between the two receivers'. And by the time she rings again—in the middle of Episode 2—he is already thinking of her as 'his Lady of the Phone' and dignifying the personal pronoun in her honour with a Rider Haggard-style capital.

Who was She? Where was She? What was She like? Was She as beautiful as he had imagined her to be?

Very much more interesting, from our point of view, is the question of what She is up to. Although before long she has Verrell deciding to return stolen rings and necklaces wholesale, the second episode makes it clear that her purpose is not just to put Blackshirt out of business.

In this chapter, we meet one Ronald McTavish, the arrogant head of the McTavish Steel Works, who has equipped his home with a multitude of electric anti-burglary devices, and who boasts to Verrell (during Ladies' Night at the Junior Arts Club) that he will send a thousand pounds to any hospital if that 'good-for-nothing crook' Blackshirt succeeds in robbing him.

Verrell has no intention of taking up this challenge.

'Undoubtedly Blackshirt would meet his match in you, Mr McTavish,' he says politely, flicking the ash off his cigarette.

But the Lady of the Phone has other ideas.

'You see, Mr Verrell, I am awfully interested in London hospitals and it would please me so very, very much if one had a cheque for a thousand pounds sent to it. You're surely not frightened of a few electrical devices, are you?'

His goddess, his commander-in-chief, is suddenly head temptress too. Later in the book,[1] she turns positively vicious. Verrell, the most susceptible of heroes, falls in love with Bobbie, the girl whose 21st birthday present he had stolen and returned back in Episode 1. He rashly describes her to the Lady of the Phone as being 'as beautiful as Aphrodite, as shapely as Venus, as enchanting as

---

[1] All the quotations in this section are from *Blackshirt* (Unwin, 1925). The Blackshirt novels are today published by John Long.

Helen of Troy'. Within minutes, he is being peremptorily commanded to steal Bobbie's opal ring.

> Verrell gritted his teeth ... 'I'm sorry, but I can't do it.'
> 'I regret to say, Mr Verrell, that you must.'
> There was a dangerous calm in her voice. She was cracking the whip now, and Verrell was feeling its lash.

No doubt a Freudian would have no trouble in detecting sado-masochistic elements beneath this novel. Not to mention a touch of female voyeurism at the end, when it is revealed that Bobbie and the Lady are one and the same contrary girl; that her house is within sight of Verrell's, and that with the aid of a telescope she can just see into his bedroom when the light is on. She watches him dress up in his Blackshirt rigout, and her omniscience about his activities derives partly from her habit of getting dressed herself and following him.

One would have thought that this telescope-trained-on-a-bedroom-window bit would have shocked the 1920s public rigid. But such things didn't bother them half as much as, for example, the thought of premature profanity.

> 'So now you know how I found you out.'
> 'Well, I'll be—'
> She placed a warning finger on his lips. 'Hush, dear. You haven't known me long enough yet to swear in front of me!'
> 'I'm sorry,' he muttered apologetically.

There are times, admittedly, when Blackshirt's gallantry seems a mite servile. But on any long-term view, how right he was to treat his Lady with such respect! From this distance, with or without a telescope, she looks remarkably like an instrument of Destiny, or at least, a numinous personification of the *Zeitgeist*. Her influence changed Blackshirt from a fastidious, but still unfashionably amoral, Raffles into a romantic, right-living society Robin Hood—the one type of desperado hero which the 1920s reading public, much of it mesmerised by top hats and Mayfair trappings, all of it strait-laced by its own sense of insecurity, was ready and willing to welcome.

Nor was it just a passport to immediate popularity that the Lady of the Phone handed out. Along with it must have gone an *elixir de vie*. Born 1923/5, yet still appearing in new novels right to the end of the nineteen sixties, old straight-souled Verrell is a powerful contender for the supreme accolade.

I am open to correction, but as far as my researches go, he is the most durable desperado of them all.

CHAPTER FIVE

In which the horizon is scanned for pirates, and Sexton Blake has cause to wonder

A L O T of the elements which made the Gentleman Outlaw what he was have now been traced to their sources. From Robin Hood, across eight centuries, came the noble bandit idea. From E. W. Hornung came the basic concept of an amateur cracksman. From Maurice Leblanc and his Arsène Lupin came the element of authoritative audacity. From Bulldog Drummond came the muscularity and the genial repartee. With Blackshirt came the beginning of a return to the straight Robin Hood ethic, and certainly a heightening of the romance.

But one or two pieces are still needed to complete the picture. The Gentleman Outlaws, as I remember them, had a certain air—of mischief, of bravado, of lounging piratical nonchalance—which is lacking in the specimens we have examined so far. Raffles had it at some moments, but emphatically not at others. Lupin, with his army of operatives in all classes and seemingly in every town and village in France, was less mischievous than magisterial. Drummond comes closest to being the actual founder of the feast: certainly there was hardly a writer in the Gentleman Outlaw *genre* who didn't help himself to crumbs by the fistful from the Sapper table. But, as we have seen, Drummond almost vied with Hannay at being a supporter, almost a secret arm, of the Establishment, and so really rules himself out as a desperado. And Blackshirt, under the deep enchantment of his Lady of the Phone, never had a chance to be a reckless buccaneer.

Locating the real point at which this buccaneer element came in is by no means a straightforward task. Some account must be taken of cross-fertilisation with other *genres*, particularly historical romance. Rafael Sabatini and Baroness Orczy were both big influences in the twenties; Sabatini was even regarded in some circles as a classic. Leslie Charteris, who was eighteen in 1925, remembers how his boyhood was spent reading *Chums* magazine stories, and then adds, significantly: 'They were a good introduction to the classics we would come on to in adolescence, from Henty to Sabatini, from Haggard to Sax Rohmer.'[1] (John Creasey, incidentally, who was seventeen in the same year, remembers mostly Oppenheim, William le Queux, Herbert Strang, Henty and Edgar Wallace. There was never much of a Sabatini influence there.)

The situation in the middle twenties can, perhaps, be roughly summed up like this. A love of law and order reigned supreme on almost all thriller frontiers, but the intense post-war demand for respectable heroes—sound chaps as distinct from daredevils, bandits, *boat-rockers*— was definitely abating. Edgar Wallace was describing underworld goings-on with growing zest, both in his novels and on the stage. Partly chivalrous villains proliferated—this was the peak period, for example, of Sax Rohmer's Fu Manchu. Blackshirt had demonstrated that, as long as the Robin Hood element was played up and the lawlessness played down, there was now a public again for a major outlaw hero. Meanwhile, partly through books and partly through the cinema, the imaginations of thousands of people—teenagers especially—were being fired by Scarlet Pimpernels, Captain Bloods, Scaramouches and the whole business of swashbuckling. As

[1] Introduction to *The Men Behind Boys' Fiction* by W. O. G. Lofts and D. J. Adley.

a result, something altogether wilder, more hell-for-leather in outlaw heroes was, so to speak, lurking beneath the water, knife clenched between his teeth, only waiting for the opportunity to break surface.

But, for a long time, he had already had a nose above water in one area: that highly coloured, human-shark-infested region which we have gingerly explored already, but which we must hastily hoist sail and head for once again. The world of Fleetway House and Sexton Blake.

Blake was no longer the only Amalgamated Press detective. For a decade or more, he had had a rival on his home ground, one Nelson Lee; and more recently, up in Edinburgh, another publishing house, D. C. Thomson, had launched one Dixon Hawke. In conception, at least, Blake, Hawke and Lee were interchangeable. Each had consulting-rooms in London—Blake in Baker St, Lee in Gray's Inn Road, Hawke in Dover St. Each had a boy assistant—Blake's was called Tinker, Lee's Nipper, and Hawke's Tommy Burke. Each had his own list of arch-villains. For some reason, Lee's adversaries tended to be geometrically grouped organisations such as the Green Triangle and the Circle of Terror. Perhaps under their influence, Lee's career suddenly went off at a tangent. In 1917, he became a housemaster at a boys' school called St Frank's, and every week until August 1933 a 20,000 word adventure appeared in which Lee, assisted by Nipper and more than a hundred named schoolboys, fought various arch-villains who, for a whole variety of odd reasons, assailed the old school.

20,000 words a week for sixteen years—creating, in the process, an entire imaginary public school, with every boy in every study in every house named and characterised—is, you would have thought, a task for a sizeable team of writers. In St Frank's case, until the very last years, it was the work of one man: Edwy Searles Brooks.

Brooks, born in Hackney in 1889, was the son of a Congregational minister who had been a well-known contributor to *The Times*. He began writing himself in 1907 and, according to his son Lionel, never earned a penny all his life by any means other than turning out stories. His career—it's here in detail in front of me, in a complete bibliography recently compiled by Robert Blythe, co-founder of the Old Boys' Book Club—is a quite extraordinary example of how torrentially prolific a star Fleetway House writer could be. In those sixteen years between 1917 and 1933, Brooks wrote nine hundred 20,000-word adventures for the Nelson Lee Library, a little matter of eighteen million words. This is getting on for half as much again as Edgar Wallace wrote in his entire crime-fiction career, and it's still only a fraction of Brooks's total output. On the side, during roughly the same period, he wrote over a million and a half words for the *Gem* and the *Magnet*. (Brooks stories about Harry Wharton & Co. of Greyfriars and Tom Merry & Co. of St Jim's were dropped in whenever Charles Hamilton was indisposed, and the famous Hamilton *noms de plume*, Frank Richards and Martin Clifford, were used to sign them. In his autobiography, Hamilton states how violently he objected to this practice, and who could blame him?) In addition to all this, Brooks is on record as having written twenty-six Dixon Hawke books for D. C. Thomson (there's another half million words there); countless stories for other boys' papers, ranging from the *Buzzer* to a hopefully titled journal called *Cheer, Boys, Cheer*; and seventy-six 28,000-word Sexton Blake adventures for *Union Jack*.

In his later life, as we shall be seeing, he wrote over sixty crime novels. I asked Mr Blythe, who is undoubtedly the world's highest authority on the subject, if he would estimate Brooks's total literary output. He came up with the staggering total of 36,135,000 published words—

which I believe makes Brooks, after John Creasey, the most prolific author known.

Since his death in 1965, he has become something of a cult figure amongst old boys' paper collectors. Many of them consider his school stories superior to Hamilton's, and copies of the *Nelson Lee Library* are getting to be as highly prized as *Magnets* and *Gems*. It isn't hard to see why. The long years of being intrepid in the face of multitudinous arch-fiends gave the St Frank's boys a truly majestic spirit of independence. They stand absolutely no nonsense from anyone. When a birch-happy headmaster comes to rule over the school (in *The Barring-Out At St Frank's*, republished 1972 by the Howard Baker Press) you feel sorry for *him*, not the boys.

Just as he was vanishing through the doorway, he was seized and pulled roughly back. His gown was torn, his mortar-board knocked off, and he was hustled forcibly into the centre of the platform.

'Boys—boys,' he gasped hoarsely. 'You—you must control yourselves! Do you realise that I am your headmaster—'

'We realise that you're a cad and a brute!' shouted Chambers. 'We don't care a snap for you any longer, Mr Martin, and we're going to give you a sample of your own brand of medicine.'

'We'll birch the beast until he can't stand!'

'Good!'

'Hold him over the table!'

'Hurrah!'

Even the enemy's complete capitulation does not incline St Frank's to mercy.

'Boys,' panted the Head. 'I-I will agree to all your terms! If you release me, I will go so far as to allow the Remove to resume its duties—Ow! Yarooh! Ow! Good heavens! Ow! Yow!'

It isn't surprising that Billy Bunter's stunts seem tame after such red-blooded rebel fare.

But, as far as this study is concerned, Edwy Searles Brooks's major achievement had little to do with St Frank's, except that it was powered by the same driving gusto that was simultaneously producing all those millions of words about japes and jollities in the Remove. It was the creation of a new kind of villain for Sexton Blake: an exuberant character called Waldo the Wonder Man who, to begin with, was not only impervious to pain but resistant to bullets, and on that account earned a living as a circus performer.

On his first appearance (in the *Union Jack* of 28 December 1918) Waldo is not only a villain, but a distinctly revolting one. Here is a moment from the account of his first arrest, given us by Nelson Lee's assistant Nipper. (This episode, by the way, is a rare instance of Sexton Blake, Tinker, Nelson Lee and Nipper all working on the same case.)

When the constable came up Lee advised them to bind Waldo's ankles with extra stout bonds. Not until this was done did Lee release his grip.

And then Waldo gave a short laugh.

'Well, I had a good run so I mustn't grumble,' he said suddenly. 'I think you hit me with a bullet, didn't you? I felt a slight jar, I believe ...'

'A jar?' I gasped. 'Oh, my hat!'

Waldo was actually bending round and rubbing the bullet wound—actually rubbing it! His forearms were blistered and burnt—scorched horribly! He ought to have been writhing in agony. But yet he picked at his burns, tearing away the burnt skin in the most ghastly fashion. And he smiled all the time ...

Fortunately for the squeamish, Waldo lost some of his phenomenal properties after a while, but by no means all of them. It was never anything to him to leap about on girders or scaffolding, even when burdened by a corpse on his back. In one much later story, while posing as a wicked lord, he allows himself to be lynched by a mob of outraged villagers, and hardly feels the rope at all. Blake and Tinker, arriving on the scene belatedly, find the crowd gone and the 'lord's' body hanging from a tree. They are about to cut it down, when—

'Don't bother!' said the corpse. 'I'll save you the trouble.'

The apparently lifeless hands went upwards to the neck, and to the amazement of Blake and Tinker the noose was pulled off with ridiculous ease, and the 'corpse' slipped its head free. Then, as springily as a trained acrobat, the figure landed on the soft turf.

'You would come and mess everything up,' said a disgusted voice.

'Great guns! Waldo!' breathed Tinker.

'I might have known it,' said Blake, the relief in his voice very apparent. 'Upon my word, Waldo, what a fellow you are for springing sensational surprises....'

There was nothing Waldo liked better than springing surprises on Sexton Blake. (And on Dixon Hawke, for that matter—he appeared in that series too, under the name Marco the Miracle Man.) In time, as one can tell from Blake's friendly tone above, he had become an increasingly welcome visitor in both Baker Street and Dover Street—because the most sensational of his surprises was the fact that, at the drop of a hat (or the lifting of a noose), he could change from a new kind of villain into a new kind of hero.

Someone very like a hell-for-leather desperado.

In the world of Sexton Blake, of course, odd things

could always happen. Amongst the odd things that were happening there in this between-the-wars era, Mademoiselle Yvonne was becoming a millionairess, with a vast organisation and all the capitals of Europe as her theatre of operations—although she always wore a locket with a portrait of Sexton next to her heart. Dr Huxton Rymer, his romantic urges now under firmer control, was turning into a dabbler in high diplomacy, playing deep games with whole nations as his pawns. Other flourishing mastercriminals included George Marsden Plummer, one of the few Scotland Yard inspectors actually to turn arch-fiend, and Zenith the Albino, a thief with snowy white hair, rabbit-pink eyes and infra-red binoculars which enabled him to see through walls—especially the walls of safes.

But none of these villains had the devil-may-care mockery of Waldo, or his astonishing capacity to switch sides. Over and over again, the laughing Wonder Man appeared as Blake's friend and ally. Once, he actually acted as Blake's understudy: another time he turned so convincingly law-abiding that he somehow got to be Assistant Commissioner of Scotland Yard. In his later adventures, he took to upstaging Blake completely, even unmasking the criminal at the end of the story. ('There's your man, Sexton Blake!' must have startled readers accustomed for years and years to Blake's own 'There's your man, Inspector!')

We shall be meeting Waldo later in this study, under yet another name. The important thing at the moment is to record the astonishingly early date of his creation (several months before Drummond's) and to suggest that, with him, the Fleetway House school came many strides closer to finding a style of hero all its own.

Thanks to Mr Blythe's comprehensive Brooks bibliography, it is possible to follow Waldo's *Union Jack* career throughout the twenties. It is surely significant that the stories appear with greater and greater frequency as we approach the romantically flamboyant thirties. If one takes the growth of Waldo's popularity as an indication of the swing in public taste, then in this table one can actually *see* the Day of the Desperado dawning.

28.12.1918	Waldo the Wonder Man
25. 1.1919	The Clue of the Five Hairs
15. 3.1919	The Case of the Stacey Rubies
13.11.1920	The Mystery of the Chinese Antique
29.10.1921	In the Grip of Waldo
10.12.1921	The Wonder Man's Challenge
8. 3.1922	Rupert Waldo—Stuntist
22.12.1923	The Flaming Spectre of Cloone
31. 5.1924	The Electric Man
6.12.1924	The Leopard of Droone
6.12.1925	The Affair of the Roman Relics
13. 6.1926	The Pauper of Pengarth Castle
20. 6.1926	The Curse of Pengarth Castle
11. 7.1926	The Great Stadium Sensation
26. 2.1927	Waldo's Wonder Stunt
5. 3.1927	The Affair of the Professional Avenger
12. 3.1927	The Case of the Second Blackmailer
19. 3.1927	The Lightning Flash Mystery
21. 1.1928	The Affair of the Bronze Mirror
28. 1.1928	The Diamonds of Devil Pool
4. 2.1928	Jungle Justice
2. 2.1929	The Case of the Shrivelled Man
16. 2.1929	The Captive of the Crag
28. 9.1929	The Case of the Three Black Cats
19.10.1929	Terror by Night
26.10.1929	The Death Snare
7.12.1929	The Frozen Man Mystery

By 1929, Waldo is suddenly (after eleven years of existence) getting close to being top character on the Blake rota.

Now it was in 1929 that Fleetway House started the companion paper to *Union Jack*, *The Thriller*—virtual launching-pad of the 1930s Gentleman Outlaw *genre*. What gave them the idea? What equipped them to play so decisive a role in the whole development of the Desperado? Surely part of the answer must lie in the decade or more which Sexton Blake readers had spent in the (increasingly tightening) Grip of Waldo.

CHAPTER SIX

In which Edgar Wallace mixes in, and Ivor Novello gnaws a bone

IN 1927, something still more significant happens in the history of the Outlaw. A character flits through, briefly—just for the length of twenty short stories—and then disappears for good. You shrug, and are about to dismiss him as being of no especial importance; but then you look around and find that, as a result of his brief appearance, everything has taken on a new perspective; the horizons of the thriller world have been quietly, subtly, but quite radically, enlarged.

He was Edgar Wallace's Anthony Smith, better known as the Mixer. Accompanied by two assistants, 'the gentle Paul and the trusty Sandy', he waged a genial, virtually bloodless war on dubious tycoons, racecourse racketeers and the like. He derived more from the Oppenheim gentleman swindler than the Raffles–Lupin–Blackshirt line: finance, remember, was the one area in which it had all along been broadly acceptable for a hero to be a rogue rather than a Robin Hood. Wallace, though, took no chances. The Mixer states over and over again that he is strictly, as he puts it, a 'rascal-skinner'. ('Hasn't every gentleman I've relieved of his surplus wealth been a villain of the deepest dye?') Just for good measure, he announces, not exactly modestly, that he and Paul are both ex-war heroes—although he follows this with a revelation, rare indeed in 1920s thrillers, that even a hero's military career can end unheroically.

'Paul left hurriedly owing to the fact that he remained

seven days in town longer than his leave allowed—and
I was kicked out of the Army most ignominiously for
punching in the eye a young person who well deserved
it.'

(The Mixer, John Long Ltd)

Equally refreshing is the commercial candour of the
Anthony Smith credo, as expounded to Pony, the villain
he encounters in the first story.

'I am out to make money,' said Anthony. 'I am the
Invincible and Incomparable moneymaker, and that is
my motto. And I've discovered that the easiest way to
make money is to take it from people of your kidney
... fellows who can't squeal and who have grown rich
on robbery.'

'The Incomparable and Invincible moneymaker.' There
is surely a touch of self-portraiture by Wallace in that
line, perhaps even a hint of wry self-parody. Wallace, by
1927, *was* an Incomparable moneymaker, although (probably because of some subconscious fear of affluence) anything but an Invincible one. This was the period when
he was beginning not only to earn phenomenally but to
spend compulsively—on the racetrack, on huge personal
suites at Claridge's, on backing plays—to such effect
that on his death five years later, he owed £140,000. A
preoccupation with money runs right through the Mixer
stories, and there are lines of the 'Cashier-counted-
out-seventy-nine-thick-bundles-of-ten-pound-notes-as-if-
they-were-seventy-nine-pounds' variety which must have
driven hard-up readers half crazy.

The Mixer remains, though, a sunny book; essentially
a product of Wallace's relaxed Golden Age. The quality
of mercy is by no means so strained as it had been in
that dark outlaw story of twenty-two years earlier, *The
Four Just Men*. The Just Men angrily dealt out death to

93

anyone who disagreed with them, regardless of whether they deserved it or not. The Mixer, by contrast, is highly discriminating in his choice of rascals to skin, and even punctilious in assessing the amount of skinning each deserves. A thief called the Dandelion (selected for treatment because of his 'penchant for whacking over the head any unfortunate person who happens to surprise him') is relieved of fifty per cent of a year's takings. A crooked bookie does not get warned off the turf because that would be 'too cruel'. On the other hand, a Mr Digle, whose speciality is swindling recently widowed women, is 'cleared out, lock, stock and barrel'. And Miss Millicent K. Yonker, an American gangstress who tries to frame the Mixer, finds herself actually—if only briefly— in jail.

All in all, the Mixer is one of the mildest, most unobjectionable heroes imaginable; and it is very tempting to think of him as pretty unremarkable. It is only when you look back on him in the light of all that came later that you realise just what a cunning achievement he was on the part of the old master storyteller. Edgar Wallace had given a still semi-puritanical public a crook hero whom they couldn't fail to warm to, because he was *as morally judicious as they were*. Anthony Smith was far from being the first crook in fiction to batten off other crooks; but there cannot have been many before him who blandly set themselves up as judge and jury to the criminal fraternity at large.

What the Mixer demonstrated was that almost any reader can revel in a crime, so long as it is made clear that it is someone else's punishment. That realisation became the plank across which all the major piratical outlaws eventually strolled ashore.

The Saint. The Toff. The Baron ... Yes. It looks as though they all owe something to the mild, half-forgotten Mixer.

It even looks as though it could be something important.

Their very *raison d'être*.

The Mixer was not the only outlaw hero created by Edgar Wallace in 1927. The same year saw the appearance of Anthony Newton, alias the Brigand.

In style, *modus operandi* and even manner of speaking, the two Anthonys are virtually interchangeable. But life is rougher on Anthony Newton: at the start of *The Brigand*, we find him being turned out into the street by his landlady with barely a half-crown in his pocket. He soon overcomes this handicap, of course, but the experience leaves him just a shade more bitter than the Mixer ever was.

His reflections as he sets out to seek his fortune by 'polite brigandage'—in other words, Mixer-style rascalskinning—give us rather a startling insight into 1927:

> The crowd about the Labour Exchange, the peripatetic organ-grinders with their virtuous military records written largely in chalk, the masked singers of aristocratic origin who 'worked' the suburban thoroughfares and earned a tolerable living from the romantic, the ex-officers who now sold beautiful water-colour paintings at the corner of West End streets, the more exhilarating fellows who held up post offices at the point of formidable revolvers, all these advertised the futility of a public school training and a military career as a means of accruing easy money or acquiring a sound sense of moral values ...
>
> (*The Brigand*, Hodder & Stoughton)

Clearly, this is a world where desperation is beginning to stalk the streets. But it is gentlemanly enough to wear a mask and greet you with a chorus of 'Overhead the Moon is Beaming', and it is driving its victims not to dark thoughts of rebellion, but to blood-red visions of romance.

One other outlaw of the later twenties has considerable significance in this connection, as well as enormous curiosity value: he achieved success in the first instance in the theatre, and then on the silver—and at that time still the silent—screen.

This hero was invented and played by Ivor Novello, and he was called—the Rat. The original version of *The Rat* was written for the stage by Novello and Constance Cox, and was filmed in 1926 by Gainsborough Pictures, after Novello had had a triumphant success with it in the West End and on tour. My own acquaintance with the character comes from reading the book of a second film, *Triumph of the Rat*, dating from 1927. This book, written by Denise Robins 'from sub-titles by Roland Pertwee', gives a very vivid idea of what the Rat was like.

He was incredibly handsome, with his pale skin, his perfect, chiselled features; straight dark brows over brown brilliant eyes; fine head; smooth dark hair brushed straight back from his broad forehead.

Quite a definite advance, that, in the direction of the dark and dashing. More interesting still, he is as slum-bred as Blackshirt, but there is no talk about his being predestined by birth for a higher station. He has arrived at one purely through his personal charm.

Pierre Boucheron—under-secretary! Since he had captured the heart of the Smart Set, he had almost forgotten that he once was the Rat—an apache of the White Coffin in Montmartre.

Pierre is no great indulger in Drummondesque repartee. (You can't be, I suppose, when the dialogue has to be

96

short enough for sub-titles.) But he does have an interesting line of advice to dish out on the subject of women.

'Cheer up, my dear fellow. Try the cold shoulder. The more I show it, the warmer they become. They're queer creatures, women, but when you know how to treat them, they are very simple.'

Before long, he is up to a trick much beloved of silent-screen heroes—betting on his own amorous capabilities. Pointing to a beautiful aristocratic woman he has never met, one Madeleine de l'Orme, he says to his discarded flame, Zélie: 'Just to prove to you what a Rat can do, I wager you Madeleine de l'Orme shall be in my arms within a month from today.'

I don't have to tell you that he wins his bet, but loses his heart to the beautiful Madeleine de l'Orme. Zélie, passionately jealous for sufficient reasons (she and Pierre were, as she puts it, 'all in all to each other' until this Madeleine business) bitterly resolves to ruin Pierre by telling the world all about him. Soon Pierre has to resign from the Foreign Office, and all the Paris newspapers are carrying the awful truth—that

he is not the gentleman of birth and breeding he made out. He is, in actual fact, an apache from the Underworld, once famous as a dancer at the White Coffin in Montmartre, and a very dangerous criminal on whom the police kept a vigilant eye when he was not under lock and key.

Madeleine, exasperated by hearing a personal account from Zélie of the bet bit, turns Pierre away too. The ex-apache is quickly in a bad way, heading straight back to that gutter from which he came, the White Coffin. And Zélie's jealousy pursues him even there: she pays a detective to make it appear that the Rat has ratted on his old associates. They fling him out—and before long, he is close to starvation.

The directors of the silent-screen era didn't believe in leaving such points unstressed. Zélie, sitting in the Casino de Paris with her rich lover, Mercereau, finds her 'restless gaze wandering to the window' and is just in time to see Pierre Boucheron 'leaning against a pillar just outside the restaurant, *gnawing a bone*'. (Miss Robins's italics.)

> She wrapped her white fur cloak about her and walked out of the restaurant, her cheeks ghastly under her rouge. . . . She had to speak to Pierre . . . to tell him she was sorry. . . .

The Rat had 'finished his bone and moved away from the window'. Zélie rushes up to him, and one can imagine the sub-titles welling up through the audience's tears, as the cinema pianist went crashing into something appropriately *pathétique*—perhaps Noël Coward's 'Parisian Pierrot'.

> 'Pierre. Speak to me!'
> 'Let me go.'
> 'No, no, tell me you will forgive me. Come back with me to my flat. Let me give you food, warmth, clothes . . .'

And one can imagine the dash, or maybe asterisks, searing the screen as the Rat said: 'Get away. Leave me alone, you ————— !'

Shortly afterwards, the Rat pays a final visit to the White Coffin, getting wounded in a knife-fight with a brute named Otto. He rushes into the street, gets run over by a car, spends four months in hospital, and when he comes out, finds it's August 1914, and is just in time 'like every other son of France, to become a soldier ready to fight to the death'.

When he is on the troop train, ready to steam away to service at the front, who happens to come along 'distributing fruit and chocolate from baskets to every carriage-ful of men' but Madeleine de l'Orme? Their eyes meet. Madeleine drops the basket, and rushes to him, 'panting, cheeks on fire'. And on an 'Oh my beloved I can die gladly now that I know you do not despise me' scene, *Triumph of the Rat* ends.

It was one of the most successful films of 1927, due largely, I suspect, to the incredible Novello magnetism, impossible to convey to people who have never seen him, and equally impossible to analyse even for those who have. Leaving that factor aside, the *Triumph of the Rat*'s triumph has, surely, quite a lot to tell us about the public, and in what direction its tastes were developing now that nine years had elapsed since the War.

The middle-twenties trends noticed in the last chapter —the trends which had been reflected in Blackshirt, and which were making Waldo's popularity spiral upwards in the world of the *Union Jack*—are now more pronounced than ever. As life steadily becomes greyer—the General Strike is just over; the Depression is already developing in wide areas of the industrial North—the public is beginning to need a touch of abandon all over its entertainment. It looks as though the Mr Smeeths are too despairing to care now if a hero rocks the boat of their traditional security: the boat is obviously sinking anyway. This 1927 public, at all events, has something in common with the 1900–13 ones: a basic longing to cut a dash, to identify with a wild, slightly dangerous hero. That does not mean that it is finding the whole idea of crime enticing, as the Edwardians had begun to do. It is consciously wholly on the side of patriotism, law and order, sweetness and light, and is far from being against Society: indeed, it is exceptionally susceptible to the glamour of the sophisticated High Life. But the female part of this public is long accustomed to being swept away by Valentino-style sheiks; the men have received, often as teenagers, frequent Captain Blood transfusions, and both are fascinated by the thought of wild places like Montmartre, of unbridled bandit passions, of knives flashing in dark streets. Apache dances are all the rage, not only in West End night clubs, but as a speciality act in seaside concert parties and even in pantomimes. They are felt to symbolise romantic allure—and everyone is fast developing a taste for everything that comes under the label of 'romance'. The great Hollywood dream machine, precision-built to gratify that taste as it had never been gratified before, is sweeping into top gear, and the talkies are only two years off. Unmistakably, the flamboyantly romantic thirties are on their way—or, to put it as accurately as possible, the romantic flamboyance which is to be the gin in the thirties cocktail (a basic ingredient of the complex, bitter-sweet, fundamentally mysterious thirties mood) is now being sloshed neat into the shaker.

Putting all these factors together, it is perhaps possible to hazard a guess as to why the young thriller writers of the later twenties and early thirties instinctively turned more to Sapper as a model, even though Wallace was the king thriller writer of the time. A flamboyant age would call for big-scale heroes, and Wallace rather specialised in small-scale ones.[1] Drummond was big-scale, both in physique and in personality; and he had his darkly dangerous side—he could dispose of a woodful of enemies single-handed, given a quiet, black night. The Drummond repartee must have looked enticingly sophisticated, too;

[1] Whatever their seminal significance, the Mixer and the Brigand were essentially small-scale creations themselves. They appeared in only one book apiece, and were just two amongst fourteen widely assorted heroes featured in Edgar Wallace books that year (1927).

and sophistication was another key ingredient of the mood that was taking shape.

Obviously, a reader outside the middle classes wouldn't be able to identify with a Drummond type as readily as with, say, one of Wallace's hard-working inspectors, or amiable nondescripts; but in an age of romance, particularly with sophistication at a premium, no thriller-reader, of any class, likes to see himself in his dreams as nondescript or workaday. From 1927 onwards, the thriller public began to close ranks: even those members of it who had hitherto disliked 'Society stuff' were now increasingly ready to accept Drummondesque man-about-town heroes, and editors were increasingly liable to insist on them. (It is worth noting that on Edgar Wallace's death, five years later, his place on the bookstalls was taken partly by Sydney Horler and partly by Leslie Charteris, both of whom were far closer to the Sapper tradition than the Wallace one.)

Despite all this, a very considerable gulf remained between the massively ugly Drummond and the hero who would completely satisfy the new romantic impulses. But it only needed one young thriller writer to find a way of bridging the gap—of adding to his flippant, Sapperish world an outlaw hero with a real touch of romantic wildness—for the most explosively popular *genre* in the whole history of thrillers to be born.

It wasn't as easy a trick to pull off as it sounds, though. You could call it the literary equivalent of crossing a bulldog with a rat.

CHAPTER SEVEN

In which we meet Leslie Charteris, and the Bandit encounters a bottle

IF, aware of this change in the public mood, you had hunted around in the late 1920s for the young thriller writer most likely to create a hero to match it, the chances are you would have overlooked Leslie Charteris.

Charteris was in those days in his very early twenties. An Anglo-Chinese, the son of Dr S. C. Yin, a Singapore surgeon directly descended from the Shen Dynasty, he had come to England at the age of twelve, in 1919, and been educated first at a prep. school near Purley; then at a public school, Rossall, near Blackpool, and finally at King's College, Cambridge. While at Cambridge, he decided he wanted to become a writer—after, the story goes, reading *Trent's Last Case* and concluding that he could write a far better book himself. Fired with this ambition, he left Cambridge after a year. Dr Yin was so exasperated that parental help stopped on the spot, so that Charteris was obliged to take any job that happened to come to hand: during the General Strike, he became a bus-driver, and shortly afterwards an auxiliary policeman. According to *The Saint and Leslie Charteris* by W. O. G. Lofts and D. J. Adley (Hutchinson Library Services, 1971):

> At one stage, he even went back to Malaya, where he prospected for gold in the jungle, fished for pearls, worked in a tin mine, on a rubber plantation and on a wood distillation plant. Returning to London, he

became a bartender in a country inn, a professional bridge-player in a club, and also teamed up with a man who ran a booth in a travelling fair.

One can only blink at these particulars. It is as though a Somerset Maugham South Sea hero had got mixed up with Gaylord from *Showboat*. And a still more remarkable fact is to come. Round about this time, he adopted the name 'Charteris' by deed-poll. (He had been christened Leslie Charles Bowyer Yin. He changed it to Leslie Charles Charteris Bowyer-Ian.) In the choice of 'Charteris', Messrs Lofts and Adley say, 'the deciding factor was when he learnt of Colonel Francis Charteris, the notorious gambler, duellist, rake and founder of the Hellfire Club'.

From these details (almost all of them, incidentally, gleaned from the invaluable *Saint and Leslie Charteris*), it is not difficult to see the strange, potentially explosive mixture which the young Charteris must have been.

Take a nature deeply inclined to swashbuckling romanticism, drenched since childhood in dreams of plank-walking piracy and scuppers running with blood. (We know that Charteris's favourite childhood reading was pirate stories in *Chums*.) Steep this nature Singapore-deep in all that the Empire, and the upper-class Englishman, was supposed to mean. (There was no Imperial outpost more snobbish or more elegantly loyal than early twentieth-century Singapore.) Add a maddening sense of being, to some degree, a perennial outsider. (What else could Charteris's mixed blood have produced in the course of a long English boarding-school upbringing?) Throw in a year of Cambridge education at the peak period of 'bright young things' sophistication. Complete with a couple of years of being broke and fighting for a living in those brink-of-depression days when half the nation seemed to be broke and fighting for a living—and

103

surely you have little need to search further for the factors which made Charteris unique as a writer and a myth-creator. You can account for both his initial driving energy and his persona of lounging elegance; both his effortless grasp of all things English and his exasperation with quite a few of them, resulting in an undercurrent of derision about the British way of life in general, and the British public school in particular. Going deeper, you can even see why that derision always stopped short of out-right contempt. Clearly, Charteris was mocking an England he had been brought up, not just to admire, but to love; and a major part of him never stopped loving it. The love created the Saint: the exasperation gave a remarkably sharp edge to the Saint's repartee: and, I strongly suspect, a hidden sense of never quite belonging anywhere—except, maybe, with the swashbuckling gods of his childhood—enabled Charteris to make the Saint a romantic myth-figure powerful enough to mesmerise the English-speaking world.

Not that the Saint was Charteris's only creation. Or, curiously enough, his most important one, in his own eyes at the time. His first book, *X Esquire*, came out in 1927, the year of *The Mixer* and *The Triumph of the Rat*. Between then and 1929, he wrote thriller after thriller for Ward Lock, each with a different hero. Distinctly odd thrillers they were, with distinctly odd heroes; but they are worth a close look, because, after all, it was from this factory, after agonies of blood, sweat and changing gears, that the first working model of a full-scale Gentleman Outlaw finally appeared.

First in what you might call the prototype parade was one Terry Mannering, and you only have to hear him open his mouth ('What cheer, brothers. Great brain hummin', Bill? I could hear it all the way down the stairs') to know that we are still deep in neo-Sapper land. Here is Terry beefily greeting the narrator, Tony, and Chief

Inspector Bill Kennedy, one of the Big Four at Scotland Yard:

'Hullo, Tony, my little one!' he cried. He gripped my hand painfully. 'And there's the toy policeman.' He neatly sidestepped Bill's right and slapped him on the back....

Five minutes later, we drew up before the doors of Mannering House.

'Dress, varlets,' said Terry, as we drew off our coats in the hall.

Apparently accustomed to this type of welcome, Tony meekly goes upstairs to change. He returns to find Terry Mannering, already 'dressed in his immaculate fashion', splashing soda into a glass. 'Here's to your silly face,' he says, amongst other things. Then, having noisily slammed the library door, he proceeds to make very Drummond-like references to one of the other guests, a wealthy Jew who, he suspects, is unaccustomed to dining in the best circles.

'And now, comrades, I will tell you the bad news ... There is at this moment resident under this roof one of the world's unique warthogs. His name is Mr Joseph Schofield and he bathes in money. You will be presented to him at dinner. I want to ask you— (a) not to comment at the key in which he takes his soup; (b) to stand by in case he gets his spaghetti tangled round his left ear; (c) to—'

At which point, or a second later, they are interrupted by the discovery of the said Joseph Schofield lying outside the library door. 'And he won't tie any more spaghetti round his left ear,' quips Chief Inspector Kennedy, on finding that Schofield has been shot dead. Shortly after this, they notice a bloody X scratched by the point

105

of a dagger or swordstick on the palm of Schofield's
hand—the trademark of a systematic killer called X
Esquire.

It turns out at the end of the story that X Esquire is
none other than Terry Mannering himself. He has been
doing a one-man Four Just Men operation, assassinating,
one after the other, a collection of businessmen who have
evolved 'the most fiendish plot in all criminal history'—an
attempt to wipe out Britain by a free mass distribution of
poisoned cigarettes.

You might think that an assassin hero takes us back to
outright outlawry on the 1905 scale. But Charteris is
extremely careful to keep Mannering almost hand-in-
glove with the police. We gather, in the final chapter, that
Chief Inspector Bill Kennedy had suspected him all
along.

'But my dear little Williams,' murmured Terry, 'why
didn't you do anything about it?'

Bill shrugged.

'The men you were killing were no loss to the
country, laddie, and I guessed you knew why you were
doing it.'

Police consideration has hardly ever, in any thriller,
gone further than that. But then Bill Kennedy is an
irregular Chief Inspector in many ways, not least in his
Flashman-like way with suspects. ('You will see behind
you, Spider, a fireplace in which is burning a large fire.
Your features are not of classic beauty, but they will not
be improved by coming into contact with the hot grate ...')

The climax of the story (and the most original thing in
the book) is the scene in which the police, after capturing
the master-villain behind the whole plot, the Hon. Basil
Strange, virtually hand him over to X Esquire themselves.

'Listen,' said the Assistant Commissioner. 'Inspector Hendersen and these two detectives will escort you back to London. You will return to your house in Mount Street. It will be watched night and day by the police, and no one will be permitted to enter it, and you will not be permitted to stir outside your door. Do you understand?'

'And on what charge am I being detained, Mr Kennedy?'

'I am making no charge, Strange.' Bill Kennedy stood in front of him with an expressionless face. 'The law will not deal with you ...'

Strange stood motionless between the two detectives.

'But X Esquire will,' said Bill Kennedy.

Sure enough, X Esquire does, in no uncertain manner. No sooner is Strange a police prisoner in his own house, than a tall, muscular man, with an Inverness cape hanging from his shoulders, an opera hat in his hand, and over his head 'a black hood, with the ends tucked into his collar', comes strolling into the room.

'How did you get in?' inquires Strange, adding, really very politely in the circumstances: 'Forgive my curiosity, but I believe I have every right to be interested.'

'I came in through the front door,' replies X Esquire. 'The watchers saluted me when I came and they will salute me again when I go.'

He then embarks on a three-page harangue detailing Strange's vile poison-cigarette plot. Strange's nerve breaks, and he grovels on the floor. This produces a bit of dialogue that is a collector's gem:

> 'You are the unworthy son of a great and noble family, Strange,' said X Esquire sternly. 'What do your ancestors, watching you now, think of you, I wonder?'
>
> Slowly Strange's face relaxed, and the mad terror faded from his eyes, leaving only frozen dread.

'I forgot myself,' he said.

Notwithstanding this disarming admission, X Esquire is implacable in carrying out the death penalty—implacable and also remarkably athletic:

And with a face of iron he broke Strange's back across a chair, as one breaks a rotten stick.

So much for Terry (X Esquire) Mannering—a hero who can fairly be described as 99½% derivative, and unpleasantly so, at that: he has all of Drummond's least attractive attributes, and misses by a mile the berserk geniality which gave the original Hugh such style. It is a relief to turn to Peter Lestrange, the hero of Charteris's second novel, *The White Rider*. Peter is much more unmistakably a Charteris creation. He has a background of disreputable buccaneering, and has even spent a year in Sing Sing. Surprisingly, his great delight is playing the piano, and on one occasion, in the course of a little flippant dalliance with the heroine, Marion, he 'got up and lounged round the piano, on which he perched himself with a quiet spring'. An ex-buccaneer who lounges? Suddenly the full 1930s Gentleman Outlaw is only a breath away.

Not that we are quite there yet with this Peter Lestrange. He is altogether lacking in the proper derisive nonchalance. His big scenes with Marion have all the solemnity of Dornford Yates.

'Peter—will you answer me on your word of honour?'
'Yes.'
'Were you in an American prison for a year?'
'Yes.'
'What for?'
His head went up.

108

'I can't answer that question.'

'Are you known to the police?'

'I suppose so.'

'And you specialise—' the scorn in the word cut him like a whip—'in bank, frauds, hold-ups, and—and dope, and murder.'

'I have.'

She wilted as if he had struck her, and with that for a second his proud self-control snapped, and he sprang towards her, ignoring her passionate resistance.

'Marion,' he pleaded fiercely. 'Wait. Don't judge me like that.'

When it is quite clear that Marion *does* judge him like that—

With a swift movement he caught up her hand and pressed it to his lips.

'Always—whatever happens—your very devoted servant, my lady.'

The next moment he was in the saddle, and the big grey, under the unaccustomed drive of his spurs, leapt forward down the hill, leaving Marion alone.

(*The White Rider*, Ward Lock)

From *The White Rider* onwards, Charteris seems definitely to have decided that a bandit hero was the thing to aim for. In 1929, he actually published a novel called *The Bandit* which has three distinctive attributes: just about the longest-named hero, the most convoluted opening sentences, and the slowest-travelling bottle in thriller history.

Ramon Francisco de Castila y Espronceda Manrique saw the bottle coming, and ducked—half a second late. It wasn't that he was taken by surprise. Having emerged with all piratical colours flying from several years' intensive experience in a career which

109

has a peculiar habit of proving fatal to those of its devotees in whom the spirit is willing but the flesh slow on the rebound, it wasn't likely that a little thing like an empty whisky bottle would catch his trained muscles and nerves and reflexes yawning.... Therefore Manrique, cool and sure of his ground, had gone on smoking a cigarette as if he hadn't a care in the world, but all the time, out of the corner of his eye, he was watching that bottle.... And now, even as he jerked his sleek head sideways and downwards, in the same infinitesimal fraction of a second that it took him to appreciate the fact that he had started to move too late, and that no possible readjustment of human reactions could make up for that lost instant of time, he realised that he hadn't got even the most anaemic ghost of an excuse....

In the next paragraph, Manrique was finally knocked out by that bottle—which is more than the public was by Manrique. It must be admitted, though, that he was a good try. Immaculate, handsome, buccaneering, cool, he really possesses all the essentials of a full-scale Gentleman Outlaw—except two. The public wasn't ready to accept a South American as a British thriller hero. And the Manrique repartee simply wasn't up to the requisite standard. Here he is, trying to talk back to a group of toughies who have taken him prisoner:

'I can see no one who looks clever here,' he said. 'It can't be Fishface and it can't be Pigface—I've met them before. I shouldn't expect much from Sheepface or Eggface over there and Horseface, over in that corner, doesn't look promising. That only leaves you and me, Harrington, and I don't think you're particularly clever ...'

(*The Bandit*, Ward Lock)

In such a situation, Drummond would have babbled

about goldfish or called them all unwashed Bolshie swine, either of which would have been a hell of a lot livelier. But then it's doubtful if Drummond would have allowed himself to be hit by that bottle in the first place.

The ill-fated Manrique was actually Leslie Charteris's fifth attempt at creating an appropriate hero for the fast-approaching thirties. Curiously enough, he had done altogether better two books earlier.

In the opening pages of *Meet the Tiger*, quite casually (he isn't even considered worthy of being featured in the book's title: the Tiger is the villain, not the hero, of the piece) a character walks on who has everything that Charteris, and his public, have been subconsciously waiting for; and it is difficult not to greet his appearance with the enthusiasm of characters in *The Glenn Miller Story* hearing That Sound at last.

Below is an extract from his entrance scene. It isn't a sensational passage; there is something absurdly nineteen-twenty-ish about its hearty gymnastic opening. But before long the mixture of languidness and action, nonchalance and authority, becomes exactly right. The authentic Charteris note is coming through loud and clear, and it is soon to blast the whole thriller world before it.

Here, then, really is our first full-scale Gentleman Outlaw.[1]

He shaved rapidly, sipping his tea in between whiles, and then pulled on a bathing costume and went out into the sun, picking up a length of rope on his way out. He skipped energetically on the grass outside for fifteen minutes. Then he shadow-boxed for five minutes. He grabbed a towel, knotted it loosely round his neck, sprinted the couple of dozen yards that lay between the Pill Box and the edge of the cliff, and coolly swung himself over the edge. A hundred and fifty foot drop lay beneath him, but handholds were plentiful, and

[1] *Meet the Tiger* (Ward Lock, 1928).

he descended to the beach as nonchalantly as he would have descended a flight of stairs. The water was rippling calm. He covered a quarter of a mile at racing speed, turned on his back and paddled lazily shorewards, finishing the last hundred yards like a champion. Then he lay on the edge of the surf, basking in the strengthening sun.

All these things he had done as regularly on the two previous mornings, and he was languidly pondering the deadliness of regular habits when the thing happened that proved to him quite conclusively that regular habits could be more literally deadly than he had allowed for.

Phhew-wuk!

Something sang past his ear, and the pebble at which he had been staring in an absent-minded sort of way leapt sideways, and was left with a silvery streak seared across it, while the thing that had sang changed its note and went whining seawards.

'Bad luck, sonny,' murmured the Saint.

Part Two

THE DAY OF THE DESPERADO
(1928–1939)

CHAPTER EIGHT

In which Simon Templar is born again, and becomes a significant rascal

FOR anyone with a taste for literary detective puzzles, the question of how the Saint got launched is, at first sight, one of the most intriguing. The facts are these.

Simon Templar first appeared in *Meet the Tiger*, published in 1928 by Ward Lock, a press with a long string of successful circulating-library authors, and, incidentally, the distinction of having also originally launched Sherlock Holmes (in *Beeton's Christmas Annual*, 1887).

The original Saint, although quite recognisably Simon Templar from his very first entrance, as we have just seen, was still only a shadow of the self he later became. He hadn't invented his skeletal-figure trade mark. He disappears from the story for a long, long time, leaving Patricia Holm to soldier on alone (which she does in surprisingly high piratical style). Pages go by without his drawling a single Saintly utterance, and some of those he does come up with are rather strained. ('Fancy meeting you!—as the Vicar said when he saw one of the leading lights of the Mother's Union dining at the Forty-Three.') And Charteris himself seems oddly lacking in confidence in him. Otherwise, why should he have given the book's title to the Tiger—and why should he have gone on trying out new heroes, faulty carbon copies though they proved to be, in his next two novels, *Daredevil* and *The Bandit*?

It is hard to resist the conclusion that the Saint wasn't an instant sensation, and was even abandoned by his creator back in 1928.

But in 1930, we find him being taken up by the major thriller publishing house of the period—Hodder & Stoughton, publishers of Sapper, Oppenheim, Buchan, Wallace, all the really big names in the field. And more than that: we find him, in a year or so, being launched in the Yellow Jacket library with more pomp and ceremony than has been accorded any other thriller hero in history.

There can be very few people who were thriller fans between the wars (or, for that matter, who were young between the wars) who didn't receive at least one of these Saintly Yellow Jackets as a birthday or a Christmas present. And nobody who received one was likely to forget it.

The first page of each book (called in the trade the 'bastard title page'—the one where you usually get the novel's name and nothing else) contained a resounding announcement—for example:

THE HOLY TERROR
THE SEVENTH VOLUME
IN THE SAINT SAGA

—followed by the Saint's haloed figure as a trade mark.

The next page stated, amidst at least three more Saint figures (and in some editions, I seem to remember that the print was superimposed on hundreds of them):

THE SAINT SAGA is being unfolded by Leslie Charteris in a series of remarkable adventures which tell of the escapades, the heroic achievements and marvellous adventures of the twentieth century's brightest buccaneer, from the time when he burst upon an astonished world to the present day.

The chronicle is yet unfinished. The Saint is still at large, and Leslie Charteris, with the shades of Boswell around him, continues his mighty task of recording for all time the amazing history of this, the most significant rascal of our day.

116

The man who has never heard of the Saint is like the boy who has never heard of Robin Hood.

There followed the actual title page, with a massive single Saint figure, and even that didn't finish the build-up. Still before you got to the story, you were treated to a page of 'Notes for Learned Readers'. In my yellowing copy of *The Holy Terror* (given to me, I see, on my thirteenth birthday, in 1940), these notes read:

1. The villains in this book are entirely imaginary and have no relation to any living person.
2. This is the 213th edition of a book in the Saint Saga and the eighteenth edition of The Holy Terror.
3. The first Saint book was published in 1930.[1] 'The Holy Terror' was published in 1932.
4. This book, by special request of the Saint, is made and printed for Hodder & Stoughton Ltd by Wyman & Sons Ltd., London, Fakenham and Reading.
5. This is the sign of the Saint.

Very spectacular, particularly Note 3. It meant that no less than seven Saint books—to give them their original titles, *Enter the Saint, The Last Hero, Knight Templar, Featuring the Saint, Alias the Saint, She Was A Lady* and *The Holy Terror*—had appeared in two years. And in the next two years—1932–4—there had appeared five more.

Undeniably, by 1932, the Saint had become the success of the thriller scene. But the basic question remains: how on earth had it happened? What was the missing link between the diffidently-presented, one-book-only hero of Ward Lock's *Meet the Tiger*, 1928, and the

[1] This means, of course, the first Saint book published by Hodder & Stoughton. The Ward Lock one is ignored. In the publishing world, dog may not eat dog, but there is rarely an enthusiastic exchange of bones.

swaggering swashbuckler of Hodder & Stoughton's deafeningly trumpeted Saint Saga, launched by *The Last Hero* (with *Enter the Saint* following, illogically, a month later) in 1930? Templar had undoubtedly undergone some kind of metamorphosis in that period, and it couldn't have been a secret process, because somehow in the course of it he had attracted a vast following and/or a fantastically confident publisher.

The mystery, for many years insoluble to me, had, in fact, a very simple answer. The Saint, by the end of 1928 all but discarded as a flop, was saved for posterity by one very significant development. In early 1929, his creator was asked to write for a publishing concern which is not exactly unfamiliar: that remarkable firm which had already given the world Sexton Blake, Wu Ling, Mlle Yvonne, Huxton Rymer, Waldo the Wonder Man and countless others, and which knew more about heroes, villains, super-heroes, arch-villains, and even arch-villain-super-heroes than any other outfit in the business—the Amalgamated Press of Fleetway House.

In February 1929, Fleetway House had launched its new paper, *The Thriller*, a 2d weekly which might roughly be described as a *Union Jack* without Sexton Blake. The controlling editor of this enterprise was one Percy Montague Haydon, whom John Creasey describes as 'midwife to the Saint and the Toff and several others'—midwife, one could almost say, to the whole Gentleman Outlaw *genre*.

Except for his time in the Army during World War I, Haydon had been with Fleetway all his life, and had risen from office boy to Controlling Editor of a large group of weeklies, including *The Gem*, *The Magnet*, *Union Jack* and *The Thriller*. He was a tall, slim man, soft-spoken, courteous and with what can best be described as a mischievously compelling manner.

W. Howard Baker, the publisher, who worked at Fleetway under Haydon for many years, has told me an anecdote which suggests that this compulsion could even become guru-like. One day Baker had a raging toothache. On his way out to get some aspirin, he bumped into Monty Haydon in the corridor. 'Is anything wrong?' asked Haydon. 'Bad toothache,' said Baker. Haydon took his arm. 'Bill,' he drawled, 'you won't have a toothache from this moment onwards. It will go away. Completely.' And, Baker swears, the pain departed that instant and did not return.

What Ezra Pound was to T. S. Eliot, what Maxwell Perkins was to Thomas Wolfe, Monty Haydon was to the youthful Leslie Charteris. Messrs. Loft and Adley tell us that 'Monty gave him [Charteris] help with practically every story he wrote for *The Thriller*.' They 'regularly kicked plots and ideas around together over innumerable three-hour lunches, usually at the Press Club'—unusual enough if Haydon had been merely editor of *The Thriller*, but phenomenal when you consider that he was controlling editor of a large group of journals, of which *The Thriller* was only one. It isn't surprising that Charteris eventually paid him the compliment of putting him into the Saint stories, as the intrepid 'Monty Hayward'. Here he is being intrepid in *Getaway*:

> Displaying remarkable agility for a man of his impregnable sangfroid, Monty Hayward possessed himself of the weapon which had fallen from the disabled gunman's hand, seized its badly winded owner by the collar, and lugged him vigorously into the sitting-room ... Then he proceeded, methodically, to handicap the wounded warrior's recovery by dragging up a massive Chesterfield, and laying it gently on the wounded warrior's bosom ...

It was rarely Charteris policy, though, to allow a second-string hero total functional efficiency. When Monty wants to gag his victim, he calls on the professional

119

expertise of the Saint's resident lady, Patricia Holm.

> She bent over the squirming prisoner, and a particu-
> larly vile profanity subsided into a choking gurgle.
> Monty watched the performance with admiration.
> 'You know, I couldn't have done that,' he said. 'And
> I've been editing this kind of stuff all my life.'
> (*Getaway*, Hodder & Stoughton)

Curiously enough, the Saint's second birth in *The Thriller* was almost as hesitant an affair as the first one had been, back at Ward Lock. It is not on record which of those Ward Lock novels had originally attracted Monty Haydon's interest, but it seems that it was something about the style of them that had appealed to him rather than any specific hero. The first story he commissioned Charteris to write for *The Thriller* featured, of all people, the Inspector who was later to be the Saint's arch-enemy, Claud Eustace Teal, and Templar didn't get a look-in at all. The first Saint offering under the new *aegis* was a serial, 'The Five Kings', in which Templar had to share star billing with no less than four other heroes.

Even after a few *Thriller* appearances in a full-scale starring role, Templar was once again dropped, this time in favour of a certain Lyn Peveril, yet another faint carbon copy believed by his creator to be an improvement on his Saint.

Precisely at what point Charteris and Haydon began to realise Simon Templar's unique qualities will probably never be known. It must have been some time either late in 1929 or early in 1930. From then onwards, Saint story after Saint story began to be featured in *The Thriller*—and presently they were being taken, usually three at a time, and rushed into hardback by the august Hodder & Stoughton to grace the same circulating-library book-shelves as Buchan, Sapper and the rest.

Surely we have here an interesting breakdown of barriers, both of age and class. Wonderful pictures are conjured up of a company chairman borrowing the latest Hodder & Stoughton from his Club library, and reading a Saint story that is already old-hat to the whistling delivery-boy in the street outside. Or stiff-collared stockbrokers on the 9.15 to Cannon Street, determined to keep up with the crimes, studying grubby copies of their sons' old *Thrillers* under cover of *The Morning Post*.

Things like that could never have happened before the thirties. But then neither, in all his glory, could the Saint. The sheer, dazzling impudence of Simon Templar, as he finally emerged in those *Thriller* episodes, is something the public simply wouldn't have taken, even in the days of *Triumph of the Rat*.

Here is a particularly interesting example of it—a passage (later republished as part of *The Holy Terror*, 1932[2]) in which Charteris is fairly savagely satirising the people who had objected to poor old Ramon Francisco de Castila y Espronceda Manrique. To mount his attack, he rather surprisingly turns the Saint into an amateur Leslie Charteris. 'During a brief spell of virtue,' it is explained, he had 'beguiled himself with the writing of a novel'—the adventures of Mario, a super-brigand of South America, which had been accepted by a publisher, and 'could be purchased at any bookstall for three halfcrowns'. Not, it appeared, that there were many purchasers. But there was definitely one, an irate reader from whom the Saint hears in no uncertain manner. Over breakfast, he reads the letter aloud to Patricia.

' "... You do not evidently understand the mentality of the English reading public. If instead of Mario you

[2] Hodder & Stoughton. Now revised and republished as *The Saint vs. Scotland Yard*. All the remaining extracts in this chapter are from the original edition of this book, which contains three stories, each taken more or less directly from *The Thriller*.

had selected for your hero an Englishman or American, you would have written a fairly readable and passable tale—but a lousy Dago who walks out of impossible difficulties and situations is too much. It is not convincing. It does not appeal. In a word, it is puerile.

' "I fancy you yourself must have a fair amount of Dago blood in you—" '

He stopped, and Patricia looked at him puzzledly. 'Well?' she prompted.

'There is no more,' explained the Saint. 'No address —no signature—no closing peroration—nothing. Apparently words failed him. At that point, he probably uttered a short sharp yelp of intolerable agony, and began to chew the furniture. We may never know his fate. Possibly, in some distant asylum—'

He elaborated his theory.

If there is a more stylish example of a writer getting his own back on a recalcitrant public, and at the same time kicking his reader's racial prejudices in the teeth, then I don't know of it.

There were no limits to the Saint's literary versatility in those early days. Not merely does he become an overnight novelist; a little later in the same story, we find that 'the continued political activities of a certain newspaper proprietor [Lord Beaverbrook?] had driven him to verse'.

'Charles Charlestone Charlemagne St Charles
Was wont to utter fearful snarls
When by professors he was pressed
To note how England had progressed
Since the galumptious, gory days
Immortalised in Shakespeare's plays.
For him, no Transatlantic flights,
Ford motor cars, electric lights,
Or radios at less than cost
Could compensate for what he lost
By chancing to coagulate
About five hundred years too late.'

122

The Saint continues to recite verses from this massive exercise in doggerel at intervals throughout the rest of the story, and he is even reluctant to stop in moments of grave emergency, such as when he notices Patricia Holm opening an odd little parcel that has just arrived through the post.

'Over that chapter of the tale
It would be kind to draw a veil.
Let it suffice that, in disdain,
Some hecklers threw him in the drain,
And plodding home—

'Excuse me,' said the Saint.

His right hand moved like lightning, and the detonation of his heavy automatic in the confined space was like a vindictive thunderclap. It left the girl with a strange hot sting of powder on her wrist and a dull buzzing in her ears. And through the buzzing drifted the Saint's unruffled accents:

'And plodding home, all soaked inside,
He caught pneumonia—and died.'

Patricia looked at him, white-faced.

'What was it?' she asked, with the faintest tremor in her voice.

'Just an odd spot of scorpion,' answered Simon Templar gently.

The Saint's nonchalance is a quality that has been imitated, and parodied, *ad nauseam*, in the past forty years. It is interesting to note that Charteris was ahead of anybody else in sending it up. Here is another bit from the same story, which appeared in *The Thriller* back in 1931:

Mr Ganniman shrugged.

'Need I explain that you have come to the end of your interesting and adventurous life?'

Simon twitched an eyebrow, and slid his mouth mockingly sideways.

'What—not again?' he sighed, and Ganniman's smooth forehead crinkled.

'I don't understand.'

'But you haven't seen so many of these situations through as I have, old horse,' said the Saint. 'I've lost count of the number of times that this sort of thing has happened to me. I know the tradition demands it but I think they might give us a rest sometimes. What's the programme this time—do you sew me up in the bath and light the geyser, or am I run through the mangle and buried under the billiard table? Or can you think of something really original?'

A couple of pages further on, he is impudently ad-libbing for all the world like a comic-strip character stepping out of his frame.

'You know, Wilf,' murmured the Saint conversationally, 'this has happened to me twice before in the last six months. And each time it was gas. Is it going to be gas this time, or are you breaking away from the rules?'

'It will not be gas,' replied Ganniman flatly.

He was as heavily passionless as a contented animal. And the Saint chattered on blithely.

'I hate to disappoint you—as the actress said to the bishop—but I really can't oblige you now. You must see it, Wilfred. I've got such a lot to do before the end of the volume, and it would wreck the whole show if I went and got bumped off in the first story. Have a heart, dear old Garbage-man!'

It is doubtful if any other major thriller writer, before or since, would have dared to take such chances with the reader's suspension of disbelief. It is certainly doubtful if any controlling editor other than Monty Haydon would have let Charteris get away with such fun and games in *The Thriller*. But in the case of Monty Haydon, one has the suspicion that he was himself the initiator of a great deal of the fun and games; that the creation of the Charteris 'anything-goes' atmosphere was, in fact, his deliberate editorial policy. If so, it was a policy of genius, because it was precisely this sense of the author's own recklessness—this feeling that you were not only reading about a mocking desperado, but were actually in the hands of one—that was the most intoxicating thing about the early Saint stories.

Neither Charteris nor Haydon were, in any case, running any real risk. It was soon very obvious that the public of the grey, depression-cowed early thirties needed the Saint so badly that nothing would have induced them *not* to believe in him. Or to surrender that all-important illusion that maybe with the help of the right tailor, maybe by continually polishing up their drawling repartee, they might, if only for a moment or two, bring themselves to resemble him. I mean, it would be quite something if one could even manage to walk along a road the way Templar did.

Down the street strolled the Saint, his hands deep in the pockets of his knife-edged trousers, the crook of his walking stick hooked over his left wrist, and slanting sideways over his left eye a filibustering black felt hat which alone was like a breach of the peace. A little song rollicked on his lips, and was inaudible two yards away. And as he walked, his lazy eyes absorbed every interesting item of scenery.

'Aspidistra, little herb
Do you think it silly
When the botaniser's blurb
Links you with the lily?'

Up in one window of the house, he caught the almost imperceptible sway of a shifting curtain, and knew that his approach had already been observed. 'But it is nice,' thought the Saint, 'to be expected.' And he sauntered on.

He sauntered on—and a great and growing public of (to quote Charteris's own delineation) 'dear bookworms, most noble fellow-drinkers, frustrated burglars, affronted policemen, upright citizens with furled umbrellas and secret buccaneering dreams' were more than delighted to saunter with him. Even though they knew—perhaps, even, because they knew—that the Saint himself would have made them the first target for his derision.

The second verse of the Saint's aspidistra ditty could be interpreted as the cruellest conceivable comment on the very people most apt to follow his adventures.

> 'Up above your window-ledge
> Streatham stars are gleaming:
> Aspidistra, little veg,
> Does your soul go dreaming?'

It has often been said—by critics who would probably go on to deny that the thirties Gentleman Outlaw was a distinctive thriller *genre* at all—that the early Saint was almost indistinguishable from Bulldog Drummond. There are, certainly, a lot of superficial resemblances between the characters. Charteris, who started, as we have seen, by being very heavily under the Drummond influence, was a long time throwing off the whole of his Sapper debt.

The Saint and Drummond were both Mayfairites and denizens of Clubland. (The Saint's club varied, but the Bruton, near Berkeley Square, is mentioned more than once.) Both men had ex-batman-type servants—Drummond's was called Denny, the Saint's, more familiarly, 'Orace. Both men moved uncannily silently at night. Both killed villains without compunction during battles, but rarely carried out cold-blooded assassinations. And both were—astonishingly enough, in the Saint's case—essentially one-woman men.

Drummond was wholly faithful to his Phyllis, whom he married after the first book, and who thereafter tended

126

to become a distressingly conventional Little Woman, forever trying to discourage him from adventuring. Templar was faithful in his fashion to Patricia Holm, who was much more of a consort in crime, a fellow-buccaneer. Patricia was quite obviously living with the Saint, although Charteris rather carefully avoids specifically saying so. She is, in her creator's words, 'imperturbably serene' about their relationship, although marriage is never on the cards and other women frequently are. 'I defy anyone,' writes Charteris in *The First Saint Omnibus* (Hodder & Stoughton, 1939), 'to discover any rift between them, or to catch her making any really bitter thrusts about his other adventures ...' This isn't surprising. Patricia doesn't even make bitter thrusts when her lover's enemies are on the point of burying her in chalk and lime. The pregnant bit of dialogue between the Saint and his lady in *The Holy Terror* when he stumbles into a 'small low vault' and discovers her predicament is wholly typical of their essentially comradely relationship throughout.

> Her eyes were open, and she looked at him steadily, with the faintest of smiles on her lips.
> 'Hullo, boy.'
> 'Hullo, lass.'
> That was all.

Another thing the Saint and Drummond had in common was a gang of friends who offered unswerving, doglike devotion to their leader. Charteris went further than Sapper in this particular. In *The Last Hero* (later, temporarily, called *The Saint Closes the Case*) there is a stirring climax in which one Norman Kent enables the Saint and Patricia Holm to escape by acting as a decoy, even though he is aware that he is saving their lives at the expense of his own, and does in fact pay this price, to the accompaniment of a positive organ voluntary of 'trumpets-sounding-on-the-other-side' prose. Charteris

127

also, surprisingly, concedes no points to Sapper in the matter of royal fervour. Drummond & Co. may have owed a passionate allegiance to the King: the Saint, in *Knight Templar* (later called *The Avenging Saint*), actually saves His Majesty's life, gaining himself a Royal Pardon for all his irregularities up to that date.

But when these points have been catalogued, the resemblance between Templar and his forerunner begins to disappear, and they are seen to be worlds apart—as far apart, in fact, as the worlds of 1919 and 1929 in which they were born. Drummond is huge and ugly, the Saint slim and elegant. Drummond is basically, as he often announces, a simple soul. He is always either massively good-humoured or massively menacing, his ham-like fists ready to sledge-hammer you on the back if you are a friend, or close round your throat in a vice-like grip if you are one of Old England's foes. Certainly, if you are an arch-fiend, he will launch into battle with you with something approaching pure exhilaration, and be ready to salute the smallest sign that your enjoyment of the fight equals his: but, aside from these sporting subtleties, his is not a complex character at all. The Saint shares this exhilaration about a fight ('*To* battle, murder, sudden death, Good Lord deliver us' he prays somewhere) but his approach is altogether more complicated. He hasn't really a great deal of good humour, as such: there is too often a rapier-thrust behind his lazy repartee. If Drummond's comedy has a lot in common with the aristocratic bumbling of Wooster & Co., the Saint's has in it more than a little of the Bright Young Things brittleness of, say, Michael Arlen or Noël Coward. In *The First Saint Omnibus*, Charteris says that it is the expression of Templar's 'own outrageous brand of philosophical indignation'—and once one grants a thriller-hero a philosophy, let alone indignation, one is obviously light years away from Sapper.

Which brings us to what is perhaps the most important thing about the Saint.

With the arrival of the thirties, as we have seen, an increasingly romantic thriller public had begun to lose interest in workaday heroes. As long as Edgar Wallace lived, his assorted heroes commanded their legions of admirers: [3] but the bulk of the new thriller writers were returning to men about town and backgrounds of Society sophistication. Undoubtedly, it was 'Depression' depression that was responsible for this trend. Society people were almost the only group left who could be convincingly portrayed as sailing serenely above the intolerable everyday anxieties, and more and more readers were prepared to pocket what class principles they had, and go along for the ride.

In the case of the Saint, though, very few class principles *had* to be pocketed. Despite his Mayfair glamour, he is hardly a class hero in the Sapper sense at all. His background is never clearly indicated. He is a man of no means, apart from his piratically acquired 'boodle'. He has no Old School Tie connections, no friends in high positions for whom he once fagged at school.

Moreover, he does things which would have made Drummond & Co. cut him stone dead in the street. He writes books about dago heroes. He not infrequently alludes to the public school in terms which (as Charteris himself puts it, again in *The First Saint Omnibus*) are 'so conspicuously devoid of reverence that it begins to look as if I might have a complex on the subject'. And he is quite liable to take violent action on behalf of the struggling workers. (In one of the most effective short

[3] Wallace, during the last three years before his death (1930-2) was mostly in Hollywood, writing such screenplays as *King Kong*. Otherwise, it is more than likely that he would have created a major Gentleman Outlaw of his own. His Mixer had already pointed the way for all the others.

stories, 'The Sleepless Knight', from *Boodle*—now *The Saint Intervenes*—the Saint ties Sir Melvin Flager, the Managing Director of the Flager Road Transport Company, to a chair in front of a cinematic teach-yourself-to-drive machine, and keeps him there for a whole weekend, virtually non-stop, lashing him with a leather strap whenever he makes a mistake in turning the steering-wheel. There are no prospects of boodle for the Saint in this enterprise: it is an entirely altruistic operation to impress on Sir Melvin the inhumanity of forcing his lorry drivers to complete long journeys with barely four hours' sleep a night.)

Finally, the Saint's relationship with Authority (Authority, at all events, as represented by Inspector Claud Eustace Teal) is several hundred degrees more caustic than Drummond's 'What ho, dear old laddie' routines with Sir Bryan Johnstone.

'You're becoming a nuisance, Claud, and I'm telling you this is where you get off ... I'm going to send you up to the sky on one big balloon; and when you come down, you're not going to bounce—you're going to spread yourself out so flat that a short-sighted man will not be able to see you sideways. Got it?'

Teal gulped.

His cherubic countenance took on a slightly redder tinge, and he shuffled his feet like a truant schoolboy ... For he gazed deep into the dancing, mocking, challenging blue eyes of the Saint standing there before him, lean and reckless and debonair even in that preposterous bathrobe outfit; and he understood the issue exactly ...

'Of course,' he grunted, 'if that's the way you take it, there's nothing more to be said.'

'There isn't,' agreed the Saint courteously. 'And if there was, I'd say it.'

He picked up the detective's bowler hat, dusted it

130

with his towel, and handed it over. Teal accepted it, looked at it, and sighed. And he was still sighing when the Saint took him by the arm and ushered him, politely but firmly, to the door.

(The Holy Terror)

It's interesting how the mildness of that last paragraph offsets the ferocity of the opening one. Literally and metaphorically ushering Teal to the door is the chief sport of the Saint throughout the early stories; scenes of what Charteris calls 'Teal-baiting' occur over and over again. It is almost as though the Saint isn't complete without Teal: as though the continual re-statement of this particular relationship with Authority—ironic mockery on the Saint's side, bafflement, resignation and, very occasionally, grudging admiration on the Inspector's— were somehow an absolute essential of the series. Remembering the decade of largely law-abiding heroes that had gone before, we can, perhaps, guess that the subconscious purpose of the Teal routines was to reassure the reader that the Saint's buccaneering wasn't taking him completely beyond the pale of respectability even now. Teal is an embodiment of the Establishment (or rather of its servants) and as long as he is there, however mournful, however disapproving, however resigned, the reader can safely identify with the Saint without feeling totally cut off from all the moral promptings of his upbringing.

For all its love of daredevils, the thirties was a time when *Cavalcade* could fill Drury Lane; when George V could still ask with his dying breath if all was well with the Empire; when children at school were expelled for showing disrespect for the flag; when, for most people, it was nice to be naughty and fun to be disrespectful but very uncomfortable to feel that one might be straying too far from all possibility of official approbation.

This is not to say that the Saint didn't represent a decisive step forward in outlawry. Compared with almost any of his post-war predecessors, he was shatteringly piratical. But he had a healthy respect—or perhaps one should say a kindly concern—for the Establishment all the time. He was forever, so to speak, courteously dusting its hat; taking care not to outrage its deepest values.

The Saint's buccaneering never really upsets the 'upright citizens with furled umbrellas' because behind it there are continual hints that the fun and games are in aid of a deeper, cosmic Uprightness. It was Charteris's genius to be able to suggest this at the very moments when he was registering the maximum of flamboyance.

'Pat, is that really what you want?' Simon asks Patricia longingly, at the romantic climax of 'The Melancholy Journey of Mr Teal' (the last story in *The Holy Terror*). 'To go on with all the fighting and the fun? To go rocketing around the world, doing everything that's utterly and gloriously mad—swaggering, swashbuckling, singing—showing all those dreary old dogs what can be done with life—not giving a damn for anyone—robbing the rich, helping the poor—plaguing the pompous, killing dragons, pulling policemen's legs—'

That is hardly a speech which shows the early Saint at his most wickedly nonchalant, but for all that it's not a bad note on which to leave him. It is one of the clearest statements of his basic creed, and reveals him for what he really was, behind the drawling mockery: absurdly English, absurdly romantic, absurdly innocent: absurdly nineteen-thirty-ish—and, by all the laws of logic, absurdly vulnerable in a darkening world where Hitler was so soon to be rampaging, and dragons beyond the reach of a million thriller heroes were getting set to take over.

By all the laws of logic, maybe. But it isn't exactly a logical epoch into which that last speech of the Saint ushers us. It is, in fact, the most fascinatingly cock-eyed period in all thriller history: the Day of the Desperado.

132

CHAPTER NINE

In which John Creasey has a déjà vu, *and Monty Haydon an honourable idea*

HECTIC, crazy, cottagey, ramshackle, fabulously pro-lific, fascinatingly cock-eyed. At one point or another, I have applied all these adjectives to the thirties thriller era; and I don't think it will prove difficult to justify any of them.

There was, as we have seen, something distinctly cock-eyed about the multiple birth of the Saint. No hero has ever arrived onstage by such a crazily circuitous route— or been elbowed so repeatedly back into the wings by his creator. And even when recognition began finally to arrive—when Hodder & Stoughton were joining with *The Thriller* in promoting Simon Templar across the whole 2*d* weekly-to-7/6-hardback spectrum of crime pub-lications—Leslie Charteris still found it difficult to make ends meet financially. Late in 1932, he took off for fame, fortune and America—returning a year or so later to find his books at last selling in Britain in tens of thousands.

For anyone who didn't achieve sales at this level, the glittering Golden Age of the British thriller was somewhat less than golden. Payment to authors, even established ones, was often remarkably low. The norm, for a thriller by a new or only relatively popular author, was around £50, and that often involved the handing over of complete copyright—in other words, sacrificing all prospects of royalties to come. Things were a little better for con-tributors to *The Thriller*: standard payment was two guineas per 1,000 words, so that for a typical story

(28,000 words—a little more than a third of a novel) an author would receive £56. But he would be very lucky if the paper took more than at the most four stories from his pen in the course of a year.

With payment so low and the demand so enormous, it might be supposed that a new thriller writer (anyone who was reasonably competent, and prepared to work like a demon for a pittance) would have been overwhelmed with opportunities. But, in fact, even to get a single story accepted was by no means an easy task. Magazine editors (Monty Haydon being clearly a notable exception) preferred to call on known names, and the old pros in the Fleetway world were so proficient at turning stuff out—remember Edwy Searles Brooks's million words a year in the *Nelson Lee Library*—that there were not many points where a newcomer could elbow his way in. Publishers had, to a very large extent, a similarly conservative attitude. Thrillers and romances streamed into the bookshops in 7/6, 3/6 and 2/6 editions from a vast range of publishing houses, but each author contributed so many new titles a year, often under such a variety of *noms de plume*, that in fact the industry revolved around a relatively small group of authors. And it would be wrong to assume that even they were making a packet.

After all, to achieve £500–£600 a year, you had to write the equivalent of a novel a month. You had to get them all accepted; you had to be prepared, in many instances, to sell your copyright and kiss royalties goodbye; and you still had to struggle to make yourself a really big name with the public, because no one press would take more than four of your books in a year, and most contracts insisted that if you wrote for another firm you had to use a different *nom de plume*. Statistics are hard to obtain, but it's a fair guess that more than half of everyone's output was published under pseudonyms.

134

Of course, as Max Beerbohm, I believe, once said, he who generalises generally lies. (A bit of word-play I have always wanted to extend by adding 'and generally realises it'.) The thirties thriller scene was a jungle where no one stretch of the undergrowth completely resembled another. Once an author *did* get a bit of a name, a publisher could sometimes be persuaded to make a special deal: and competition between publishers was so fierce that it wasn't impossible to play one off against another.

Basically, however, the fact remains that being a popular thriller writer in the nineteen thirties called for something quite exceptional in creative stamina, and even stamina wasn't everything. Just to get started in the game at all, you had to have some pretty rare additional qualifications.

Publishers required from you an ability to pack your story with what was called 'action'. In practice, this usually meant constructing the narrative to allow at least one hold-up at gunpoint and/or murder attempt and/or discovery of a corpse every five pages. And as if that wasn't difficult enough, you were expected to be *au fait* —or to give the impression of being *au fait*—with man-about-town Mayfair. This second requirement was at least as important as the first: indeed, it was the real Open Sesame. Dennis Wheatley, for instance, had not the slightest trouble in getting his first manuscript, *The Forbidden Territory*, accepted in 1933, and surely it is not irrelevant that he had been the director of a Mayfair wine merchants. The man-about-town merry-go-round was something he was in a unique position to understand: the cellars of his firm had supplied a lot of its merriment, and probably imparted not a little of the spin. There may not have been much West End wit about Wheatley's thrillers—his sustained success derives basically from a talent for darkly dogged storytelling allied to a Cecil B. De Mille imagination—but the ease with which he arrived

135

in print in the first instance must have had more than a little to do with his air of writing as though he had a magnum of champagne at each elbow. (And before long, it is only right to add, he had reason to order up magnums by the crateful. *The Forbidden Territory*—an aristocracy-triumphing-against-the-Reds epic in which the Duke de Reichleau and friends carry out a secret invasion of Russia to rescue a friend from Siberian imprisonment— had to be reprinted seven times in its first seven weeks.)

Stamina and a veneer of sophistication: these, then, were the essential credentials for an aspiring early-thirties thriller writer, and the tragedy was that if you had a working-class background you could very easily be trapped in a vicious circle, endlessly exhausting the one in a struggle to acquire the other. Hour after hour of midnight oil was burnt by beginners seeking a way to serve up a corpse with a knife in its back not only every few pages, but unfailingly in accordance with a vast, elusive set of table manners.

Out of the acute agonies of this kind of battling was born one of the major thriller writing talents of our time —that of John Creasey.

Creasey was the son of a motorcoach body-builder and carpenter—a man who knew something about writing, having contributed technical articles and drawings to *The Coachbuilder*. There were nine children in the family; Creasey was the seventh. He was educated first at Fulham Elementary School and then at Sloane Secondary, Chelsea.[1] It was during his last years at Fulham Elementary that he began submitting poems to magazines, at the age of ten. He was already writing stories in 1920, at the age of twelve, and had collected 743 rejection-slips before the age of seventeen, when he sold his first short story for 3 gns. Perhaps, for a moment, he thought he had arrived;

[1] Now absorbed in another school.

he promptly went on to write his first full-length book, a romantic wartime adventure, and started sending it around. But it was five years and ten books later when he had his first novel accepted—by Andrew Melrose in 1932—and it was 1936 before he succeeded in earning a living from his pen. During the period 1927-36, the peak of the Depression years, Creasey worked in an endless succession of dead-end jobs in somewhat uninspiring settings: the stock room of a tube carriage manufacturer, the office of a dairy supply company and so on. He was a factory sweeper at one period, a temporary postman at another. Quite a lot of the time he was unemployed, usually after some boss or other had caught him writing stories during working hours. It is interesting to look at a photograph of the young Creasey. The eyes come blazing out of the sheet with a sort of 'Love On The Dole' intensity, produced not by starvation but by sheer frustration. It is obvious that the struggle to break into this crazy 1930s thriller world, with its scores of publishers, dozens of magazines, unlimited opportunities all blocked by an insistence on ridiculous criteria, left a more than ordinary mark upon him. 'More than ordinary' is right. The boiling internal frustrations of those years pressure-cooked his creative energies to the point that he has since become, quite simply, the most prolific writer in the history of writing. Five hundred and twenty-three books was his total output by 1968; by now the 560 mark has long been passed. And the extraordinary thing is that more than four hundred of his novels are either in print, or on their way back to being in print, at this moment. Even the very early Creaseys being considered in this chapter are selling, and selling in their tens of thousands, on the paperback counters of 1973.

The same applies, of course, to virtually the entire Saint Saga, and to a great deal of Dennis Wheatley. We are, in other words, no longer dealing with half-forgotten thrillers and time-dishonoured heroes, but with works which publishers and public alike are demanding as eagerly now as when they first appeared. (In some cases, considerably more eagerly.)

To put it grandiloquently, we have not only crossed the frontier into the magic thirties; we have entered the mysterious region which it is one of the prime purposes of our expedition to investigate. The Zone of Durability.

'The magic thirties.' To anyone steeped in the studies of left-wing sociologists, the very phrase must seem a contradiction in terms. What could be called magical about this era of depression, deprivation, hunger marches, class division, smug bourgeois snobberies, open fascist tendencies, and from 1933 onwards the steadily growing menace of Hitler? There are a number of answers. One is the background *awareness* of magic, or at least of mystery in the heart of life, possessed by almost every thirties writer, of almost every *genre*. It was the age, after all, of Dunne's *Experiment With Time*, of Jeans's *The Mysterious Universe*, of J. B. Priestley.

As an introduction to the latest edition of his first book, *Seven Times Seven*, Creasey describes how he felt on the day of its first publication, 22 January 1932. A fascinating vignette of life at the height of the Depression, this description ends with something which few contemporary characterisers of the thirties would have thought of adding, and yet which is peculiarly typical of its time: a moment of mystery, of *déjà vu*.

That morning I rushed to the library in Brentford, near my home, and was overjoyed to find a good review in *The Morning Post* ... Soon, however, I had to come down to earth. Being out of work, I had to cycle to the local Labour Exchange to 'sign on'. I could hardly wait to tell my family about the review, but sadly, when I arrived home, everybody was out. I hadn't yet

138

seen a copy of the book but the manager of the nearest
3d-a-week library had promised to get me one. Hardly
daring to hope he had it, I went in: and had one of
the greatest shocks of my life. Years before the book
had been written, I had arrived home after a day of
looking for work, slumped in an armchair and 'seen' a
book without an author's name or title, but with the
shadow of a man with his arm upraised, obviously in
fear. Now I saw it again: the jacket drawing of *Seven
Times Seven*! My cup was running over ...
(Introduction to *Seven Times Seven*, John Long, 1971)

Seven Times Seven is a fast, exciting story, but reading
it is liable to give thriller fans a slight *déjà vu* sensation
themselves. Here we are in the same Sapper-orientated
world that we encountered in Charteris's *X Esquire*, complete with a hero of the Bulldog Drummond breed, and
an opening scene featuring the time-honoured breakfast-
serving butler.

'Domkins,' demanded Peter Augustus Marraday,
'what day is it?'
'Friday, sir.'
Peter Augustus surveyed the small breakfast tray
which was placed before him with a slightly bored air
of resignation. Beneath and beyond the tray were
bedclothes. In front and above the tray were the recognisable parts of Peter. These comprised a mop of corn-
coloured hair, a smooth forehead ... and a large nose
which in its early days had been a nose in a thousand,
but which was now reduced to the ordinary as the
result of contact with a hard, vindictive fist ... Beneath
his face was a vast chest which a décolleté suit of pink
pyjamas immodestly revealed ... He was massive,
muscular and masterful ...

A paragraph or so later, a human touch arrives which
is typically Creasey (Marraday becomes worried about

Domkins's salary being in arrears); but it is not until his second novel, *The Death Miser*, published by Andrew Melrose in the same year, that Creasey's individuality begins to show itself unmistakably. The hero this time is the Hon. James Quinion, and the paragraph in which he is first described is arresting, to put it mildly.

He was a vast man, uncommonly broad of shoulder and long of limb, but his clothes—at the moment he wore a suit of silver greys—fitted him too perfectly. They spoke of affectation, and the perfumed cigarettes, the scented oil that he used for his hair and the complete correctness of every small item of his everyday apparel bespoke the dandy. In a small man, these things might have passed unnoticed, but in the huge Quinion they were incongruous to the point of repulsion.

It almost looks as though in that paragraph we are witnessing a war between Drummond-style muscularity and Charteris-style elegance, with Creasey coming down heavily on the side of the former. One page later, Quinion has divested himself of his silver greys, and become a 'large-limbed, clear-eyed young man' striding rapidly across the Sussex Downs wearing 'a disreputable sports jacket, a pair of flannels that would have disgraced an under-gardener, down-at-heel brogues and an open-necked shirt'.

It is just as well that he is dressed for action. One and a half pages later he is fighting a fiend who is trying to whip the heroine's dog. Within the following fourteen pages, we find him at the heroine's cottage, puzzling over a mysterious pool of blood; being fired at through the window; being attacked by a vicious villain whom he laughingly nicknames 'Funny Face'; being held up at gunpoint by the arch-villain, and finally seeing the story's first body 'topple slowly to the ground, falling on the

140

floor with a sickening crash'. In the book's first eighteen pages, then, we have had two fights, an attempted murder, a hold-up at gunpoint, a pool-of-blood discovery and a toppling corpse—plus an intriguing variation on the Man About Town hero, and the most hate-provoking villain-type known to English fiction, a dog-whipper. Creasey was certainly getting the measure of the market now.

But action isn't all there is to *The Death Miser*. It turns out that the Hon. James Quinion is leading a double life, fooling his relatives that he is an idle dandy, when in reality he is an agent of the British Secret Service, an organisation suddenly re-Christened Department Z. We go with Quinion to meet the head of this Department —and suddenly there occurs a passage which is as impor-tant to a Creasey connoisseur as Simon Templar's first stroll down the beach is to a Charteris lover.

Chapter Six
MR GORDON CRAIGIE
No one who entered the sparsely furnished room in which Gordon Craigie spent eighteen hours out of the twenty-four worried much about the apartment or the appointments. Craigie was perhaps the least-known man in England; he might be concerned in a motor accident, but his name never appeared; he might give an opinion which would change the whole trend of diplomatic relations between one Power and another, but his name never appeared. At the secret conclaves of the Inner Cabinet, he was spoken of as 'Z' ...

Craigie was less a personality than a presence, creat-ing an atmosphere as he sat, immobile, in a swivel-chair in front of a polished desk which at no one time held more than one file of papers ...

The room itself was unremarkable, being furnished very much after the manner of most offices, but possess-ing a brown leather armchair, a gas-ring and a cabinet containing the necessities for minor creature comforts, next to the fireplace ...

One thing with which every visitor was cognisant was that the walls of the room were steel-lined, that its one window was fitted with unbreakable glass, and that its one door could not be opened without Craigie pressing a button.

(*The Death Miser*, now published by John Long)

We have entered an Inner Sanctum, one of the few memorable Inner Sanctums of crime fiction, and what happens inside it is unmistakably Creasey, just as Craigie himself is unmistakably a Creasey creation.

Dozens of writers—Le Queux, Buchan, Laurence Meynell, Sapper—have conducted us into the presence of some Great White Chief of the Secret Service. But not a Chief who stays eighteen hours a day in the same bed-sitter-like office, making his own coffee on a gas-ring. Who puffs endlessly at a drooping meerschaum, slings a well-filled tobacco pouch at you by way of welcome and, no matter what world problem may be pressing on his shoulders, is always a mine of information about your own particular concerns. If you want to know the identity of the villain who bopped you on the head last night near the Kingston Bypass, someone will have quietly telephoned Craigie with the facts. If you want to know whether it is all right to go ahead and make love to the girl with hazel eyes and creamy white shoulders whom you met in Chapter One, then Craigie is the man to tell you. If he says 'no' and you decide to rebel, then he will accept your resignation from the Department with troubled grey eyes but a gentle, understanding smile. He smiles only to indicate sympathy. If you venture to make a joke (and, in these days of facetious repartee, woe betide any hero who didn't, repeatedly), Craigie's lips will barely twitch at the corners, and he is quite likely to reply 'Get out'. On the other hand, if at any time you come into his office in a depressed state—say, dead tired, having had only five hours' sleep in three days—he will invite you

142

to loosen your collar and sit in his own swivel chair; and after you have dropped off, he is liable to stand looking down at you for nearly five minutes before turning away with a smile on his lips, thanking the Goddess of Fortune for bringing Department Z such an employee. And if you are concerned about whether the nation can save itself from a gang of foreign agents, armed as they are with this poison gas for which no antidote is known to man, then the knowledge that Craigie is prowling round his office night and day is in itself an assurance that somehow Britain will worry through.

Worry through. That is the key point. Creasey had found in Craigie the first of his gentle, obstinate *worriers* —and for the first time on paper he had found himself. Craigie, he has told me in a letter, was the first of his characters who really mattered to him. He seemed rather surprised when I wrote back and said that Craigie was a character who had always mattered to me, and, I fancied, to quite a few thousand others. I wonder how many Intelligence recruits during the War went into Whitehall expecting to meet a Gordon Craigie. It is extraordinarily hard to believe that, at least at the height of the blitzes, there wasn't someone like him there.

Craigie appears in all the Department Z books. (There have been thirty of them to date—and it is one of the shortest of Creasey's eleven major series.) Over the years, he has acted as a combination of nursemaid and guru to an endless succession of wounded, dog-tired, or otherwise troubled heroes. He is seldom onstage for more than two or three chapters per book, but it is his scenes that one remembers; his 'presence without a personality' that dominates the series. The last thing that you could call him is a desperado, and technically he has no place at all in this study, except for the fact that his sudden appearance in *The Death Miser* was a moment no review can, or should, resist celebrating: the moment when a master thriller writer, after meeting to the letter all the commercial requirements of his day, first rises to the full height of his individual talent and becomes, not just an entertainer on everybody else's terms, but the maker of an enduring myth that is all—or mostly all—his own.

Not that Creasey, still broke and often on the dole, was in any position to refuse other people's terms if they were offered. In 1933, the year after *Seven Times Seven* and *The Death Miser*, a well-known editor came into Creasey's life, and gentle, obstinate worriers were not what he was looking for.

Monty Haydon had decided that the creator of Peter Augustus Marraday and the Hon. James Quinion was just the fellow to cook up a new-style hero, a sort of aristocratic Saint.

CHAPTER TEN

In which the Toff is far from Saintly, but the Baron is not without his scruples

N O W an aristocratic Saint is, basically, a flat contradiction in terms. The whole point about Simon Templar is that he was an outsider. Elegant, certainly; immaculate, of course; wealthy, yes—through ill-gotten boodle; but a prop of the Establishment, or even a real Society man about town, never. Make the Saint the Hon. Simon Templar, give him an honestly inherited fortune, supply him with a Jeeves-like butler, and you kill the character stone dead. The piratical humour becomes a genial Captain's orders from the quarter-deck; the indignant philosophy a sort of Top Person's in-joke; the drawling nonchalance an assertion of class superiority, and nothing more.

Creasey, I suspect, ran headlong into this sort of difficulty the moment he started to write for *The Thriller*. His first *Thriller* story, 'The Black Circle',[1] is a queer mixture of styles. It begins resoundingly, but with such overblown rhetoric that at any moment one expects the author to break off and start declaiming 'There's A Little Yellow Idol'.

> In the murky saloon bars of the East End of London, and the countless grimy doss-houses in the side streets and alleys branching from the Thames, where the scum

[1] Later lengthened from 25,000 to 60,000 words and published as the novel *Introducing the Toff* (John Long, 1938).

of the earth get drunk and the chief topic of conversation is crime, they called the Hon. Richard Rollison the Toff.

Touching their forelocks, no doubt, at the thought of him, like the respectful scum of the earth they were.

The Toff, we are told in the next paragraph, 'came down from Cambridge with half a million and a hatred of dullness'. He 'travelled the world's farthest corners; and from the dopedens of Shanghai, the dives of San Francisco and the cesspools of Marseilles trickled fantastic stories of his speed on the draw, his uncanny accuracy with a knife, the punch like the kick of a mule which he carried in both hands ...'

Fine. So now we've got a combination Tom Mix, Rat, Bulldog Drummond and Lord Peter Wimsey; but there is no sign yet of the impudent nonchalance that had made the Saint the Saint. As a matter of fact, this element never arrives in the story at all. The Toff, when he appears on the scene in person, is a fast-moving and effective hero, but no great shakes as a humorist.

The Toff grinned, deciding that it was time to break the spell.

'It looks,' he drawled irritatingly, 'as though I've spilled the salt in the gravy. What's the trouble, Achmed?'

He wondered for a moment whether the Egyptian would keep back his rage, and he moved the bulge in his pocket suggestively. It had a steadying effect.

'So you know about the Circle, do you?' breathed the Egyptian.

The Toff beamed.

'But you're smart. Not many men would have guessed that already!' He winked at the girl. 'Great minds are about us, Annabelle.'

And he said other things flippantly ...

(*Introducing The Toff*)

146

That's the general standard of repartee. Compare that with anything in peak-period Charteris, and you will see why Creasey himself refers to the early Toff as a 'rather heavy-footed Saint'.

It is impossible, though, to dismiss Richard Rollison quite like that. Dazzling impudence may not be his forte, but right from the outset he has a certain style of his own.

We have had a moment from the Saint's initial appearance in print. Here is one from the Toff's. Some gunmen blaze away at his car, and puncture one of the tyres. You would have thought that this terror of the Underworld, this man whose speed on the draw freezes Frisco, whose accuracy with a knife coagulates the cesspools of Montmartre, would have leapt into a blaze of dynamic action. Instead, he stumbles forward, losing his grip on his gun and banging his nose on the dashboard. After he has watched the enemy drive off into the night:

'It might have been a lot worse,' he consoled himself, dipping into the toolbox for the jack. He had a habit, when alone, of talking aloud, usually in the plural. It fortified him.

He started to take the wheel off. 'We ought to have the spare wheel on inside a minute,' he told the world at large, 'and then we shall see what they wanted to stop us from seeing. And it looks as if we shall be busy in the not too distant future.'

(*Introducing The Toff*)

What has happened there is surely something very interesting. Instead of the flashy super-hero which Monty Haydon's editorial specifications laid down, Creasey's subconscious has obstinately come up with an altogether different character—a character who is, in a way, closer to Gordon Craigie than the Saint. Those two paragraphs suggest a cheerful, really rather unassuming young man,

147

unsure enough to need to talk to himself aloud to keep his spirits up; quirkish enough to choose to do it in the plural—you would almost say, something of an introvert. A man who, considering that this is part of his spectacular arrival-in-print sequence, is behaving extraordinarily mildly.

The Toff has gone on to do a lot of impossible things in the course of 54 books and forty years, some of them with a considerable flourish. But inside him, all the time, there has been this other Rollison, as mild and reflective as his outer self is dashing and impulsive. And this inner Rollison, often more than a little unsure of himself, is the diametric opposite of the self-sufficient Saint. It is significant that the Toff is very rarely a lone wolf; almost always —in the words of the Barbra Streisand number—'a person who needs people'. Equally significantly, as the series has gone on, the people he has needed have come from all classes: the manservant Jolly, Bill Ebbutt and his East End gang (an adult equivalent of Sherlock Holmes's 'Baker Street Irregulars'), Inspector Grice, the formidable Aunt Gloria and many others whom we shall be meeting later.

The only one of these resident characters to appear in the first Toff story is Jolly, and he barely speaks more than half a dozen lines. But the hallmark of the Toff series—a sort of two-way protectiveness—is there from the outset. The Toff always gets anxious about other characters, especially, of course, the heroine. (Even the very young Toff is rather paternal towards females.) Before the end of most of the Toff stories, there comes a point when the other characters return the compliment, and begin to feel anxious about *him*. No hero more often gets knocked out by explosives, or injured in car crashes; and when the Toff is in hospital (or more frequently a nursing home) all his friends rally round ...

The need to get involved with, to rope in, other people

148

is an unusual characteristic to give a desperado. But it is highly typical of Creasey, and in the case of the Toff it was a stroke of genius. Self-contained, the Toff could hardly have avoided becoming, in the course of time, an exasperating symbol of class dominance As he is, you could almost call him a symbol of human interdependence.

The more one considers the subtlety of this concept, and the evidence that part of it was present in Creasey's subconscious from the start, the harder it becomes to write off the early Rollison as 'a rather heavy-footed Saint'. Indeed, in one or two respects, the Saint begins to seem a slightly heavy-footed Toff.

While researching into the early Toff stories, I spent a fascinating lunch-hour with Mr Fairman, the keeper of the archives at Fleetway House (now IPC Magazines Ltd). He took me down to the vaults to look through some file copies of the *Thrillers* of the Haydon heyday. These are housed, incidentally, in an underground stronghold that would not make an inappropriate setting for the climax of the next Bond screen epic. The only approach is by means of a fire-escape-like structure descending into a kind of man-made gorge between Farringdon Street and the railway line that runs from Ludgate Circus to Holborn Viaduct. At the bottom of the steps, you look up and see rearing above you a miniature cliff-face of blackened brick, as thick with soot as the inside of any railway tunnel. The next moment you are in a concrete fortress—once housing the *Daily Mirror* printing presses, later an air raid shelter—as elaborate as a stretch of the Maginot Line; and five or six corridors later, there is actually a strongroom door, a foot thick, to be negotiated before you are allowed into the dusty presence of Fleetway House's hallowed past.

I concentrated on the *Thriller* file for 1933, the year

149

the Toff first appeared. I was interested to discover what sort of company he had kept on that occasion; who were the other writers and heroes taking part in the Monty Haydon Flying Circus of desperadoes. My eyes were assailed by a fantastic parade of images, as informative as they were nostalgic. Here was an early Saint trade mark, the skeletal figure sloping-shouldered, with an elegant *insouciance* entirely missed by the chirpy, squared-up later versions. Here was an artist's impression of the early Saint himself. Ivor Novello profile, languidly drooping cigarette—it could have been a still from *Triumph of the Rat*.

Other writers, other heroes. I noticed a lot of authors familiar from my own boyhood thriller reading in the very late thirties—Geo. E. Rochester (creator of Grey Shadow and the Flying Beetle), John G. Brandon, Hugh Clevely (creator of the Gang Smasher and Maxwell Archer), James Ronalds, Francis Gerard. Some of the guest appearances startled me. Sydney Horler was there with a weirdo character called Rubber Face, whether hero or villain I hadn't time to see. Peter Cheyney was in with a Lemmy Caution serial. (It must have been one of Lemmy's earliest appearances in print. Good God, was he a Monty Haydon discovery too?)

But the hero of heroes in *The Thriller* of 1933, the character who seemed to be featured in more stories than any other, wasn't a new boy at all, but A. J. Raffles, resurrected from his Boer War grave by Barry Perowne.

The Saint and the Toff, then, were not merely remote descendants of old A. J., but in direct week-by-week competition with him—or, at any rate, with his 1930s alter ego.

There appears to have been quite a Raffles revival in the thirties, perhaps sparked off by the Ronald Colman film of 1930. It is tempting to start spinning theories around this. The thirties love of daredevilry has so far seemed essentially idealistic, opposed to the pompous and priggish sides of respectability, but not to law and order. Following in the footsteps of the Mixer, the Saint and the Toff only broke the law to bring greater law-breakers to book. But was this changing? Was public taste spiralling back on itself, returning to exactly the same disguised disgust with the *status quo* that had inspired the original fervour for Raffles back around 1900? Had the Depression and the hunger marches created a despair, not only about respectability, but about the law and all that it stood for?

Some aspects of the always-complex thirties lend support to such assumptions. You could argue that the Bright Young Things certainly registered a *fin de siècle* degree of restlessness and boredom, and that the success of the gangster movies suggests a love of violence for its own sake. But both the Bright Young Things and the gangster movies were only superficially tough: basically, they were highly romantic. 'Someday I'll find you, moonlight behind you' hummed the Bright Young Things: 'Don't fight this thing, kid, it's bigger than both of us' breathed the gangsters to their molls, angel choirs taking over from tommy-gun rattles on the soundtrack. In the thirties, forbidden waters could generally only titillate if they flowed from a rosily floodlit fountain.

Not that romance was the only thing the thirties expected from its entertainment. Equally sought after was elegance, smoothness, glamour, impudence and gaiety—all with an underlying warmth: style with a capital S and a hat on the side of its head. Most 1930s readers would, I suspect, have found the original Bunny a depressing prig, and the original A.J. a disturbingly cold fish at times. What they wanted—whether Mr Perowne gave it to them or not I can't say, but certainly his illustrators did—was a *new* Raffles, made, so to speak, in the 1930s image: a lounging, immaculate Raffles bursting

151

with bright, bitter, brittle wit, and smiling mockingly to hide a very gently broken heart.

In 1935, a competition to find a contemporary Raffles was presented by two publishers, George G. Harrap in England and J. P. Lippincott in the United States. The prize offered was £1,500—a lot of money in those days when payment for a single novel was often around £50 —and, to quote the *Daily Dispatch*, the entrants included 'novelists of established repute in every corner of the globe'.

What was plainly called for was a story not only of action, but of very considerable polish and sophistication. It was the very last thing, you would imagine, which could be won by the creator of the anxious Craigie and that mildest of jesters, the Toff.

Creasey himself didn't think he had much chance of winning at the outset. In the autumn of 1935, hard up and once more on the dole, he read about the competition, and on an impulse, wrote the opening chapter of a book called *Meet the Baron*. He believes now that he wrote it more with Monty Haydon in mind than the competition. He had no plot, to begin with: all Creasey's plots, he has told me, 'come as he writes', which must mean that he leaves it to his remarkable subconscious to come up with whatever it feels the situation requires. On this occasion, the result was so unlike previous Creaseys that it was as though a new author had taken over. An author who shows no immediate interest in gun battles or *Thriller*-style action; an author who might, for that matter, never have read Hornung, Leblanc or Graeme. *Meet the Baron* starts in a country manor, where Colonel Bolton and Lady Mary Overnden are idly discussing the difficulties Lady Mary is having with her daughter, Marie.

The trouble with Marie Overnden seems to be that she is something of a gold-digger, and is on the point of discarding her latest boy-friend, who has gambled away

152

a fortune, and is now reduced to an income of £1,000 a year. This young man, one John Mannering, has just 'a seven-room bungalow, one servant, two acres of land and two horses', but nothing more.

'He could give up things—one of the horses,' says the Colonel, 'as a man inspired'. But Lady Overnden doubts if that will satisfy her daughter, and Lady Overnden is right. That night, 'beneath the spreading branches of the oaks that bordered the lake in the Manor grounds', John Mannering proposes—and is icily refused.

Mannering takes it very well. He swings round with 'a bitter humour in his eyes, but a humour for all that'. Next day, he takes 'the morning train to town'.

It is left to Lady Overnden to sum up the situation to the Colonel.

'She broke something in Mannering—I know, I saw it this morning: in his eyes, on his lips. Oh, he *took* it all right—on top, only on top.'

The Colonel 'grew suddenly wise. He slipped his arm round his lady's shoulders and let her cry.'

That was all there was to this first chapter: a smooth, elegant Country House romance episode, a little reminiscent of non-Bulldog-Drummond Sapper, the Sapper of *The Man in Ratcatcher*, or perhaps of Warwick Deeping, a very popular romantic novelist of the time. Creasey stopped there, and showed the story to Monty Haydon —who was unimpressed, to put it mildly. Then a job came up, and John Mannering's matrimonial setbacks went clean out of Creasey's mind. (Out of his conscious mind, that is. Not out of his subconscious one, by any means, as events will show.) Perhaps *consciously* Creasey had a feeling that for once his insight had led him astray. I doubt if he had ever written nine pages before without a hint of mystery or menace. And if it couldn't even be considered as a £58 story for *The Thriller*, what chance was there that it could win a £1,500 international contest?

By December 1935, Creasey was out of a job once more: he ran through twenty-five jobs altogether in those lean early years. To make ends meet, he got work as a temporary postman helping with Christmas deliveries. On the morning of Christmas Day, 1935, he cycled miles home through the snow to his home in Southall, just in time to join the family for Christmas dinner. It was while browsing through some books after this dinner that he suddenly remembered the competition, and became fired with a new determination to enter it. It wasn't so easy now, though. The closing date was 31 December, six days away. Entries had to be at least 80,000 words—and a 5,000-word opening chapter was all he had.

But he was jobless, with time on his hands. For the last six days of 1935, he must have used every minute of it. He finished the remaining 75,000 words of *Meet the Baron* by the afternoon of 31 December itself, and cycled the nine miles to London, delivering the typescript just as Harrap's were closing. In July the following year, he heard that the judges (who included Dennis Wheatley and Leonard R. Gribble) had awarded him the prize. The only disappointment was that it had been reduced to £1,000, an American magazine which had offered U.S. serial rights having in the meantime closed down.

Now this is, of course, the kind of dramatic story which all biographers crave for. It's almost rags-to-riches, and you've got snow and Christmas and a touch of the Dick-Turpin's-ride-to-York thrown in. My own suspicion, though, is that something rather deeper than a Holly-wood-style success episode was going on. I think that Creasey's creative subconscious—in terms of productivity alone, the most remarkable in the history of writing—was beginning to demonstrate its full strength, insight and cunning. My belief is that in the autumn it had started to show Creasey a revolutionary way to handle the Amateur Cracksman theme; but the result promised to

154

be so different from the action thriller normally demanded by the publishers of 1935 that he had dropped the project. It remained, though, in his subconscious, which went on working on it and perfecting it—and then impelled Creasey to start writing when the schedule was so tight that his conscious mind had no chance to argue; could only, so to speak, take direct dictation.

Certainly, *Meet the Baron* does not read like a book written in six days. The characterisation is subtler, the dialogue sharper, the plot more ingenious, the action more intricate than in anything Creasey had done before. And, perhaps because so much of it originated direct from his own subconscious, there is another factor present, too: the sense that one has stepped into a different world altogether from those of the Toff and Department Z.

It is a rare gift in crime fiction, this ability to create, not merely distinctive characters, but distinctive *worlds* for them to live in. Many crime writers, particularly in the thirties, had more than one regular hero: but they do not offer more than one world. John Dickson Carr's Gideon Fell and H. M. are rather different heroes; so are Peter Cheyney's Lemmy Caution and Slim Callaghan; so are Buchan's Hannay and Leithen. But both Fell and H. M. inhabit a Dickson Carr universe, where bodies are rarely found elsewhere than in locked rooms; Caution and Callaghan may differ slightly in their wisecracks, but both drink neat Bourbon first thing, before they even get around to shaving; Hannay and Leithen are both Buchanite in their love of cold baths and long tramps across moors. The same atmosphere, the same way of putting things, the same attitude to events, generally runs through the whole of a crime writer's works, as personal and as recognisable as a signature. But this is not the case with Creasey. The Baron is as different from the Toff—or at least the early Toff—as if he had been created by an entirely different mind, with a different attitude to life,

155

a different approach to writing, even a different sense of humour. The author of the Baron is interested in all the things that the author of the early Toff is not: the fundamental motivation of the hero, the actual mechanics of crime, the technicalities of being a bandit, the human reactions of the police. The Baron, unlike Raffles, Lupin and Blackshirt, does not step onstage fully proficient in the arts of safebreaking, a wonder hero all set for Exploit No. 1. He is simply John Mannering, a 35-year-old man about town (for once, a convincing man about town) who has been jilted by a gold-digger, and is fed-up with being hard-up. (As, indeed, Creasey must have been by this time.) He plans his entry into crime coolly, as a step-by-step operation, and he is a man who cuts his coat according to his cloth. He spends the last of his dwindling capital in creating a reputation for affluence, and consequently becomes the member of a set gravitating around the smartest parties. He secretly discovers the names of various old lags and pays them to give him instruction in such things as lock-picking and safe-breaking, but meanwhile he is only adept at quick snatches of small stuff. He is good at whipping the odd brooch off a dowager duchess's corsage, for example, after he has organised a failure of the lights in a ballroom. The original Raffles would have had considerable contempt for him, because he was technically a guest at the parties, and cared nothing if his victim was the hostess. He goes to particular pains to get himself invited to one glittering occasion: the wedding of the gold-digging Marie Overnden. While lounging nonchalantly round the table where the wedding gifts are on display, he spots a £5,000 pearl necklace, a gift to the bride from Lady Kenton, a dowager whose corsage he once de-brooched. Lady Kenton herself is standing beside him at the time, and happens to stumble across the table. Mannering gallantly helps her to her feet, in the same moment swiftly pocketing the pearls. In

156

the ensuing scene, he acts with a majestic effrontery that takes him right up into the Lupin class.

Seeing that there is rather a mess in the room—two gold-backed hairbrushes, a set of carvers and a glass bowl have all been swept on to the floor by the stumbling dowager—he turns to a man he now knows to be a plain-clothes policeman.

'You'd better check the presents, and make sure everything's here,' he suggested, and the man grimaced, but nodded in agreement.

'I don't suppose anything will be missing, sir, but if anything does happen it'd be safest. There have been several people in and out.'

'That's just it,' said Mannering. He offered the other a cigarette, and smiled to himself as his hand inside his pocket brushed against the pearls. 'Do you need any help?'

The Yard man was beginning to wonder if the other was a colleague ...

'No, thanks,' he said, refusing both the help and the cigarette; 'we'll manage all right. Be best to shut the room for half an hour, though. Would you mind—'

'I'll see Colonel Belton,' promised Mannering.

(Meet the Baron)[2]

And, of course, he strolls out of the room, pearls in pocket. The writing may be quiet, but if that isn't style, in the full Gallic sense of the term, what is? It is not surprising that that French Jack-of-all-arts, Jean Cocteau, pronounced the Baron his favourite character in crime fiction.

At this point, incidentally, the plot thickens. There is a search, and a dummy necklace is found in the pocket of an innocent young American, Gerry Long. The Baron does not understand this development, but it is against

[2] Currently available in a Lythway library reprint.

157

his code that anyone else should be arrested on suspicion for one of his, the Baron's, crimes. To clear Gerry, he writes a letter to the press, which is again Gallic in its brevity, pertinence and polish:

'I have been working against the police for some months, without the slightest cause for worry. At the house of Col. George Belton I took the pearl necklace that has since caused so much publicity and speculation. My method was simple, which may explain the ease with which the burglary was accomplished. But simplicity begets monotony. It occurs to me that this letter may stir the police to greater efforts to apprehend THE BARON.'

The most interesting thing about the Baron *is* this code of his. It is significantly different from the code of any previous cracksman in twentieth-century crime fiction, and reflects the ways in which the ideas of the new thirties thriller writers—one could call them *The Thriller* writers —were significantly different from those of most of the authors of previous decades. Ten years before, in *Black-shirt*, a great fuss had been made about the hero's gentlemanly status, and Verrell repeatedly felt guilty about his dishonesty.

There is very little agonising about dishonesty in *Meet the Baron*, and the question of behaving like a gentleman scarcely arises at all. It rarely enters John Mannering's head that he might be Letting Down His Class, or that, on occasion, his glorified form of pocket picking might be labelled Abuse of Hospitality. Abstract questions of chivalry do not intrude unduly, either. (He will rob a rich woman as cheerfully as a rich man, and the girl who has jilted him he will rob most cheerfully of all.) In the first Baron book, at least, no one ever suggests—and he does not even suggest to himself—that it would be more honourable for him to do a Decent Job of Work. In all

158

this, his standards roughly—though only roughly—parallel the Saint's.

Nothing could illustrate more clearly the complex nature of the 1930s public. Here is an age when thriller-readers of all classes favour Society heroes. Yet, in the minds of those readers, right-wing class compulsions are infinitely weaker than they were. On the other hand, the left-wing (to extreme left-wingers, bourgeois) insistence on the puritan ethic of earning a living is considered rather a boring point to bring up. It looks as though the thirties reading public knew how to keep the prigs of left *and* right at bay.

But while the Baron is not remotely concerned about whether he is behaving either as a gentleman or as a good citizen of Britain, 1935, he is passionately particular about things to which Raffles and Lupin would hardly have given a thought. Before committing any crime, he asks himself again and again whether his victim can really stand the loss. He robs only people who can afford to replace the stolen item many times over. When on one occasion he knocks out an armed guard, he barely sleeps until he reads in the papers that no serious injury was sustained. (His own favourite weapon is that rather un-likely contraption beloved of 1930s thriller writers, the ether pistol.) He will go to any lengths to see that no innocent person is accused of one of his crimes. And at the end of *Meet the Baron*, although half-fainting from a bullet wound himself, he spectacularly saves the life of an Inspector, one Bill Bristow, even though Bristow had been on the point of arresting him, and the Baron knows well enough that the Inspector is a cop first and foremost, and will not spare him from arrest in return.

The Baron's ethos, then, discards pseudo-chivalry and 'noblesse-oblige' compulsions, and yet contains no serious element of anti-Establishment anger—only anti-society-gold-diggers anger. It slices through the 'pseudos' and

159

irrelevancies and brings us to the bedrock of simple, irreducible romanticism. The one question that concerns him is: *Am I, as a human being, doing serious harm to any other human being?*

Put like that, it's rather shaking. It is so obviously more, rather than less, demanding that any class-conscious Gentleman Outlaw's code.

At the beginning of the last chapter, we met John Creasey struggling vainly to break into the thirties thriller scene, at any level. It seems only right to end this Creasey sequence with a picture of him breaking out all over it, at every level.

Department Z novels from Andrew Melrose ... The prizewinning *Meet the Baron* and a sequel, *The Baron Returns*, from Harrap's ... Detective novels from Cassell's ... Cheap bookstall romances from the humble Fiction House ... Sports novels, schoolboy air thrillers, even a Western—the list of John Creasey's books published in his first big year, 1937, devastatingly includes them all. Just for fun, here it is in full.[3]

1. *Hardbacks (priced around 7/6)*
   Dept Z novels (Andrew Melrose Ltd)
   Carriers of Death
   Days of Danger
   Baron novels (under the name Anthony Morton—Harrap Ltd)
   Meet the Baron
   The Baron Returns
   Detective novels (under the name Michael Halliday—Cassell Ltd)

[3] Extracted from 'A John Creasey Bibliography' by R. E. Briney and John Creasey—*The Armchair Detective*, Minnesota, Oct., 1968.

Three for Adventure
Four Find Danger
Thrillers (under the name Peter Manton—Wright & Brown Ltd)
Stand by for Murder
Murder Manor
Western (under the name Tex Riley—Wright & Brown Ltd)
Two Gun Girl (3/6)
Romance (under the name Henry St John Cooper— Sampson Low)
Chains of Love

2. *Juvenile hardbacks (priced 2/6 or 1/-)*
The Black Biplane
The Secret Aeroplane Mystery
The Air Marauder
The Mystery Flight
The S.O.S. Flight
(Publisher: Sampson Low)

3. *Original paperbacks (priced around 6d)*
Sporting novels (under the name Patrick Gill— Mellifont)
The Fighting Footballer
The Laughing Lightweight
Thrillers (under the name M. E. Cooke—Mellifont)
The Moving Eye
The Rover
The Hadfield Mystery
Romances (under the name Margaret Cooke— Fiction House)
Troubled Journey
False Love or True Love?
Romance (under the name Elise Fechamps— Fiction House)
True Love

4. *Fourpenny thrillers in paperback* (*app. price*)
   Murder by Magic (Fleetway House)
   The Mysterious Mr Rocco (Mellifont)

In addition, there were Toff stories in the *Thriller* and at least one Sexton Blake.

John Creasey has supplied me himself with a fascinating footnote on 1937. In the June of that year, he wrote two novels (each of 70,000–80,000 words) in a single week. 'And on the Saturday afternoon,' he adds proudly, 'I played cricket!'

Now when Creasey wrote at that rate, his subconscious was usually cooking up one of its distinctive worlds. Sure enough, one of the novels in question was *Secret Errand*, the first of the series of thrillers he published under the name Norman Deane. These Deane books were a new departure for Creasey: spy stories written in the first person. Their protagonist, to begin with, was one Bruce Murdoch, and during the War years they featured the Withered Man, von Horsell, who was for me the most memorable villain of the 'Ach-Himmel—because-of-you-I-haff-been-reprimanded-by-the-Führer' brigade. A number of the Norman Deane novels are back in print; the rest are scheduled for republication in the next three years.

The other product of that busy week was *The Speaker*, the first of the Patrick Dawlish adventures written under the *nom de plume* Gordon Ashe. There have been more than fifty of these to date, and new ones are still appearing. Dawlish is a hero of the Bulldog Drummond school, although in fact he resembles Drummond no more closely than the Toff resembles the Saint or the Baron Raffles. It would be interesting to explore why, but in 1961 Dawlish became Deputy Assistant Commissioner for Crime at Scotland Yard, and 'Britain's delegate to a world Police Convention in constant session', and if that doesn't rule a hero out for consideration as a desperado,

162

I don't know what does. But there is no reason why I should not salute his creation in passing, and frankly confess my awe of his creator.

Twenty-five novels published in a single year.

Two distinctive worlds—each the basis of a long-running thriller series—created in one week.

To achieve the former, you've got to be an unusual author, almost certainly one trained in some such frenetic forcing-house as the nineteen thirties.

To achieve the latter, you've got to be John Creasey.

CHAPTER ELEVEN

In which 1066 arrives in 1937, but everything gets more modern all the same

IT was in 1937, the year of what the Americans would call the 'blossoming forth' of John Creasey, that Monty Haydon's *Thriller* found the third and last of its major desperadoes: Norman Conquest, the creation of one Berkeley Gray. This time, Monty Haydon hadn't searched the circulating library shelves for an up-and-coming author: he had turned to one of the hardest-working and most distinguished resident writers of Fleetway House itself. Berkeley Gray was none other than Edwy Searles Brooks, the man who had spent sixteen years writing 20,000 words a week about St Franks for the *Nelson Lee Library*, and who had created that pioneer piratical desperado, Waldo the Wonder Man, back in 1918. It can be said that Norman Conquest *was* Waldo the Wonder Man, updated and groomed for stardom by the same editorial hand that had so brilliantly groomed the Saint, but had somehow never quite succeeded in dusting down the Toff.

Unlike the Toff, Norman Conquest was wholly an extrovert hero, unmistakably from the Simon Templar stable. Indeed, in his previous incarnation, he had been horsing around the paddock ten years before the Saint was even dreamed of.

Let it not be thought, though, that there was anything about Norman which was remotely behind the times. If there was one dominant characteristic of the first Conquest stories, it was a relentless determination to be absolutely modern; nineteen thirty-ish through and

164

through. It isn't difficult to understand why, if one puts oneself in Edwy Searles Brooks's place. Here he was, pushing fifty. He had spent his entire professional life churning out words by the million for Fleetway House papers. No one except Frank Richards (Charles Hamilton) himself had come near to equalling the Brooks output on the schoolboy story front, and there are still heated arguments going on about which of the two produced the most. But whereas Frank Richards's fortunes were still riding high, with *Magnets* and *Gems* selling in their thousands every week, Brooks's *Nelson Lee Library* had folded back in 1933. Whispers may well have been going round that he was out of touch, past his prime. All the floodlights in the Fleetway boys' paper arena were, in any case, being focused on *The Thriller*, and on Monty Haydon's performing troupe of young authors, who were doing things and going places in a way that no Fleetway boys' paper writer had been known to do before. By 1937, for example, Leslie Charteris was well established in America, and the first Saint film (*The Saint in New York*, starring Louis Hayward) was already on a Hollywood studio floor. Young John Creasey had carried off the £1,000 cracksman prize with the Baron (not a *Thriller* character—through no fault of Creasey's) and the Toff was shortly to appear in hard covers. Plenty of other Haydon authors were becoming familiar names in the circulating libraries, too. How had they achieved all this? By cashing in on the current craze (it was by 1937 almost a mania) for buccaneering desperadoes. But if there was anyone in England who ought by rights to be benefiting from this craze, it was surely Edwy Searles Brooks. Not even Bulldog Drummond had appeared in print when he had first created the mocking Waldo.

I am only guessing that Brooks's thinking ran along these lines, of course. But all through the first Conquest stories one can surely hear the voice of an old pro saying

165

to himself 'By heaven, I'm going to show these youngsters a thing or two on the subject of laughing desperadoes.' And by heaven, show them he does.

I have read several thousand thrillers in my time, of all types, *genres* and eras, but never have I come across anything that matched the sheer high-spirited gusto of the first Conquest books, *Mr Mortimer Gets the Jitters*, *Vultures Ltd*, and *Miss Dynamite*. (Published in hardback by Collins from 1938.) All the energy that had driven Brooks through sixteen million words of St Frank's stories, all the experience gleaned from nineteen years of Waldo's Wonder Stunts in *Union Jack* and its successor *Detective Weekly*, was now poured into Norman Conquest, the indomitable '1066'. No words can describe this hero of heroes better than his creator's. Chapter 1 of his first story begins:

> As Norman Conquest strode along the empty country road his feet crunched in the deep snow, and he sang. There was a laugh in his lilting baritone voice and a deadly purpose in his heart.
>
> (*Mr Mortimer Gets the Jitters*, Collins)

The laughing desperado bit is thus established right from paragraph one. Later on the same page the buccaneering build-up begins. We are told that 'nine out of ten of his blood corpuscles are of the exact shape, size and description as those that flowed so recklessly on Flodden Field in 1513'. Norman's ancestors, 'long known as the "Lawless Conquests", had fought under the Percies in the Border Wars'. When he was seventeen, we learn later, he had run away from home and for eight years had knocked about 'on practically every corner of this earth —including Cochin-China, Siberia, Borneo and Wigan'. A rather curious list, but all the best places had been pre-empted by earlier Haydon protégés—the Toff, as we saw, having bagged in one sentence the dives of Frisco, the dopedens of Shanghai, and the cesspools of Marseilles.

On page 2 the serious laughing begins. Norman, still striding along and singing (that bloodcurdling piratical ditty, 'Whistle While You Work', as a matter of fact—highly topical since it came from Disney's *Snow White*, just released) turns a corner and sights his enemy's country-house headquarters. 'He interrupted his song,' we are told, 'with a gale of mischievous laughter that struck the face of the building and came echoing back to him like a broadcast by the BBC Male Voice Choir.' Now that in itself was daringly mischievous: it just wasn't done in those pre-Band Waggon days to make jests about the BBC. But it is a few pages later, when the villainous owner of the house, Geoffrey Mortimer, has captured Conquest and surrounded him with thugs, levelling guns, that Brooks really begins to show his style.

Norman politely asks if he can smoke. Since there are no less than four guns covering him, the thug leader, a man called Burton, thinks it safe to give permission.

Norman laughed, and lowered his arms.

'Aren't you taking a big chance?' he asked, as he leisurely opened his cigarette case. 'This gasper I'm going to light, for example. How do you know it isn't charged with poison gas, or something? Or this automatic lighter,' he added, deftly producing the article in question from his waistcoat pocket. 'Supposing, when I press the catch, it doesn't burst into flames, but gives a terrific report? ...'

He flicked the lighter and it burst into a little flame.

'That's funny,' said Norman, frowning. 'I'll try again.'

'Cut out the comedy!' snapped Burton impatiently, with a wave of his gun. 'I've had enough—'

Norman held out the lighter at arm's length, and flicked it again, and there was a blinding flash and a deafening, ear-splitting detonation.

167

A beautifully judged triple-take, that, which rivals even the best getting-out-of-hold-up performances of the Saint (who had, incidentally, been using exploding cigarette tricks since 1931). Within seconds, of course, it is Conquest who has a gun, and the thugs who have parted with theirs. And any readers who are so conventional as to imagine that a tying-up scene is coming next simply don't know their Gay Desperado.

He stepped forward and swiftly pocketed the lethal weapons. 'Now, boys, we're going to be busy. Ever done any furniture removing? I don't like the way that bookcase is placed.' He waved his gun towards a massive piece of furniture which stood flat to the wall. 'I think it would look a lot better across the corner.'

The crooks, their ears 'still ringing with the sound of bullets which had whistled almost through their hair', heave and tug at the heavy bookcase until at last it stands in the required position. Even the arch-criminal Mortimer joins in.

'All you've got to do now, customers,' says Norman, his eyes, naturally, 'full of mocking mischief', 'is climb to the top of the bookcase and drop in to the triangular space at the back ... I could, of course, make Nunky yank those curtains down and tear them into strips and bind you up. But this business of binding up crooks is out of date, and not always satisfactory ...'

At one stroke, customers, the Saint, the Toff and all the other binders and gaggers of defeated opponents are put firmly in their place. It's curtain up on a new age now that 1066 is here. And don't imagine I'm being wholly ironical. The twelve-year-old boy who defended Norman Conquest against all comers at school lives on inside me still, and is liable to keep my impartiality under serious pressure throughout this chapter. Even my present self unreluctantly concedes that few heroes were quite so effective as

168

1066 when at bay—when, for instance, being tied up in noisome cellars. Later in *Mr Mortimer Gets the Jitters*, the crooks fling him into a brick-sided pit, ten feet deep by eight feet square, the walls 'covered with wet filth and slime'. Burton is again the chief thug, although his boss, the cringing Mortimer, is quivering in the background.

With a heave he hoisted Norman upright, and then bound his wrists securely to the iron ring in the wall.

'You won't see the water rising, but you'll feel it!' he said tauntingly. 'But there's nothing you can do about it, see? And when it's all over you won't be marked. We'll leave you nice and quiet until the pubs are closed. Easy enough, then, to fish you out and drop you into the river.'

While speaking he had removed the gag from Norman's mouth.

'You've got a nice night for the job,' said Norman coolly. 'Plenty of fog and murk. By the way, my lungs are in first-class condition. Think it's wise to remove the doings?'

The affable professionalism of that is surely wholly delightful. Nor does it desert Norman when the crooks depart. He sings lustily as the trap door slams behind them, carries on singing until the water is rising past his knees, and then comments severely: 'An ingenious sort of trap, but medieval. If these thugs knew me better, they'd realise how they'd insulted me. I've got out of better cellars than this with a hairpin.'

He doesn't have a hairpin with him on this occasion, but he does have a wristwatch with a flexible metal band, concealing three steel blades with teeth like fretsaws. (An item which has been quite fairly introduced earlier in the story: to get a hero out of a flooding cellar with a gimmick not previously mentioned is unthinkable in a good thriller. It is as bad form as concealing a vital clue until the denouement of a detective story.) With the

169

aid of the saw, he is out of the cellar in a paragraph, and ringing the arch-villain, Mortimer, at his home within two pages. He does not ring just to tell Mortimer that he has escaped from his clutches. By that time—such is the pace of the early Conquests—he has set Mortimer's riverside warehouse (full of stolen dope) ablaze.

'Cheerio, Blot! You'll be seeing me,' he says by way of farewell, and this is no less than the truth. Less than an hour later, when Mortimer is hurrying back from a quick, frantic visit to the scene of the fire, Conquest, now disguised as a newspaper boy, is sidling up to him to proffer a copy of an evening paper with a faked 'Stop Press' designed to panic him into believing that he is wanted by Scotland Yard. It really isn't any wonder the man gets the jitters.

Pace and modernism—that was the formula which Brooks stuck to for all he was worth. He supplied Norman with a heroine, Joy Everard, who is as unmistakably 1937-ish as 1066 himself. She walks onstage immediately after the three thugs have climbed over the bookcase in the hold-up scene, an 'absurdly tiny slip of a thing' wearing 'a neat three-quarter-length coat and skirt of astrakhan cloth'. Her face is 'full of a curiously elfin charm, with eyes as dark and lustrous as dewdrops in the night'. It is love at first sight, in full Hollywood style, and then some.

'Hullo, Pixie!' said Norman, smiling.
She smiled in return, and all the lights in the room seemed dim by comparison. She looked at Norman, and saw his gay, dashing, cavalier assurance, and her answer was as inevitable as the four seasons.
'Hullo, Desperado!' she said simply.

A few pages later she is leading Norman towards her racy MG two-seater. 'Jump in. We'll drive to London; you can have a few hours' sleep at my flat, and then—'
Now this suggestion, in 1937, was scandalous enough
170

to freeze any hero rigid, or perhaps one should say frigid. Back in 1935, John Mannering had nearly had a blue fit when the heroine, a girl artist called Lorna, insisted on spending a night in his flat to look after him when he had sustained a bullet wound. Conquest is less shaken, but only slightly.

'I suppose you've got an aunt, or some such useful article, knocking about in the background?'

'No; I haven't any people at all, and I'm the only occupant of the flat,' she replied; and she turned her face towards him and smiled. 'You're not afraid of me, are you?'

'I rather thought,' said Norman, 'that you might be afraid of me.'

She shook her tiny head.

'Isn't it funny?' she replied, suddenly becoming serious. 'I've never known any man in the whole world I would trust. I've known you only about an hour, and the thought of not trusting you is too silly even to discuss.'

That was the key thing about the Gentleman Outlaws: in treatment of women at least, they were gentlemen to a man. Sex appears in the Conquest books rather obliquely, but it is a persistent undercurrent for all that, and occasionally a deafening torrent. In the third Conquest book, *Miss Dynamite* (Collins, 1939), Norman meets a beautiful villainess, Primrose Trevor—'an opponent worthy of his steel', says the blurb at the beginning, although to judge from one or two of their encounters the metal gets a little molten at times.

Norman's chin, after a brief struggle, ceased looking like a lump of granite, and became jellified. He could no longer resist the sweetly appealing lips which quivered so temptingly just beneath his. He took a swift nose dive. His lips pressed down upon hers; and she, far from withdrawing in simulated innocence, gripped

171

his arms with passionate fervour, pressed her quivering body close to his, and gave him the works.

What kind of works Miss Dynamite gave Norman isn't entirely clear. But after two minutes 'the marrow in his bones turned to molten larva, and his wits, what remained of them, were scattered some miles over the Essex border'—and in a 1930s thriller, prose couldn't get much more torrid than that. Joy, it should be mentioned, is by no means as acquiescent as the Saint's Patricia Holm to these extracurricular activities on the part of her desperado.

'So this is the charming little prairie flower that Norman's fallen in love with!' thought the girl, as she deftly emerged from her hiding place and ran to the door. 'Primrose, my foot! Her name's Poison Ivy!'

(*Miss Dynamite*)

Speaking of sex, one of the thoroughly modern things about *Mr Mortimer Gets the Jitters* (an element that is, in fact, strikingly reminiscent of *Thoroughly Modern Millie*) is its dabbling in White Slavery. In the second part of the book, a fiend called Sir Nicholas Glibley has the unpleasant, but in thrillers somewhat prevalent, practice of sending boatloads of beauties out to Buenos Aires.

This part ends spectacularly with an episode which, even if filmed today, would bring roars of protest about violence. And it isn't entirely sexless either. Norman Conquest, clad only in vest and underpants, swims out to the Glibley yacht as it is gliding through an estuary with three luscious lovelies and Joy all prisoners on board.

Reaching the deck, he streaks 'like a muscular ghost for the bridge'. Then:

'I thought we'd meet here, Sir Stench,' said Norman Conquest, with a laugh that nearly froze the surrounding atmosphere.

Sir Nicholas Glibley who stood beside the wheel, where he had been frantically urging the captain to make all speed, turned with a staggering roll.

'Good God! Conquest! It's impossible—'

'Not many things are impossible to a man with a purpose like mine,' interrupted Norman, his words slashing through the air like swordthrusts. 'Pardon me one moment.'

Crash!

Before Sir Nicholas could even come out of the bewilderment which Norman's move had occasioned, something which felt like the bows of a destroyer hit him on the chin. He sagged to the planks in a heap; and Norman, taking no notice of the captain's expostulations, seized that outraged man by the scruff of his neck and the seat of his trousers, and dropped him on to the deck below. If he escaped with only one broken leg he was lucky.

While the captain lies on the deck twitching convulsively, various members of the crew start rushing towards the bridge. Conquest fires two shots 'with such deadly accuracy' that two of the men lose their left ears. The others scuttle away. 'Like lightning' Norman turns, grips the wheel, and plunges the bows of the yacht into the hulk of a nearby wreck. Every man on deck is flung headlong, except Norman, who goes to the top of the bridge ladder, and commands them all to jump overboard.

'If any of you sons of Belial can't swim, it's too bad! Go to it, rats!' he yells, and shoots dead the one man who fires back.

As the crew jumps, Conquest uncoils a length of rope which he finds handy, passes it over Sir Nicholas Glibley's shoulders and draws it tight. Glibley is recovering consciousness.

'Listen, Conquest,' he babbled. 'Be sensible! I'm willing to make terms—'

'We don't talk the same language,' interrupted the Desperado. 'I don't need you for some minutes, so I'm going to put you where I can find you.'

173

He hoists 'his palpitating victim over the edge of the bridge-rail where, immediately below, was the sea' and pays out the rope until his victim's head is only just above the surface. He leaves him there while he rescues the girls ('I shall have to ask you to excuse the undies, ladies') and on his return he finds that the yacht has unexpectedly listed to starboard, and that Glibley has been drowned.

'And the Desperado looked down, and his conscience gave no twinge.'

There is something strongly reminiscent of a James Bond film in scenes like that. And as a matter of fact, in general terms, Conquest seems to me the character closest to James Bond of all the thirties heroes.

This may seem a pretty curious conclusion. Fleming was obviously more of a literary artist than Brooks; Bond was conceived as a 'blunt instrument' of the Secret Service and has, at first sight, very little in common with a Laughing Desperado.

Nevertheless I am convinced that Fleming, at some period in his past, however brief, must have been either a Waldo or a Conquest fan. The evidence is purely circumstantial, but look how it builds up.

In the first place, there is the fact that Bond and Conquest both had much-stressed numerical aliases. In the second place, there is the love of mechanical gimmickry. Listen to Joy Everard checking that Norman is properly kitted out for one of his earlier assaults on Sir Nicholas Glibley:

'Got your cigarette-case?'
'I'm never without it,' he replied, carefully opening the case at the hinge side and selecting a smoke ...
'Your wrist watch?'
'All present and correct.'
He touched a hidden catch in the flexible metal band ...

'Gun?'

'Comfortably on the hip,' he replied, patting his pocket.

'Then you seem to be set for any kind of trouble that breaks loose.'

(Mr Mortimer Gets the Jitters)

In the third place, there is the tendency for Brooks's villains to go in for spectacular torture effects—although Brooks took care that nobody actually got hurt, least of all the elfin-faced Pixie:

She heard a series of strange clicks, and the sounds came from various spots near the floor. Then, looking down, she saw jets of steam spurting upward like a series of miniature fountains. The temperature of the room rose rapidly. They were giving her the heat, and it would go on and on until—

(Until, as a matter of fact, Glibley suddenly realises that Joy is 'worth big money to us—big money!' and orders an underling to 'go in there and get her out—if one atom of her beauty is harmed I'll kill you!')

Circumstantial evidence, yes. A lot of thrillers of the thirties had, in varying degrees, the elements that I have been describing: Sax Rohmer, whom Fleming acknowledged as an influence, had the arch-villains and the torture scenes; a lot of secret service stories had numbered agents, although the numbers were rarely flourished, and cigarette gimmicks were not unknown even to the original Raffles.

But take all these things together, and add one more fact—the fact that in one of the early novels Conquest is turned into a gilded statue and threatened with death through pore-suffocation just as a character is in *Goldfinger*—and it no longer appears quite so ridiculous that Bond may have had a touch of Norman ancestry.

Certainly we can say that 1066 was the 007 of 1938–8.

CHAPTER TWELVE

In which the Desperadoes come thick and fast, and it looks as though the Saint deserves his halo

W E have now arrived right at the end of the nineteen thirties; at the closing hours of the Day of the Desperado. There is time for one last quick look round before the dusk sets in.

The Saint is now a cult figure in Britain, and a growing success in the States. The second and third Saint films (*The Saint Strikes Back* and *The Saint in Palm Springs*, both starring George Sanders) are now on release. Charteris is being besieged by interviewers and by requests for personal details about the Saint. In *The First Saint Omnibus* (1939) he delivers what is probably the most often-quoted statement which a crime writer has ever made about his creation. (Though possibly it is rivalled by Chandler's 'Down these mean streets a man must go ...' explanation of Philip Marlowe.)

'I have been trying,' Charteris says, 'to make a picture of a man. Changing, yes. Developing, I hope. Fantastic, impossible—perhaps. Quite worthless, quite irritating, if you feel that way. Or a slightly cock-eyed ideal, if you feel differently. It doesn't matter so much, so long as you feel that you would recognise him if you met him tomorrow.'

Later in the same piece, he goes on, downright sentimentally (but, compared with today, these were downright sentimental times): 'I have done all this, frankly, because I love him. Over all these years, he has grown into me, and I have grown into him, so much that there may ... be some excuse for a confusion of our identities.'

176

Over all these years ... In fact, the Saint had been going, as a public institution, for less than eight years when that was written. But so much had changed, both in Charteris's life and the Saint's, that looking back in 1939 it must have seemed half an eternity.

Templar's development had passed through three clearcut stages. In Stage 1, he was what may be called the *Meet the Tiger* Saint: piratical, romantic, energetic, prone to healthy skipping on beaches, but not considered a major hero, even by his creator. Stage 2, beginning around 1931 in the *Thriller*, introduced the Very English Saint whom we met in Chapter Eight: rakehell, impudent, eccentric, outrageously versatile, eternally versifying, prone to telling long stories about such characters as Aristophanes the bow-legged bedbug, and the most dazzling stroller along pavements in fiction history.

The Stage 3, or Anglo-American, Saint was born in 1934. Charteris had been away in America (where he had wowed the Yanks with 'The Saint in New York' in the *American Journal*) and was now back home again writing for the *Thriller*. In the first *Thriller* story after his return, 'The Simon Templar Foundation',[1] the Saint is subtly different, although nobody notices except Patricia Holm.

> 'You're older,' she said quietly ... She could not have pointed to a grey hair or a new line on his face to prove her statement ... [but] she knew him so well that the lazy quirk of the unscrupulous freebooter's mouth told a story of its own, and even the whimsical smile that lurked in his eyes could not deceive her.
>
> 'It isn't my fault if you develop these psychic powers, old sweetheart,' he said.

The new Saint is older in the sense that he is smoother,

[1] Published in hardback in *The Misfortunes of Mr Teal* (later *The Saint in London*); Hodder & Stoughton, 1934.

less flamboyant and (to my personal regret) a lot less outlandish than the old one. But he is still as adept at some things as ever, most notably at prodding Inspector Teal's ever-protuberant stomach; and he has one advantage over the old Templar—the more or less constant companionship of the dumb minor gangster, Hoppy Uniatz. Hoppy is one of Charteris's happiest creations—even if he is a little close to a Runyon type.

Simon had a difficult problem to ponder, and he was inclined to share it.

'Tell me, Hoppy,' he said. 'Suppose a bloke had some papers that he was blackmailing you with ... What would you do about it?'

Mr Uniatz rubbed his nose.

'Dat's easy, boss. I'd bump de guy off, sure.'

'I'm afraid you would,' said the Saint. 'But suppose you did bump him off—those papers would still be around somewhere, and you wouldn't know who was going to get hold of them next.'

This had not occurred to Mr Uniatz. He frowned gloomily for a while; but then he brightened again as the solution struck him like a ray of sunshine.

'Why, boss,' he said. 'I know what I'd do. After I'd bumped him off, I'd look for de papers.'

'And where would you look for them?' asked the Saint.

'In de guy's pocket,' said Mr Uniatz promptly.

'And suppose they weren't there?'

Hoppy sighed. The corrugations of worried thought returned to his brow. Thinking had never been his greatest talent—it was one of the very few things capable of hurting his head ...

'I dunno,' he said. 'It looks like we better not bump off dis guy, at dat.'

(*The Misfortunes of Mr Teal*)

It is interesting that right through the nineteen thirties, Leslie Charteris maintained strong links with Monty

Haydon and the *Thriller*. As late as 1938, he was still writing stories directly to *Thriller* length; and as long as the *Thriller* itself survived the Saint was still surrounded by the old familiar supporting cast. Teal, Patricia Holm, 'Orace, Monty Hayward, Peter Quentin and now Hoppy Uniatz—the Mark III Saint foregathered frequently with them all. Charteris himself speaks of the whole crowd quite emotionally at the end of *The First Saint Omnibus*, and there is no hint that within two to three years a Mark IV Saint will be created who will be all but cut off from their companionship for good. Why this happened is a fascinating question, but it belongs to the War period—the night after the Day of the Desperado—and so does not concern us yet.

Let's turn instead to Creasey's Toff. He has been developing significantly, too. In his opening adventures, back in 1933, he had been an aristocratic scourge of the East End: but now he has become something much more like its champion. In *Here Comes the Toff*, obviously written in '39 but published in 1940, a high-life girl called Anthea asks Rollison if he will take her slumming. His reply is gentle (the Toff is always the gentlest of the desperadoes) but in its way quite withering.

'Anthea, the East End has many points I like but you wouldn't ... Parts of it you'd call dirty and smelly. You'd think the people unspeakable, you'd consider the shops lousy, you'd find the children call after you, you'd get tired because you couldn't get a cab to take you from corner to corner, your shoes would be so thin that they'd wear through on the cobbles—yes, there are plenty of cobbled streets left, my sweet, don't imagine Lancashire has a lien on them. You can't *look* at the East End. You've got to be part of it, and it takes years to get acclimatized. Be wise, and stay this side of Aldgate Pump.'

(*Here Comes the Toff*)

179

It could be objected that the Toff is still speaking of the East Enders rather as though they were restless natives in some aboriginal village, but his sympathy for them is clear, and his superiority the reverse of smug. Smug is the last thing Richard Rollison could ever have been, anyway. That fundamental lack of self-sufficiency— always his saving grace—is as apparent in *Here Comes the Toff* as ever. Here for once is a hero who does not ask for advice just to enable the author to write in a bit of explanatory dialogue. He asks for it because he really needs it—and surprisingly often he takes it, too.

His behaviour towards his man Jolly is typical. Jolly, originally, was probably intended to be a cross between Jeeves and the Bunter of Dorothy Sayers's Lord Peter Wimsey stories. But Creasey is not a writer to sustain a conventional master–man relationship, even on a serio-comic basis, for long. Rollison and Jolly give the impression that they are only playing a game of being master and servant. In reality, they are increasingly obviously friends and equals; and Jolly is often the more dominating of the two.

'If I dare say so, sir, you have waited too long already. Waiting is quite satisfactory in some cases, when you know what is coming and where to expect it. In this case, the complete mystery which surrounds the activities of Kohn and the woman Cardew makes it imperative for you to weigh in, sir, with all you've got. I hope I have made myself clear, sir.'

'Abundantly so,' murmured the Toff dryly.

'I trust,' went on Jolly with some anxiety, 'that I have not caused offence, sir. I am a little perturbed by the possibilities as I see them, and ...'

The Toff put a hand against Jolly's cheek and pushed his face gently aside.

'You're worth a fortune, Jolly, at least I acknowledge it.'

(*Here Comes the Toff*[2])

The Saint, the Toff, the Baron, Norman Conquest—these only head the list of thirties desperadoes. They do not by any means complete it. Amongst the ones that I remember particularly well, there were, cheek-by-jowl with the Saint in Hodder & Stoughton Yellow Jackets, Sydney Horler's hearty, Soccer-playing Tiger Standish and the same author's angry cracksman, Nighthawk. The latter not only stole the jewellery of dubious society ladies, but was not above scrawling 'WANTON' in their own lipstick across their pillows as they slept. Elsewhere there was Frank King's Dormouse, a gentleman crook afflicted by a droopy eyelid, and consequently the only hero to carry nonchalance to the point of actually looking half-asleep. Sexton Blake's friends-cum-adversaries included the monocled, drawling (I should say drawlin') 'R.S.V.P.', not so much the Robin Hood as the Arthur Augustus d'Arcy of modern crime. (His creator, John G. Brandon, called him 'A.S.P.' outside the Sexton Blake books.) In the *Thriller*, usually in a serial at the back, British thriller-readers were introduced to the Shadow, a really novel desperado who had studied under some species of guru and acquired powers of levitation, invisibility, and Heaven knows what else. (The Shadow, and a rival character, the Spider, had a fabulously long run in American pulp magazines, and are currently becoming subjects of cult interest here in Britain.)

The publishers Herbert Jenkins had quite a long-running success with Wyndham Martyn's Anthony Trent, a very commanding gentleman crook with a really extraordinary degree of sensitivity. In one novel, *Trent of the*

---

[2] John Long, 1940—currently available as a Lythway reprint.

Lone Hand, he finds himself living near Sing Sing prison. But the atmosphere makes him miserable.

'How can there be any real peace of soul near that home of misery and unrest? On the non-material plane nothing ever dies. Think what an aura must surround Sing Sing, where so many men sit, and have sat, during so many years, hating—hating—hating. Hating laws and the police; hating companions who have double-crossed them; hating the women for whom many of them have robbed and murdered; worst of all, hating themselves and despairing of hope in this world or mercy in the next. Think of all the hate force these poor devils have set in motion. I'm psychic enough to be affected by it. We shall not stay here much longer.'

Trent is, in fact, often downright psychic.

'A few minutes ago I proposed that we go outside and smoke a cigarette before turning in. I deterred you from going within a minute of having made the proposition myself ... I had very suddenly the feeling—no, I'll call it the knowledge—that outside in the garden danger lurks. That's why you're not going, Swithin.'

From Methuen's, there was Cecil Freeman Gregg's Harry Prince, the closest character in the *genre* to a contemporary anti-hero.

Prince had made his début in *The Ten Black Pearls*, published in 1935. It was subtitled 'A Tale Without a Moral', and Harry, writing in the first person, explains bluntly that he is a thief and proceeds to recount his exploits without apology.

Or, rather, *almost* without apology. At the end of the story, someone (a Judge, as it happens) tells him he must be mad. Prince replies with a statement that shows him to be not merely rational, but suffering from that essential adjunct to fictional crackmanship in the nineteen thirties, a broken heart.

'No, sir, if I were mad, I shouldn't remember; I should not be haunted with dreams of Estelle as she was when I first married her; I should not feel so utterly alone in Britain's teeming millions; I should not feel that the world still owes me something despite the fact that I have wiped my own slate clean of those who have wronged me. If I were mad, then I should have no regrets that I am not on the side of the angels.'

(The Ten Black Pearls)

A rather sombre hero, Prince, foreshadowing a lot of the fiction of the nineteen forties; the book has a sort of Nigel Balchin downbeat. He is an interesting oddity in an essentially optimistic *genre*, and a reminder that there were strong counter-currents about in the second half of the Golden Age of the thriller. The heyday of the laughing desperado also saw the birth of the colder, greyer worlds of Simenon and Eric Ambler, and the arrival of the first Hammetts and Chandlers on British bookstalls. It is interesting, incidentally, that the 'hard-boiled' thriller *genre*, so different in style, philosophy and feeling from the desperado one, nevertheless originated in much the same way. The American pulp magazines like *Black Mask*, which launched Hammett and Chandler, could be regarded, at a pinch, as the Transatlantic equivalents of the *Thriller* and *Detective Weekly*. It is fascinating (although some would consider it bordering on the irreverent) to speculate about how different Chandler and Hammett might have been had they begun their careers under Monty Haydon instead of *Black Mask*'s Joseph T. Shaw.

But to get back to the desperadoes. A short list of the remaining significant names would include Michael Arlen's Gay Falcon (about whom eleven films were to be made in the course of the 1940s); Richard Essex's Lessinger; Harman Landan's Picaroon, and Louis Joseph Vance's Lone Wolf, an American desperado whose creator died in very strange circumstances. The best known, perhaps, of all the American desperadoes was Frank L. Packard's Jimmie Dale, who had been around since 1917, and had had Blackshirt-type trouble with a beautiful female blackmailer six years before Blackshirt was invented. (Dale's menacing lady communicated by letters, though, so he was spared that incessantly ringing phone.) The most remarkable thing about Jimmie Dale was that he had not one alias, but two. Half the time he was a gallant gentleman cracksman known as the Grey Seal: on other occasions, he 'slouched through New York's gangland' as Larry the Bat.[3]

There were innumerable other desperadoes, many of them equally fascinating, but we must close the list somewhere. In any event, listing the multiple variations which the nineteen thirties played on the Gentleman Outlaw theme will bring us no closer to understanding the phenomenon of the theme's appeal. Here he was, the same fellow, staring up at you from the jackets of a dozen books a week, every week of the year: debonair, immaculately evening-suited, often top-hatted, given to light laughter, expressing himself in a flippant drawl, always above and contemptuous of, and yet basically on fairly friendly terms with, the law. Why in the world didn't people get tired of him? What were the roots which this myth somehow tapped deep in the public's subconscious? What did he mean to the distraught, hard-up, hard-pressed, increasingly fearful public at this particular point in history? It cannot be denied that it must have been something important.

Perhaps the first thing to establish is just how wide the Gentleman Outlaw's public was. It has been said—by Nicholas Blake amongst others—that before the Second

<hr />

[3] *The Adventures of Jimmie Dale* by Frank L. Packard (Tom Stacey, 1972).

World War detective stories were read by the middle classes and thrillers by the working class. There is some evidence to suggest that, to put it mildly, this is a considerable over-simplification. In *The First Saint Omnibus*, Charteris sets out to reply to readers who have asked why he so often makes cracks about public schools. 'Since,' he writes, 'what I proudly call my fan mail statistics reveal that a large percentage of my most faithful readers are either past or present members of some British public school, there is no explanation I could give that would not expose me to the undying hatred of just about as many readers as it would deathlessly endear me to.' Consequently, with what he calls 'that sublime genius for equivocation and diplomacy which was so tragically stolen from the world when my first publisher accepted my first novel', he tells a harmless story about a master not appreciating his literary style.

Clearly, then, the Outlaws reached a pretty heterogeneous audience, whatever its precise constitution may have been. We are back to the question: what did the Outlaw *genre* mean to that public, and how did it help?

One answer that is too obvious to be ignored is the snob element. These were *Gentleman* Outlaws; much was made of their evening suits and Mayfair addresses, of their instant acceptability at grand houses, and the like. Whether the middle or the lower classes made up the bulk of the readership, it is likely that most readers wanted to rise in the world, and here was an opportunity to do so, vicariously, merely by opening the pages of a book. Personally, though, I feel that the appeal to snobbery can be over-stressed.

What was so attractive to me about these heroes (and I began circulating the circulating libraries as early as May 1940, the day *The Thriller* ceased publication—a disaster which was to me comparable with the Fall of France) was the fact that they were their own men. They belonged to no organisation, worked at no job, got their income (invariably referred to as 'boodle') nefariously but according to a strict personal code, and were, in fact, private enterprise personified. In modern terms, they were on a level with the Establishment, but at the same time thumbed their noses at it. Identifying with them put you in a unique dream position—acceptable at all levels, liked at all levels (it was important that you should be secretly admired even by the police) and yet a law absolutely to yourself. You were, in fact, *in a class of your own.*

Looked at in this way, the Gentleman Outlaw is an intensely interesting psycho-sociological development. On his first appearance, in the very late twenties, it had seemed as though he was a throwback, infuriating to a sociological observer. Hadn't Edgar Wallace broken the class barrier and brought the thriller to the people with his 'ordinary-man' heroes? What business, then, had the ordinary reader, a few years later, to start showing a preference for the elegant Society hero after all?

But on any serious analysis, it is quite obvious that the thirties Gentleman Outlaw *wasn't* a Society hero in the pre-Wallace sense at all. He was no Oppenheimish slave to *maîtres d'hôtels*; no Buchanist Establishment figure respected by the Right People across the Empire; not even a classbound officer-type like Drummond. Beneath that rakishly tilted topper, he was actually the most truly universal myth since Robin Hood—upper-class in his elegance and drawling impudence, middle-class in his sturdy independence, working-class in his increasingly basic human creed. The Saint's anger against public schools and capitalist labour exploiters, Nighthawk's fury against high society, the Baron's scorn of *noblesse oblige* concepts: there are examples all over the *genre* of the Gentleman Outlaw forgetting that he's a Gentleman, and becoming much more like a spokesman for everybody, a glorified man in the street. Insofar as it was Leslie Charteris more than anyone who initially gave the Outlaw this universality, it looks as though the Saint deserves his halo.

Once it had got over its initial, peak-of-the-depression-era revulsion from the workaday, there was, as a matter of fact, nothing the thirties liked better than glorifying the man in the street. This was the age of *Mr Deeds Goes to Town* (1936), the Frank Capra movie starring Gary Cooper—the epitome of the ordinary private citizen getting up on his hind legs to put the whole rotten world to rights. This was the age, for that matter, of the Chaplin masterpieces *Modern Times* and *City Lights*; of books like John Steinbeck's *Grapes of Wrath* and William Saroyan's *Daring Young Man on the Flying Trapeze*; of popular songs like 'Underneath the Arches' and 'Tenement Symphony', all of which invested the humdrum with an almost mystic grandeur. It was part of what you might call the cult of the Little Man: a feeling that the ordinary individual was really *extra*ordinary at heart, a unique being, rooted in mystery, who had to be true to himself rather than to the imposed values of any clique or class. It was no accident that the *Daily Express* cartoonist Strube represented the nation not by a massive John Bull figure, but by a small bespectacled surburbanite; or that the leading comedians of the day should have been the George Formbys and the Arthur Askeys. At the very end of the nineteen thirties, the Little Man achieved what I always feel was his apotheosis at the curtain fall of J. B. Priestley's 1939 life-after-death extravaganza, *Johnson Over Jordan*. The soul of Johnson—perhaps the finest part ever played by Sir Ralph Richardson—is facing an afterlife in some unimaginable fourth dimension. There he is standing calmly at the edge of the universe, about to set out for the ends of eternity, but he is still unmistakably the Little Man, staunchly bowler-hatted beneath a myriad stars. It is impossible for me to watch this scene

187

without feeling that it is not only the spirit of Johnson I am seeing, but the real spirit of the nineteen thirties, the only decade there has ever been which preached that to be an ordinary private individual is potentially the most exciting thing on earth. (Or beyond it.)

The message, it is true, was preached only fitfully, largely by middlebrows. To the intellectuals, it was bourgeois rubbish, and it was drowned often enough by strident propaganda on behalf of those least private of all individuals, the organised masses of the extreme right and left.

Nevertheless, it remains an important strand in the literary and entertainment worlds of the thirties, and deserves to be remembered at least as often as the sight of Fred Astaire whisking Ginger Rogers off on a Hollywood staircase to Paradise.

Which is not to deny, of course, that the thirties *did* have a weakness for romantic stylishness and glamour, as we have already seen. This—and their love of lounging impudence—remained characteristic to the very end.

The elegant top-hatter on the one hand; the mystically endowed, staunchly independent Mr Everyman on the other. These were two of the main dream images with which the people of 1936–9 fortified themselves to face the menacing music of a world gone more than slightly mad.

In the Gentleman Outlaw, *and nowhere else*, the two myths met and coalesced. This, surely, was the real secret of his appeal, and the factor that differentiated him decisively from Raffles, Drummond and most of his predecessors.

The thirties Gentleman Outlaw was uniquely *of* the thirties because, for all his elegance and bonviveuring, for all his buccaneering wildness, he was, at heart, a Super Little Man.

Part Three

THE AWKWARD WAR
(1939–1945)

CHAPTER THIRTEEN

In which the son of Blackshirt goes to war, and is back before he's started

THE Second World War proved to be the most hazardous period in the whole history of the desperadoes. Only a handful of them survived it at all, and most of the ones that did emerged somewhat unlike their former selves.

There is probably no better way of illustrating the assault course of traumatic complications which now lay in every desperado's path than by returning to the story of Bruce Graeme and Richard Verrell, alias Blackshirt.

We left Blackshirt, you remember, back in 1925, repenting his wicked life as the Raffles of the twenties and on the point of proposing to his telescope-wielding Lady of the Phone. In the second book of the series, *The Return of Blackshirt*, Verrell actually marries his Lady, but, immediately after the ceremony, they are both involved in a rail crash: Verrell receives a blow on the head, loses his memory, and returns to cracksmanship. There is an ingenious reprise of the earlier book in which his Lady has to take to the phone and reform him all over again.

At the end of *The Return of Blackshirt*—which, like the original *Blackshirt*, sold a clear 1,000,000 copies— Richard and his Bobbie are reunited, though like all good showmen Graeme holds this up until the very final paragraph:

She went over to him, and, bending down, placed her lips upon his. The seconds ticked by; neither moved. Incredible as it seemed, this was their first real kiss

191

since the few words had been spoken which made them
man and wife. So their lips clung, and the flame of
love burned brightly. He smiled up at her, and then
closed his eyes.

He was happy.

(*The Return of Blackshirt*, 1927)

He was happy, but no longer, of course, anything resembling a Raffles. In the words of his creator, he 'settled
down to a more orderly and domestic life—save for the
several occasions when he donned his old, familiar black
shirt for the sake of his country and risked all—his life,
his happiness, his reputation—in order to combat and
defeat the machinations of foreign spy organisations'.
Those occasions were recounted in a long series of
books—*Blackshirt Again*, *Alias Blackshirt*, *Blackshirt
the Audacious*, *Blackshirt Counter-Spy*, *Blackshirt Inter-
feres* and *Blackshirt Strikes Back*—appearing all through
the later twenties and the thirties. In addition, Graeme
had embarked on two other regular crime series, one
featuring a detective, Theodore I. Terhune, and the other
two Yard men, Superintendent Stevens and Inspector
Allain. Under the pseudonym David Graeme, he had also
written four 'Monsieur Blackshirt' books—historical
novels featuring an ancestor of Verrell's who swash-
buckled in seventeenth-century France.

But he was beginning to have serious trouble thinking
up new ideas for Verrell himself. Blackshirt was, you might
say, the pioneer Durable Desperado: consequently Graeme
is the first of our authors to have to grapple with the
peculiar difficulties inherent in the very fact of durability.

Just before the War (by which time he was feeling that
he had reached the very end of invention where Blackshirt was concerned) he met a young girl who had once
been a Blackshirt fan. He goes on:

'When she said she was no longer one, I asked her

192

why. "He is too old by now," was her reply. In other words, she was aware that when the first of the stories was written, it was soon after the First World War, in 1923, to be exact. She did not have to be a mathematical genius to add sixteen to 1923 and make Blackshirt a man of forty or over, and therefore a man of great age! Then she added: "Couldn't you write books about the son of Blackshirt? After all, he was married in 1923, wasn't he?"'

As a matter of fact, *The Return of Blackshirt*, in which Verrell marries, did not appear in hardback until 1927: it must have been published in a magazine considerably earlier. Assuming that Blackshirt and Bobbie both met and married in 1923, they could have had a son in 1924, who would have been fifteen in 1939. Just a little novelist's licence has to be allowed, however, for what Graeme actually did: he created a grown-up Anthony Verrell, an RAF hero complete with DSO, DFC and bar, who made his bow in *Son of Blackshirt*, published by Hutchinson in 1941.

Bruce Graeme writes that he never considered Anthony Verrell a success as a character. Some things about Anthony, though, are distinctly refreshing. It is a nice change to meet a hero in this *genre* who eschews the almost obligatory cigarette and favours a nauseous pipe (called Agnes). He is also interestingly eloquent about what makes a desperado a desperado:

'I love the thrill of finding myself in a dangerous predicament, and the deep satisfaction of contriving to reach safety again. There is no comparable sensation, unless it be the first drop of water after days of raging thirst, or a warm bed when one is feeling cold and miserable.'

In his own way, too, he has considerable style, if not

193

overmuch modesty, as this snatch from his first conversation with the heroine shows:

'Is this trouble something a man could tackle?'
'Not any man.'
'Only one that was reckless, daring, adventurous?'
His eyes danced; his heart sang. 'I am ready.'

Surely there is nothing wrong with the idea of a between-the-wars desperado having an offspring who becomes a pipe-smoking RAF type. It seems now an eminently sensible way of bridging the gap between two neighbouring, but colliding, decades: a wholly attractive variation on the theme of Continuing England. And logically there would be nothing in his Air Force commitments to stop Anthony Verrell having Blackshirt-type adventures. He could encounter arch-fiends on leave, or perhaps have special permission to go absent from some Gordon Craigie of the Air Ministry ...

These, however, are the reflections of someone writing thirty-two years after the event. The situation seems to have appeared in a very different light to Bruce Graeme at the time. With the Battle of Britain a recent memory, the worst of the blitzes actually in progress, and fighter pilots getting killed at a sobering rate every night, he must have felt that it would be in dubious taste to feature one who lounged about being a desperado in off-duty hours. *Somehow the War had to be got rid of*—and what better way of doing that was there than projecting the stories into the future, making out that victory was already won? Shifting the date to an unspecified future would also overcome any difficulties about Anthony's age.

Hence we find that *Son of Blackshirt*, written in 1940 and published in 1941, opens with the paragraph:

The small private room was gay with colour, with

flowers and above all with light; light which streamed freely out through the curtained, but unblacked-out windows.... In fact many pleasing luxuries of which Europe had been deprived were present in the room ...

Anthony Verrell, his gallant wartime career contained in a few retrospective paragraphs, is on his way to celebrate the Armistice 'by dining at the Chez François in Wardour Street'.

Here, then, we have the strangely adult Son of Blackshirt, at the end of a war which in fact is only just beginning, starting his adventures by celebrating the Armistice in a novelist's phoney peace. And those are only the first of the complexities and convolutions with which the book eventually confronts the reader.

Take a deep breath. You might as well have the rest. Here is the story of *Son of Blackshirt*, as it is recapitulated in the second Anthony Verrell adventure for the benefit of new readers. Anthony, we read, had passed up that Armistice celebration party 'for the sake of a pair of unfathomable violet eyes'. Thereafter:

> What a night that had been! ... He had transformed himself into an ersatz cracksman, and had broken into and entered the old Tudor home of Lady Redbrook, widow of the first Earl of Redbrook. Once in the house, disaster had overtaken him. He had tripped over a cat, knocked his head against a wall ... On recovering, he had found himself imprisoned in a priest's hole. While looking for a means of escape, he had discovered the diaries of Ralph Rowen, afterwards the first Earl of Redbrook. Compelled to wait till morning, Tony had read the diaries through, to make ... incredible discoveries. His father, Richard Verrell, was none other than the missing son of the first Earl of Redbrook ...
> (*Lord Blackshirt*, Hutchinson, 1942)

At last, then, that old, old mystery of Richard Verrell's

parentage has been solved. When, in *Blackshirt*, he had changed from 'a slum-bred grub into the polished, educated gentleman of the West End' Graeme had added, significantly: 'perhaps, for all he knew, the ultimate position to which he had been predestined by birth'. Now it is revealed that he had most emphatically been predestined for that exalted state.

I may be wrong, but I doubt if a writer of the nineteen thirties thriller school would have let Verrell turn out to be a lord. The Toff excepted (and we have seen the factors that made him a special case), the thirties desperadoes had either obscure or nondescript family backgrounds, as befitted characters who were half men about town, half the man in the street. But Blackshirt is essentially a nineteen-*twenties* hero, and it is fascinating that his birth mystery should be solved, here in the forties, in a way that is typical of nineteen twenties thrillers— even, remembering *The Northing Tramp*, of Edgar Wallace ones.

But to return to young Anthony, still rummaging amongst those diaries in the priesthole. Before long, he begins to discover why the first Earl of Redbrook had never tried to contact his missing son and acquaint him of his heritage. The detective who had traced Verrell on behalf of the Earl had done too thorough a job: he had also found out that Verrell was the notorious Blackshirt.

The unfortunate Anthony is consequently faced with a second disturbing discovery. His father is not only an Earl, but a celebrated cracksman. At first, he is profoundly shaken. ('How could he ever again join the company of decent, upright men? How could he meet the unwavering eyes of Stephen, of Edward, or Jerry three of the finest chaps in the world? How could he dare speak to Penelope? ...') Gradually, however, his own desperado blood begins to tell—he has even inherited crooksman's eyes from his father, which have stood him

196

in good stead as a night fighter—and he ends by deciding that he is downright proud of his old man.

Tony pictured his father; tall, lithe, slim, the personification of healthy manhood; in his imagination he gazed into his father's eyes, and saw as he had seen so often in reality, a pair of eyes that were honest, whimsical, humorous. And Tony laughed gladly, as the last doubt deserted him, never to return ...
(Son of Blackshirt)

He decides, in fact, to carry on both sides of the family tradition, and become Lord Blackshirt—the title of the second book in the Anthony Verrell series, published in 1942.

Richard Verrell himself never puts in a personal appearance in the *Son of Blackshirt* books. We have here, in other words, a unique instance of a desperado being laid up, for all the world like some 1923 Rolls Royce, all through the Second World War—or, rather, all through the odd, imaginary peace in which the stories were set.

It is a distinctly awkward, complicated situation. But then, as we shall be seeing, for almost all the durable desperadoes, it was a distinctly awkward war.

CHAPTER FOURTEEN

In which Norman Conquest goes to war, and appears to sign a separate peace

W H Y, though, *was* it quite so awkward?

One would have thought, on the face of it, that a war would have provided a natural setting for dashing desperado-like activities. After all, the Boer War had been Raffles's salvation, and the memories of World War I trenches—particularly of lone Hun-strangling sorties into No Man's Land—had been Drummond's continuing background inspiration all through his four rounds with Carl Peterson.

Why, then, did World War II leave so many of the thirties outlaws flopping about like fish out of water?

The reason, surely, is that their basic attitudes were drastically different from the officer-type heroics of their predecessors. As we have seen, *they* were really Super Little Men, glorifications of the ordinary private citizen. And the ordinary private citizen of the nineteen thirties had not been over-enamoured of the prospect of war. Thriller after thriller of the late thirties (to say nothing of the *Daily Express*) had given him to understand that war was a despicable contrivance of millionaire pluto-crats, in which Britain should have no part. He had been petrified by the alarmist visions of bombing in such films as *The Shape of Things to Come* (1936); he had turned out in his thousands to applaud Chamberlain the peacemaker in 1938; he had listened in to the same Chamberlain's 'it-is-evil-things-we-shall-be-fighting-against' broadcast of 3 September 1939, with a chill in his heart rather than a cheer in his throat, and although he would have been the first to agree that something had to be done about Hitler, he relished not one whit the prospect of going into the forces and being marched and ordered about. And sure enough, we find these feelings instantly reflected in that most typical of thirties super heroes, Norman Conquest.

'The Second World War had not affected him as it had affected so many other adventurous young men', we are told. His 'hatred of the Nazis was a negative hatred'. War to him was 'a drab dirty business and much over-rated as a pastime'. Most significantly, 'he had no enthusiasm for service which entailed routine and discipline and the taking of orders from somebody Higher Up ... In all his battles with the Ungodly he had worked alone ...'

Here, surely, is the crux of the matter. The thirties Gentleman Outlaws could serve in the forces only at considerable peril to their own super-hero status. If they became officers (as several, in fact, did), they were inviting readers to identify with the officer class, which some of those readers would feel to be a kind of betrayal. If they became privates, the Top Hat bit went for a burton, for a start, and credibility became strained on almost every count.

(The mind boggles at the thought of a corporal saying 'Take that cigarette out of your mouth, Templar, and stand to attention when I talk to you.' Clearly, that sort of thing would come high on anyone's list of Literary Situations That Should Never Be Allowed To Arise.)

Bruce Graeme's subconscious had obviously sensed this double danger when he had made Anthony Verrell not just a RAF officer, but an *about-to-be-demobbed* RAF officer; but that had involved a kind of cheating, a somewhat facile bypassing of the war.

Edwy Searles Brooks, with the cheery bluntness of one

of his own St Frank's boys, at least met the situation—
and all its difficulties—head-on.

In 'One-Man Blitzkrieg', the last story commissioned
by Monty Haydon before the *Thriller* died,[1] the war has
has been going on for months, and here is Conquest still
out of uniform—to the undisguised disgust of apple-
cheeked Inspector Bill Williams.

'I suppose you know you've let me down badly,
don't you? Soon after the war started the Chief and
I were talking about you, wondering why you hadn't
been up to any of your usual mischief, and I bet him
a level quid that you were in the Air Force or the Army
... How have you managed to evade service all this
time? ... Hell, when there's a war on, Conquest, every
man has got to pull his weight.'

This, of course, no citizen, however private, would wish
his hero to deny.

'I haven't been as idle as you apparently think,'
growled the Desperado. 'I'm not going to tell you what
I've been doing because my lips are sealed.'

'Well, I'm damned glad to hear it,' said Williams
warmly, his manner becoming cordial. 'Sorry I was
wrong about you, Conquest ...'

'You're not altogether wrong,' interrupted Norman
impatiently. 'I've had no heart in the job I've been
doing ... I've always hated hole and corner stuff ...'
He shrugged. 'You know me, Bill. Attack has always
been my strong point. Now, if they'd let me invade
Germany single-handed, I'd show them something!'

What happens next is deeply revealing. Conquest goes
home to 'Underneath the Arches', the flamboyantly

[1] The story was advertised as a forthcoming attraction in May,
1940, but the *Thriller* stopped before it could appear. It finally
arrived in print in 1942, lengthened into the novel *Six Feet of
Dynamite* (Collins), from which the bulk of the extracts in this
chapter are taken.

eccentric residence which he and Joy Everard have built under the arch of a railway viaduct. (He and Joy are still, incidentally, unmarried: they live together as 'partners in crime', in love with each other but with their precise sexual relationship left in the reader's mind, after the fashion set by the Saint and Patricia Holm.) There is a blitz, and Underneath the Arches receives a direct hit. Norman, with his assistant, the Cockney tramp Mandeville Livingstone, finds Joy under a mass of woodwork, 'unconscious, bleeding, a pitiful little figure'. Norman, 'his senses reeling', carries her out. She is alive, but it was a very near thing indeed.

Livingstone had seen his virile young master in many a battling mood, but never had he seen such fury on any human face.
'They nearly killed her, the Godless hellspawn!' said Norman, between clenched teeth. 'If it's the last thing I do, Mandy, I've got to have a crack at them!'

In other words, this private citizen's hero has had to be given a *private* reason for getting really involved in the War. And once he is involved, it is still essentially a private fight. He undertakes to go into Germany single-handed, and rescue an old personal friend of his, one Spots Paige, an inventor who is being held by the Nazis in a concentration camp.

Conquest is given this assignment by Sir Huntley Tring, head of Dept M 101B in Whitehall. But there is no suggestion that Conquest is *under orders*. He is not even summoned to some mysterious London HQ. On the contrary, Sir Huntley comes to visit *him*—and is treated with something less than the deference normally accorded to Secret Service chiefs in fiction.

'You talk too much, Brother Tring,' said Norman briskly. 'I'm sold, so why all the explanations? You've probably got some plans ...'

201

It soon becomes clear that Brother Tring's function in the story is not to inspire awe, but to register it.

'Knowing that you will be going to almost certain death, you agree to make the attempt?' asked Sir Huntley, a look of admiration joining forces with wonder in his expression. 'Observe, Conquest, that I am making no attempt to minimise the insane peril ...'
'What, again?' snapped Norman, almost savagely. 'For the third time, when do I start?'

By now, Sir Huntley is almost grovelling.

'I am sorry. I won't try your patience any further. We hope to get you going in a fortnight.'
Norman laughed, with the old gay lilt in his voice. 'What's the matter with you, Brother Tring? Are you completely nuts? What's the matter with today ... this afternoon ... now?'

In fact, there is a week's delay, while the Desperado becomes fluent in the German language by listening to gramophone records night and day. And then (to quote Brooks's own words) it's 'Look out, Hitler—here comes Norman Conquest!'
The news naturally shakes the Third Reich to its foundations. Listen to Baron Kurt von Rattenblut, second-in-command to Heinrich Himmler, talking to the commander of the concentration camp where Norman's friend is imprisoned:

'You do not know this man Conquest. He is the mad Englishman incarnate! ... We have records of all his exploits on our files. As cunning as a snake, as wily as a fox, he succeeds where a thousand men might fail ... We knew of his coming, and we took our precautions ... Yet this young hell-hound escapes us in the first ten minutes, and God knows what dances he will lead us before we take him again.'

And so on, and so forth. In a Conquest thriller, the entire supporting cast—Scotland Yard inspectors, Secret Service chiefs, monocled *schweinhunds* alike—all end up in the 1066 fan club. It is part of the fun, and the fun—as befits this last story to be written under the auspices of Monty Haydon's *Thriller*—is fast and furious. But one thing spoils it: the German hell-camp—into which Conquest blithely charges in a borrowed tank—is Buchenwald. The moment the eye hits that name, the bestial reality collides with the amiable myth, creating a queasy emotional fug through which even 1066's laughter sounds hollow, echoing and drab. There are ways of getting wartime thriller heroes in and out of Germany, and even in and out of hell-camps, without uneasiness resulting, but Brooks's way is not one of them. Look out, Norman Conquest—Buchenwalds and Gay Desperadoes don't mix.

It rather seems as though Brooks was quick to realise this himself. Or perhaps Baron Kurt von Rattenblut had a quiet word with the Führer, and it was decided that *Gott's blutt*, the only way to deal with this mad Englander was to sign a separate peace with him. At all events, in subsequent Conquests the war has been banished from the scene. There is no mention of Underneath the Arches, or what happened there. Norman and Joy are inexplicably ensconced in the penthouse of a brand new Park Lane skyscraper called Conquest Court.

What are we in now, then? Another phoney future— or is the situation stranger? For the rest of the war, and on into the peace, Norman seems indefinably different. In *The Conquest Touch*, we find him climbing scaffolding with the ease of a monkey ... and suddenly there is a scene which sharp-eyed readers will find curiously familiar. While posing as a wicked lord, Norman allows himself to be lynched by a village mob. Inspector Williams and his sergeant, arriving on the scene belatedly, find the

crowd gone and the 'lord's' body hanging from a tree.
The Inspector is about to cut it down, when—

> 'Don't bother,' said the corpse. 'I'll save you the
> trouble.'
>   The apparently lifeless hands went smartly upwards
> to the neck; and to the amazement of the Scotland
> Yard pair the noose was pulled loose, and the 'corpse'
> slipped his hand free. Then, with the springiness of
> a trained athlete, the figure landed on the soft turf.
>   'You would come along and mess everything up,'
> said a disgusted voice.
>   'My God! Conquest!' Williams swore violently.
> (The Conquest Touch, Collins)

The scene is practically word for word the same as
the one in *Village Vengeance*, the Waldo the Wonder
Man story that appeared in *Union Jack* in 1934. Not
exactly word for word, of course. What you see above
is a celebrated process in action: a process known in
Fleetway House circles as 'de-Blakenising'. Waldo's name
has been changed to Conquest's wherever it appears;
Sexton Blake and Tinker have given place to Inspector
Williams and his sergeant, with appropriate alterations
in the dialogue.

Williams does not say 'Upon my word, Waldo, what
a fellow you are for springing sensational surprises.' He
says, 'I might have known that you'd be up to some
of your blasted jiggery-pokery. Curse you, Conquest!'
and so on. Nor has Norman suddenly sprouted Waldo's
phenomenal neck muscles. He grasps what appears to be
the skin of his neck and peels it away—revealing an
ingeniously moulded steel collar. He is, incidentally,
better at repartee than Waldo was. 'I was just going to
let myself down,' he tells Sexton—sorry, Inspector
Williams, 'when I saw your car coming, and so I thought
I'd hang around ...'

With one exception, all the Norman Conquest novels

published between *Six Feet of Dynamite* and the close of the nineteen forties turn out to be rewritten Waldo the Wonder Man adventures. Everything is breezily updated as far as it can be—but that doesn't prevent some very singular anomalies. *The Conquest Touch*, for example, contains what seems to be an attack on the extravagance of aristocratic Bright Young Things living in a mad whirl of gaiety—and it appeared at the height of the austerity era, in 1948.

Still, there could hardly be stronger proof that Norman Conquest and Waldo were basically one and the same desperado—that desperado whose imperviousness to bullets had first daunted Sexton Blake (or, rather, Sexton Blake and Nelson Lee) in the pre-Drummond days of 1918, and whose snowballing success in the twenties had first conditioned Fleetway House editors—Monty Haydon in particular—to be on the lookout for buccaneering heroes.

It is sometimes tempting to dismiss Norman Conquest as a poor schoolboy's Simon Templar. But in fact, without the long-running Fleetway House career of the Waldo–Conquest Laughing Desperado, it is quite possible that there would have been no launching of the Saint at all.

Our desperadoes seem, then, to be falling on strange times, in every sense of the word. Graeme projects Blackshirt, plus son, into the future. Brooks, after one merry brush with Buchenwald, sends 1066 back in spirit to 1934 and earlier.

It would be a relief, after all this, to escape from bizarre developments for a while. But now we have to catch up on the adventures of Simon Templar himself, and—as the Hodder & Stoughton blurbs so often proclaimed—nothing ordinary ever happened to the Saint. Certainly there was nothing ordinary about what happened to him during the Awkward War.

CHAPTER FIFTEEN

In which Simon Templar goes to war, and virtually goes it alone

ALL through the nineteen thirties, Leslie Charteris had increasingly made America his home. When World War II started, he was in Hollywood, and decided to stay there: a decision which made the Saint's immediate position more complicated than that of any other desperado. Here was the war ravaging Europe, threatening Britain. Here were the Saint's British fans (my teenage self amongst them) expecting their hero to wade in spectacularly against Hitler, perhaps even raiding Berchtesgarden. Here were the Americans, from now onwards the main Charteris public, still uneasily neutral. And here was Charteris himself, five or six thousand miles away from blitzes and blackouts and even the rudimentary first-hand knowledge of the hostilities possessed by the Saint's youngest British fan.

It looks as though Charteris, far more than Graeme or Brooks, had a reason for excluding all mention of the war from his stories; and he had a ready means of doing so. He wouldn't have had to project the Saint into any mythical future. Over in America, there was all the peace that any desperado could want in which to continue his escapades undisturbed.

Charteris didn't play it that way, though; I suspect that that deep romantic streak in his nature simply wouldn't let him.

The Saint in Miami, the one book he wrote when he was uncomfortably perched on the sidelines in the still-neutral U.S., is a war thriller throughout, and even ends on a note of homespun propaganda urging America to come in. (A Western old-timer called Sheriff Hoskins orates: 'I reckon if enough rabbits ganged up together an' got properly mad, they could put a bobcat on the run. Most times the folks in this country are homelovin' and peaceful as rabbits—but it seems to me that the time for a little gangin' up an' gettin' mad has moren' come.' After two pages of this he tells the Saint: 'I got to go. But I'm hopin' more of our folks will start gangin' up before it's too late. Mebbe I jest sorta like you, son.' 'Maybe it's mutual, Daddy,' says the Saint. And as befits an English ambassador, to say nothing of a descendant of A. J. Raffles, he puts 'out his own strong grip'.

Since the Saint can't come to the war, the war is brought to the Saint in the form of a dastardly Nazi plot right there in Miami, a spectacular affair featuring a German submarine (for the Saint to blow up in the last chapter) nosing around offshore. The Nazi villain, incidentally, is refreshingly more articulate than most members of thriller fiction's *Gott in Himmel* brigade. He taunts the Saint (who, at that point in the story, is tied up in a cellar—the standard fate of desperadoes, in peace or war) with an eloquent statement of the Master Race's creed.

'I should like a particular thought to cheer your last moments. You, in your unimportant dissolution, are only a symbol of what you represent. Just as you have tried to fight us and have been outgeneralled and destroyed, so everyone on earth who tries to fight us will be destroyed. The little damage you have done will be repaired; your own futility cannot be repaired. Console yourself with that. The rest of your tribe will soon follow you into extinction, except for those whom we keep for slaves as you once kept inferior races. So you see, all you have achieved and all you die for is nothing.'

207

Nobody in a Saint novel, of course, is ever allowed to upstage the Saint, particularly not on account of a little thing like eloquence. The Saint, his eyes 'unmoving pools of sapphire', comes back with:

'All that you and your kind will destroy the world for is no more in history than a forest fire. You'll bring your great gifts of blackness and desolation; but one day the trees will be green again and nobody will remember you.'

The trees will be green again ...
Was it an accident, I wonder—or was it some message from the collective unconscious, channelled across eight centuries of English mythmaking, which made Charteris put such a precisely appropriate metaphor on the lips of the *Robin Hood* of Modern Crime?

For the long-term aficianado of Simon Templar, *The Saint in Miami* is a deeply nostalgic book.
Here, for the last time, is the Saint of the nineteen thirties, complete with full supporting cast. He is, it is true, the relaxed, Mark III (or Anglo-American) Saint; but he is as carefree and debonair as ever. Worry, we are told on the second page, is something 'quite external to him. If it ever touched him at all, it was in the form of a perverse and irresponsible worry—a small inkling worry that life might one day become dull, that the gods of gay and perilous adventure ... might one day desert him, leaving nothing but the humdrum uneventfulness which ordinary mortals accept as a substitute for living.' He is lying on a beach, that most typical of all Saint settings, and trickling 'sand through his fingers on to the arm which Patricia was using as a pillow for her spun-gold hair.'
Not only Patricia Holm, but Peter Quentin (one of

those gentlemanly sidekicks of the Monty Hayward type) is around, to act as a foil for the Saint's repartee and to keep up the banter whenever the Master is offstage. There is also Hoppy Uniatz ('Cheese, boss, it's a sea-soipont' he says on first sighting the submarine) and there are references in plenty to absent enemies like Chief Inspector Teal.

In other words, it's a standard Saint story; as Charteris himself once put it, 'the mixture as before'. There is no hint anywhere that someone is about to drop the cocktail shaker, and that the mixture will never be served again. In the next story, and the next, and the next—and, indeed, except for a few isolated and rather awkward interludes, for the rest of the entire Saint series—Simon is doomed to soldier on alone.

There isn't really a great deal of mystery about why this happened, although it has baffled Saint fans for a lot of years. For reasons that seem to have been partly emotional, partly technical, the Saint stories underwent a major change of course around 1942. From what he writes in *The Second Saint Omnibus*, it seems clear that once America was in the war Charteris felt uncomfortable about running a super-hero with so many ordinary people fighting and dying for their country in real life.[1] He set out on a considered policy of *scaling down* the Saint. ('He had to lose some of the spurious grandeur I had endowed him with when the going was easy, and there were not so many real-life heroes to compare him with.') Simon was to be presented as an ordinary (well, comparatively ordinary) federal agent fighting saboteurs up and down the country, and nothing more. (Mind you, Charteris is as careful as Brooks to see that his hero is never

[1] 'No personal St George slew that dragon. It cost the blood and agony of millions, and brought forth heroism that made everything I ever wrote about the Saint seem childish.' *The Second Saint Omnibus.*

put in the position of having to obey orders. The Saint's wartime boss is an obscure Washington high-up called—or, rather, code-named—Hamilton, who is rarely allowed to be more than a laconic voice on the phone; and Templar's treatment of him is every bit as peremptory as Conquest's was of Brother Tring. 'Hullo, Ham,' he says into the telephone in one story. 'I'm going solo for a few days. I want a private plane to go to the nearest field at Stornfield. Organise it for me, will you? I'll be at the airport in an hour.')

In changing his hero from a swashbuckling privateer into a semi-public, semi-private eye, Charteris is also moving the Saint more into line with the prevailing thriller fashion. This isn't the Day of the Desperado any more. The *Black Mask* genre has proved all-conquering, and in Britain and America alike it is the day of the quick-moving investigator in slouch hat and mackintosh; the day, in other words, of the Philip Marlowes, Lemmy Cautions, Mike Shaynes—the type played by Humphrey Bogart in main feature films, and by Lloyd Nolan, William Gargan & Co. in the B ones. The movies had already shifted the Saint some distance in this direction, as it was. The Saint, as portrayed by George Sanders between 1938 and 1940, had been a smooth, slightly bored investigator rather than an impudent buccaneer. (This is not a reflection on the late and very much lamented Sanders. It was just that George never could help being George.)

Now the differences between a 1930s desperado adventure and a 1940s private-eye thriller are more than superficial. They are structural, affecting the way the story works from beginning to end.

If you are describing the exploits of a Drummond character who is making war upon an arch-fiend of the Peterson type, then your story is the account of a quasi-military campaign. A large supporting cast is a help rather

210

than a handicap; your hero can deploy them as a captain deploys his platoon. But if you are featuring a fast-talking investigator, rushing from scene to scene and quizzing suspect after suspect, you want him to be as unencumbered as possible. The pace and the build-up of tension in this type of story depends on the balancing of suspects, the counterpointing of partly revealed motives. Regular characters—old friends from the past whose motives are beyond suspicion—may be nice to have around as sentimental souvenirs, but like most souvenirs they do tend to clutter up the place.

Thus the streamlined Mark IV, or next-best-thing-to-a-G-man Saint, has his regular acquaintances restricted to Ham and a rather colourless Inspector, one John Henry Furnack.[2] It isn't surprising that his new life seems to get him down.

> The Saint's fingers combed through his hair. The piratical chiselling of his features looked quite old in a sardonic and careless way ...
>
> (*The Saint Steps In*)

A rather interesting quote, that. Fans often complained that George Sanders never looked remotely like the real Saint. But in that passage (and more than a few parallel ones from the war adventures) the Saint seems to be looking awfully like the real George Sanders.

Perhaps it's his curious sex life that's bothering him most. With Patricia virtually faded out, he is now free to have a fresh girl in every story, but the end is nearly always a melancholy walk-off into the sunset by the Saint.

> 'You will be coming back, won't you?' she said.

[2] Furnack, a good-hearted American cop, *is*, in fact, from the past (he first appeared in *The Saint in New York*) but he has made only spasmodic appearances in the series. Furnack has his moments, but he isn't a patch on Claude Eustace Teal.

'Very soon, I hope.'

He had so many meanings in his mind that he couldn't help which one she chose from his voice ... He wanted to believe that he might be going back there some day. There was no harm in hoping.

(The Saint Steps In)

The number of young women whom the Saint is hoping to meet again some day must be astronomical, and his address book the size of the *Encyclopaedia Britannica.*

The sex game in popular fiction was now being played to rather complicated rules. By the war years, the thriller had come a good 50% of the way towards the permissive society. It had reached the point where sexual relations were freely permitted between the hero and any number of girls—provided that they were referred to half-jokingly, and happened before the beginning or after the end of the story. It was during the actual course of the narrative that the complexities arose. A female character, particularly if she was a villainess or deeply suspected, could now be quite specifically seductive, and even reach the point of lying on a bed, wearing only a flimsy nightie; but it had to be made quite clear that nothing actually happened between her and the hero on that particular occasion. The author couldn't get away with a line like 'his fingers reached towards her creamy white breasts' followed by a hasty row of asterisks—not, at any rate, in the thrillers I read. At all costs, the hero had to be prevented from setting knee on that bed. Sometimes a scream or a pistol shot echoed through the house at the crucial moment. More often, in the nick of time, there suddenly came to the hero a dark suspicion that the lady was using him, or worse, that someone was using *her*: compelling her to act the seductress against her natural instincts to further some arch-villain's scheme. The thought of such a horrendous possibility never failed to put him off her instantly.

It came over him like a wave, like a tide turning back, swamping and stifling him and dragging him down, and he had to strike out and fight and be clear. He put his hands up and seized her wrists and tore them away from round his neck ... He threw her off him so roughly that the bed caught her behind the knees and she sat down foolishly, her liquid eyes still fastened on him and her hair a disordered cloud of spun honey round her face.

'Good night,' he said, 'and give Daddy my regards.'

He went out, crossing the living-room quickly, and closing the door on the landing.

(*The Saint Steps In*)

All this is not to say that the basic Saint was entirely lost in those wartime novels. Every now and again a moment comes when the years and the pressures of war melt into nothing, and the Saint Eternal takes over from his new utility incarnation as nonchalantly as though nothing had changed at all since 1932.

At the climax of 'The Sizzling Saboteur', one of the two stories in *The Saint on Guard*, 1945,[3] the villain makes that fatal little error of judgement common to so many Charteris arch-crooks: he leaves the Saint tied up in a cellar. The Saint, and for good measure, a beautiful Russian spy (called, believe it or not, Olga Ivanovitch) are suspended by their wrists from two overhead boiler pipes, with their feet only just touching the floor. There is a bit of dialogue in which Olga reveals that the head of the Nazi sabotage organisation in the United States is one Seigfried Maris, and suddenly we get the first sign

[3] Hodder & Stoughton, publishers of all the books quoted in this chapter.

that the old what-the-hell daredevil is on his way back to us. Simon is surprised at Olga's news. 'Comrade Maris has been offstage far too much,' he complains. 'It is not fair to the readers ...'

Better is to come. The Saint crosses his left leg over his right, but 'not with the idea of striking an elegant and insouciant pose'. He is feeling to see if the Ungodly, who have officially searched and disarmed him, had by any chance overlooked the little knife strapped to his leg beneath his right sock. They had, of course. And so the rest is easy. All the Saint has to do now is (a) slide off his socks and shoes; (b) twist his body and balance himself on one foot, swinging the other leg lithely up to kick his hand ('I always knew all those years I spent in the Follies Chorus would come in handy' he says contentedly); (c) get the knife firmly wedged between the big toe, and the next one to it, on his left foot; and (d) swing the leg, 'aiming the razor edge of the blade between his left wrist and the pipe'.

At the crucial moment, he drops the knife—but the rope has been frayed enough. One mighty heave, and he bursts free.

> He regained his balance without a waste motion, and fell to attacking the knots that bound his right hand.
> 'I must be slipping,' he said. 'I used to do things like this just to warm up ...'

George Sanders had stopped playing the Saint some years before this book came out. Which is a pity, really. I'd have given a good deal to have seen how he tackled *that* little scene.

CHAPTER SIXTEEN

In which the Creasey battalion goes to war, and the Toff meets a real policeman

FOR John Creasey, it can by no stretch of the imagination be said that the '39–'45 conflict was an awkward war. No one who was a thriller fan at the time can fail to remember how all-pervasive Creasey novels were in the circulating libraries. It would not be too much to say that he provided many a thriller addict with as much as 50% of his reading material all the way from Dunkirk to the doodlebug era. Not that all the fans realised that Creasey was the founder of so much of the feast. Under his own name he was publishing a mere five or six novels a year. There were usually two Department Zs, a couple of Toffs, and a double-length (120,000-word) novel about Department Z5, headed by one Dr Stanislaus Alexander Palfrey. It is when you add the aliases that the fantastic scale of the Creasey industry becomes clear.

As Norman Deane, he sent Bruce Murdoch into battle with Hitler's super-agent the Withered Man around once a year; under the name Gorden Ashe he rarely failed to produce two Patrick Dawlish adventures; as Michael Halliday he turned out cheerful whodunits, without a series hero, again twice a year, and in 1943 he started writing a further book a year under another whodunit alias, Jeremy York. In addition to all this, he was doing an average of three Westerns a year (*Masked Riders*, *Guns on the Range* stuff) under the names Tex Riley and William K. Reilly; and as Anthony Morton he was still, to some extent, in business with the Baron.

It is well known that the Churchill government co-opted Dennis Wheatley on to their joint planning staff to get a thriller-writer's-eye view of how the war could be won. It is a wonder to me that a similar invitation wasn't given to Creasey. It would require a complicated fold-out chart to do justice to the scale of the operations in which Creasey characters were involved throughout the hostilities.

Britain itself was protected by Gordon Craigie's Department Z, which had seen the war coming from a long way off (*The Mark of the Crescent*, 1935) and was in a fine state of preparedness. But Z was essentially a counter-espionage concern, a save-Britain-from-disaster unit: as long as Craigie paced and smoked and worried, twenty-four hours a day in that cosy Inner Sanctum, you knew that somehow Britain would survive. It was in order to carry the war to the enemy that Creasey created, in 1942, his Department Z5, headed by Dr Palfrey. Palfrey —much given to smiling faintly and twisting a finger round a strand of his hair—was really a gentle worrier in the Craigie mould, but a young and mobile one. By the time Dept Z5 came on the scene, Russia and America were in the war, and Palfrey's team was thoroughly cosmopolitan, containing an elegant Frenchman, a wisecracking American and a genial Russian giant called Stefan Andromovitch. Reading one of their adventures —and, because of their epic length, they took a little reading—gave you a literally *super*-patriotic glow. It was the same emotion that came over you when you listened to all the national anthems of the Allies being played on the radio. (Which they were, incidentally, every Sunday, for a solid quarter of an hour before the nine o'clock news.)

With Craigie looking after defence and Palfrey's unit conducting endless combined raids in Europe, Creasey's war still had room in plenty for more individualistic

216

enterprises, such as Scarlet Pimpernel operations across
the Channel to rescue super-scientists and such from the
Gestapo. These were normally entrusted to Patrick Dawlish, the huge, hard-hitting neo-Drummond created back
in that busy week in July, 1937. Dawlish became a star
figure in M15—a department left with little enough to
do, one would imagine, with so much of the action being
grabbed by Z and Z5. And for special, sporadic counter-
espionage offensives (such as supporting the newly
formed Home Guard against a Fifth Column run by von
Horsall, the Withered Man) there was yet another Creasey
department on call—S1, run by a plump little man called
Pinky from a quaint converted cottage near Sloane
Square. When asked by Bruce Murdoch why he doesn't
move his headquarters nearer Whitehall, Pinky explains:
'You addle pated young pup, use what brains the good
Lord gave you. I chose it because no one in their senses
would think I really work in it. Most spies have sense.'
(*The Withered Man* by Norman Deane, Hurst & Blackett,
1940.)

It may be wondered how Creasey was able to send
heroes into and out of Nazi-occupied Europe without
seeming to cheapen the real-life heroisms of war. I think
the answer lies in the fundamental vulnerability of all
Creasey's heroes. Creasey is incapable of creating a
reckless daredevil in the Charteris–Brooks sense: his
heroes, even the most dashing of them, agonise, blunder,
worry: they don't saunter in to sort out Hitler, they are
Britons (or, in the case of Dept Z5, gallant allies) with
their backs to the wall, inviting you to identify with them
in 'seeing it through'. Creasey was never at his happiest
in the 1930s. His particular trick is always to involve you
with his heroes through sharing their difficulties, and this
is probably why he had to wait until the 1940s before
really coming into his own.

It is interesting to see what happens to Creasey's most

217

1930-ish hero in the totally changed conditions of 1943. We left John Mannering, alias the Baron, back in 1935. He was, you remember, emphatically the Raffles of that decade—an elegant, implacable thief with daringly ungentlemanly standards but the most advanced humanitarian code of any cracksman in fiction. What had originally motivated him was a broken heart—broken twice, actually, in the same novel. In Chapter One of *Meet the Baron*, Mannering was jilted by a society gold-digger because of his lack of funds. In the course of the book, he met a girl artist, Lorna, who became his life-long love. In the final chapter, he found that Lorna could never marry him: she was secretly married already—to a blackmailing wastrel who would not divorce her, and who held over her head the fearful threat that he would tell the world about their wedding unless he was constantly supplied with funds. It was basically because he could not marry his Lorna that the Baron's bitterness against the world, and his consequent career of crime, continued unabated for the rest of the thirties.

But the Mannering we met in *The Baron Comes Back*, 1943, has undergone more than a few changes. He has retired from crime and actually joined the Army. What is more, Lorna's secret husband has been killed off in an air raid, and so she and John are free to marry at last, and indeed they do just that, at a registry office, on the last page.

Perhaps, in the new, 50%-permissive climate of the wartime thriller, the old secret-blackmailing-husband routine had looked outdated. Or perhaps it was just that Creasey took pity on John and Lorna, and felt that, as (to quote the book) 'the day of the Baron was over', there was no point in prolonging their plight.

It is rather an awkward book, *The Baron Comes Back*. Mannering fights against a curious gang smuggling some stolen jewels out of occupied France, and trying to frame him in the process; but even Creasey's storytelling skill cannot make us forget that there is a war going on, that the police have more important things to do than arrest (or fail to arrest) jewel thieves, and that maybe it is time Mannering was roped in by Dept Z, Z5, S1, M15 or some other unit at the Creasey campaign headquarters. Creasey must have sensed these psychological objections. He wrote about other characters under the Anthony Morton pseudonym during 1943 and 1944, and the next time the Baron comes back, it is virtually the end of the war.

With the Toff series, the Inspector West series, the Dr Palfrey series, the Bruce Murdoch (vs. the Withered Man et aliis) series, the Dept Z series and the Patrick Dawlish series all going full blast, John Creasey was offering his wartime public a solid half-dozen different thriller worlds, each with its own regular characters, each with its own particular style and tone, each developing from book to book and year to year. From the point of view of this study, of course, the most important is the world of the Toff. What happened to Rollison during the war years is, indeed, one of the most interesting examples of desperado development we have yet encountered.

Creasey made no bones about taking the Toff into the Army: he is Major the Hon. Richard Rollison almost from the beginning of the war. But, perhaps to prevent any reader feeling that his hero had become irrevocably a member of the officer class, Creasey goes to considerable pains to establish that the Toff is no ordinary toff. With the exception of his stern but lovable Aunt Gloria, a formidable cross between Lady Bracknell and a typical 1940s WVS Commandant, Rollison finds most of his relatives loathsome. They don't appreciate *him*, either. His Aunt Mattie (ill in bed from eating some tainted black-market salmon) calls him an 'annoying beast'.

'You've even shooed me out of the flat to see one of those funny little friends of yours from the East End. If you prefer men like that to people of your own kind ...'

The Toff's relationship with the East Enders is now, indeed, a closer one than ever. He has taken more than a few hard-up families under his wing financially, and in his capacity as desperado has rescued many good-hearted Cockney folk from the toils of villains. Consequently, he is now turned to instinctively by anyone 'east of Aldgate Pump' who is in any kind of trouble at all. It must be admitted that these East End characters in the Toff stories are just a little hard to take nowadays. At the drop of a hat (or a titfer) they start talking like Cockneys out of a Hollywood musical.

'Hullo, Liz,' Rollison said as he reached the bar. 'Aren't you old enough to retire yet?'

'Watcher me old cocksparrer. 'Ow are yer?' She extended a work-grimed hand and Rollison took it firmly. 'Strewth, I never expected to see yer, strike me.'

When Rollison hints to Liz that he will help her husband fight the gang that has beaten him up, her 'eyes glow'.

'Strewth, that'll warm 'is 'eart, that will. Cor bless my soul, 'ave I been wantin' to hear that!'
(*The Toff Goes to Market*, John Long, 1942)

Sometimes, when this sort of thing goes on for pages, you can't help feeling that Cor luv a duck, you won't 'arf be glad when Mister C turns it up. But the sheer warmth with which these Cockneys are described makes the best of them, in the end, extraordinarily memorable. Bill Ebbutt, the wheezy, asthmatic fight promoter, with his Salvation Army wife and his gymnasium full of lads ever ready to rush to the assistance of 'Mister Ar', has become, over a quarter of a century or more, almost as real

220

to me as Gordon Craigie. And in point of fact, the prob-
lems facing Creasey's wartime East End are depicted
with a documentary realism very rare in the thrillers
of the time. Liz and her husband in *The Toff Goes to
Market* are being menaced by a crook called Barbecue
who is a chilling composite portrait of the actual Home
Front villains of the war. He runs a combination blackmail and protection racket; his gang beats up small pub-
owners who won't buy his illicit whisky at £5 a bottle.
In addition, to finance his black-market purchases, he
buys blitzed buildings from their owners at rubble-bottom
prices, and sells them to land speculators. His profits
(precisely detailed—£759,607 19*s* 6*d* in a single trading
year) enable him to live it up in a West End hotel as
almost a 'Churchill of crime'.

The job of tackling operatives like that is, of course,
in the direct tradition of the desperado hero. The Mixer,
the Saint and Conquest would all have had fun giving Mr
Barbecue a roasting. The Toff, though, doesn't handle
the situation quite their way: he works in much closer
association with the police. Creasey, tiring of the endless
Desperado-versus-Stupid-Cop routine, introduced into the
Toff books very early in the war years an ascetic-looking
Scotland Yard man called Grice, who is not only a reasonable and believable policeman, but not even above calling
on the Toff for assistance.

> 'Rollison, the scope and extent of buying on the
> black market is increasing much too fast. I think one
> of the centres is in the East End. I've been seriously
> considering getting in touch with you—you can help
> more down there than any man living. If we can per-
> suade the War Office to grant you leave, will you drop
> everything and work in with us?'
>
> (*The Toff Goes to Market*)

The appearance of the mild and friendly Grice marks

a major turning-point in Creasey's career. Once he started writing about believable policemen (the most believable, in this kind of thriller, since Edgar Wallace's) he found he couldn't stop. Within a year of Grice's first appearance in the Toff series, he had created Inspector 'Handsome' West, the hero of a 40-novel saga which still continues; and in 1955, he developed West into perhaps the most human Yard man in all crime fiction, the celebrated Gideon. (It is Creasey himself who traces Gideon's descent back through West to Grice. Personally, I am inclined to think that Bristow, the benign Inspector whom Mannering rescues at the probable cost of his own freedom at the end of *Meet the Baron*, 1935, has a claim to be considered the father of them all.)

The wartime world of the Toff, then, is an endlessly fascinating mixture of contradictory elements, in which the past and future of the thriller itself seem somehow to be entwined. There is Aunt Gloria, representing the good old aristocracy, so beloved of thriller writers for all this century. There is the Jeeves-like Jolly, reminder of the once-strong link the thriller had with comic literature of the Wodehouse type. There are the 'wotcher-me-old Cock-sparrer' Cockneys, unexpectedly acting as a channel for Creasey's first experiments in social realism. There is Superintendent Grice, forerunner of Gideon and the serious, believable Yard men of the next decades. And in the midst of it all is the Toff, himself as extraordinarily divided a character as ever.

On the outside, the Toff is forceful, dynamic and emphatically tough. In *The Toff Goes to Market*, he follows a fire-raiser all the way home from a blaze. He knocks the man unconscious on his own doorstep, and drags his body into the house. When the man recovers, he finds that the Toff is about to set light to a pile of furniture.

'Stop! Stop that!'

The other's shout was frenzied. He moved from his chair, but with his free hand the Toff pushed him back. He groaned, and Rollison stood up without setting the paper on fire, and opened his lips for the first time.

'Doesn't death by fire appeal to you?'

'Don't—don't do it!' Blackie's voice was high-pitched, his face was working. 'You must be mad—mad ...'

'I'm under a strain, perhaps ...'

Rollison took out his revolver and slowly and deliberately turned it so that he held it by the barrel. He made a feint for the other's head. 'I mustn't hit too hard. If there's enough of you left, they might realise it was no accident ...'

Rollison soon has Blackie telling him all he wants to know. And this technique of the Toff's—he calls it 'psychological terrorism'—is equally resolutely applied to the arch-villain Barbecue.

But at home, in between actual confrontations with the enemy, Rollison is a wholly different man. He potters around hesitantly trying out theories on people, and all the other characters in a story often combine to reproach him for the way the case is going. Aunt Gloria will call him 'Richard' instead of 'Rolly', which always worries him. Grice, infuriatingly smug once he has made a big arrest (usually of the wrong man), will start hanging up the phone in a huff in mid-sentence, which worries him more. And even Jolly can be needling at times:

'So all we have to do is find the murderer, sir; yes,' said Jolly mildly.

'Oh, go and wash up,' said Rollison irritably. 'That was sarcasm to the nth degree.'

(*The Toff Goes to Market*)

One way or another, Creasey usually gets you concerned about the Toff before the end of a story. But there is not much need to be sorry for old Rolly. He emerged in 1945 a far stronger and more personable character than he had been in 1939.

Which, I rather think, means that he, alone of all the durable desperadoes, did not merely survive, but *won* his Awkward War.

Part Four

THE GREAT TIME ROBBERY
(1945–1972)

CHAPTER SEVENTEEN

In which most of the Desperadoes become good citizens, and the Saint walks about in a dream

ONCE the War was over, it might have been expected that the Gentleman Outlaws would immediately revert to type, and become their old mischievous, buccaneering, devil-may-care selves.

They didn't do this, though, for the simple reason that they couldn't. The mood of 1945 was as different from that of the thirties as if six decades, instead of six years, lay in between.

The thirties mood had leant itself to gaiety, romantic flamboyance, elegance and wit—or at any rate as much wit as an author could contrive—because underlying it had been a quasi-metaphysical attitude: an attitude best expressed, perhaps, in that familiar Rodgers and Hart line, 'So don't be serious: *life's too mysterious.*'

It would be very hard to find a line *less* descriptive of the mood of the second half of the forties. Immediate post-war Britain was bedevilled by economic crises, fuel shortage, power cuts and intensified rationing. It was haunted by imminent threat of war with Russia, and stunned by the twin horrors of Hiroshima and the realisation that ordinary people had been slaughtered by the million in Hitler's death-camps: an operation that wouldn't have been possible without the acquiescence (and, in some cases, the connivance) of thousands of other ordinary people. Notwithstanding the evidence which also abounded of ordinary citizens having shown invincibility —in the Resistance movements, for example, and the

London blitzes—the cult of the Little Man took a beating from which it has not recovered to this day. The fundamental post-war outlook, in fact, was almost: 'We've got to be serious, because *nothing's* mysterious'—which could pass as a crude definition of the early existentialist ethic. What has been called 'the black light of the twentieth century' had been switched on full, plunging into shadow virtually all the things that had compounded the real magic of the thirties: its mysticism, its warmth, its innocence, in other words its *reasons* for gaiety. A thirties desperado waving a mocking salute to the 'gods of gay and perilous adventure' was just a little *de trop* in the age of *It Always Rains on Sunday* and *The Naked and the Dead*.

The class situation was as difficult as the mood one. The Gentlemen Outlaws may have basically represented the man in the street, but their trappings had always been those of high society. Now joining (or being on a level with) high society was far from being a fashionable dream. The arrival of a Labour Government in 1945, the almost universal refusal of people returning from the forces to entertain the idea of domestic service, and swingeing taxes on unearned income combined to turn men-about-town into anachronisms overnight—and who wanted to identify with an anachronism, still less a pseudo-anachronism?

Mayfair elegance had not quite lost its century-old hold over the imaginations of the public, as a matter of fact: as we shall be seeing in a couple of chapters, it was to return in strength in the early fifties under a new name, 'Gracious Living'. But for the time being, the rich had to be shown as quaint, charming keepers-up of stately homes, graciously at bay before the forces of progress, as in the enormously successful Anna Neagle films like *Spring in Park Lane*. Even in Hollywood, top-hat sophistication had temporarily lost its sparkle: it is a

228

very wan and lugubrious Fred Astaire we see in *Blue Skies* (1946).

In addition to all this, we have, for the second time in this study, to take into account the background of a savagely war-ravaged Europe.

In 1918, this had produced a compensatory demand on the part of the British thriller-reading public for 'sound-chap' heroes. Its effects this time were more complicated.

The black existentialist mood, crossing from the Continent, gave a further lift to the 'sombre realism' school of thriller writers: it was widely maintained that the only thrillers worth considering were those by people like Simenon, Chandler, and Eric Ambler.

It is often assumed that the immediate post-war mood was cynical: the phrase 'couldn't care less' comes to us from roughly this period. But disillusionment didn't reach any depth amongst the general public until towards the tail end of the forties. In the social if not the sexual sense (the joyless rape-upon-rape saga *Forever Amber* was the best-seller of the time) the public of 1945-9 was earnest almost to the point of priggishness. The solemn voice of the Iron Chancellor, Sir Stafford Cripps, promising tax reliefs only 'within the lifetimes of most of us', was listened to with grey masochistic relish, and this really sums up the mood of the hour.

What was basically most admired was an ability to face life glumly but unflinchingly, rather in the style of a Nigel Balchin or Neville Shute hero. The one thing nobody could stand was the idea of a hero larking about irresponsibly.

Quite plainly, then, the drawling buccaneer type was at every kind of disadvantage, and had the desperadoes been nothing but that it is doubtful if they would have survived.

But there had always been a second side to their natures, the Robin Hood, humanitarian side, and it was this aspect that the authors began instinctively to stress.

There is a very significant passage at the opening of *The Toff on Ice* (John Long, 1947) in which Aunt Gloria delivers a half-hour lecture on the Toff's Lack of Purpose:

'You, the liveliest man in London, a man consulted a hundred times by the police, a man who really did some good in his own way, who spent his money well, who showed every sign of having a conscience and not wanting to wallow in luxury provided by his forebears, a man whom every newspaper in the country regarded as first class news—'

'Steady!' pleaded Rollison.

'But it's all true!' declared Aunt Gloria vigorously. 'There was real spirit in you. I've heard it said that you looked on life as a crusade—'

'Oh, no!' gasped Rollison with a horrified grimace.

'But I have,' said Aunt Gloria firmly, 'and it was true. You adopted many poor people of the East End, and they loved you for it; you did more than any man to smooth out the difficulties between petty criminals and the police; you had more influence than any man in London in the East End, and ...' She paused and looked at him as if she were daunted by the thought of what she wanted to say.

He did not look away from her, but his eyes were narrowed and the lips were pressed tightly together. She drew a deep breath and went on:

'Well, you *have* asked for it. You're throwing away everything you've built up because you fell in love with a married woman.'

Clearly, Amber not withstanding, the Permissive Society has not quite arrived as yet. Rollison pulls himself together after Aunt Gloria's lecture, which is just as well: this new age has sterner trials in store for him. Within a year or so, Creasey's publishers, John Long,

230

began to get complaints that the Toff was not actually *earning* his living. From then onwards, for quite a while, clients had actually to pay him for his services. This, a very awkward business, was always handled by Jolly, of course, but it somehow altered the tone of the books and Creasey was glad to drop it as soon as he could.

This demand that heroes should be provided with a respectable means of support was met by different authors in different ways. Bruce Graeme would have had no trouble with Blackshirt: Verrell had always been a successful crime novelist in his spare time. (Though this is rather an academic consideration at this point, because no Blackshirt book appeared between 1945 and 1950.) Edwy Searles Brooks got Conquest and Joy Everard wedded and officially bedded at last (in the slightly unfortunately named *Mr Ball of Fire*, 1946) and they acquired a comfortable legitimate income by renting apartments in their Park Lane skyscraper, Conquest Court. Finally, in *Career for the Baron*, 1947, John Mannering set up his celebrated Mayfair antique shop, Quinn's.

From this point onwards, he moved against a background of grave appreciation of beautiful things ('Immediately after lunch he went to Christie's for a preview ... a Chinese oil lamp of the Fourth Ming Dynasty caught his eye' and so on) and awed respect began to alternate with stubborn suspicion in the eyes of Inspector Bill Bristow, always my personal favourite of Creasey's human policemen.

I asked John Creasey direct whether this major development in the Baron's life had come about through pressure from a priggish public. He replied that there had been no question of pressure at all. 'John opened that shop because Lorna wanted him to. It was as simple as that.'

231

I stood corrected (as gently and firmly as a Dept Z agent being put right by Gordon Craigie). Nevertheless I can't help feeling that, in being so determined to get John to settle down, Lorna was being wholly typical of the girls of that period. This Austerity era was, above all things, a time for stopping nonsense; for taking life seriously; for quietly and sensibly getting on with the job. Even the job of being a desperado.

In a serious world, the Saint was, in certain respects, becoming more serious too. It was just after the Second World War that the Saint Club was founded, which assisted first of all the Invalid and Crippled Children's Hospital in Plaistow, and later the Arbour Youth Club in Stepney. This (to quote Messrs Lofts and Adley) was one of the toughest areas in East London, badly blitzed during the war, where 'facilities for recreation were almost non-existent'. The Youth Club provided dozens of teenagers with a place to go in the evenings. Money for it came entirely from Saint fans, and an appeal for funds appeared at the end of every Saint book, prefaced by that celebrated Charteris sentence which I have quoted already about upright citizens with furled umbrellas and secret buccaneering dreams.

Charteris was not often in England, though, to direct these Saintly activities personally. He was now on the point of becoming a U.S. citizen, and busy completing his conquest of the American public. In 1945, a coast-to-coast Saint radio programme was launched in America, and a Saint strip cartoon was syndicated by the *New York Herald Tribune*.

In the first post-war Saint book, *The Saint Sees it Through*, Templar is still the Mark IV Saint, the tough Federal investigator working for Ham. (Very tough, as a matter of fact. At the climax of *The Saint Sees It Through*, 'in the pellucid knowledge of what they were
232

and what they had done', he shoots two torturing villainesses in the region of their respective navels. Not many reviewers took much notice of the Saint, but I can distinctly remember one asking if it wouldn't have been more gentlemanly to have aimed a few inches higher.)

But by the next Charteris book, *Call for the Saint*, in 1948, it is clear that the old Mark III Saint is trying to stage a comeback. In 'The Masked Angel', one of the book's two novellas, we actually meet Patricia Holm again (understandably a slightly acid Pat) and even Hoppy Uniatz is around. What is more, Inspector Fernack is becoming so Teal-like that he is almost an acceptable substitute for the real Claud Eustace.

> Inspector Fernack did not sit down. In fact, he looked more as if he might easily rise into the air, from the sheer pressure of the steam that seemed to be distending his chest.
> For the same routine was going to be played out again, and he knew it, without being able to do anything to check or vary its course. It was all implicit in the Saint's gay and friendly smile; and the bitterness of the premonition put a crack in his voice even while he ploughed doggedly onwards towards his futile destiny....
>
> (*Call for the Saint*, Hodder & Stoughton)

It could hardly be made plainer that the Saint is back in the cop-baiting business, and it looks as though the war is now fading like a bad dream behind him, leaving him very little altered. Appearances, though, are rather deceptive. Charteris is abandoning the attempt to bring the Saint closer to a Chandler-type investigator, but he is not really able to turn back the clock, any more than anybody else is, in this post-war era.

The Mark III Saint turns out, in fact, to be back with

us only for a one-book stand. In the next volume, a collection of short stories called *Saint Errant* (1949), we meet the Mark V, or Cosmopolitan, Saint: a smooth, relaxed, essentially solitary figure, always on the move around the world, rarely seeming to live anywhere but in hotel rooms, and only once appearing in anything longer than a short story. We shall have to get used to this Mark V Saint. He will be around for all of fifteen years; and although there's something a little lost and melancholy about him, now and then, it has to be admitted that he's a lot closer to the Saint Eternal than the Mark IV Templar ever was.

The most startling of the Mark V Saint stories is one of the very first of them: 'Dawn', the climacteric story in *Saint Errant*.

It is twilight in the Sierras, and the Saint is by himself in a log cabin in a pine forest. Suddenly a man enters, hatless and coatless, and stares blankly at the Saint.

'I never dreamed you here,' the man said. 'Who are you?'

'You dropped a word,' the Saint said. ' "I never dreamed you *were* here" makes more sense.'

'Nuts, brother. You're part of my dream, and I never saw you before. You don't even have a name. All the others have, complete with backgrounds. But I can't place you. Funny, I—look here, you're not real, are you?'

'The last time I pricked myself, I yelped.'

'This is crazy,' the man muttered.

It gets crazier. The man keeps talking about a girl called Dawn. He produces a circular fire opal blazing 'with living beauty—blue, green, gold, cerise, chartreuse' —and the Saint 'gasped with reverent wonder as he looked at the cameo head carved on the unbelievable gem'.

'There is beauty to which one can put a name,' thunders Charteris, the shades of Rider Haggard surely around him. 'There is beauty that inspires awe, bravery, fear, lust, passion. There is beauty that softens the savage blows of fate. There is beauty that drives to high adventure and to violence.' The face on that stone was 'the lily maid of Astolet, the lost loveliness that all men seek and never find, the nameless desire that haunts the ragged edge of sleep, that curls a lovely smile and sends vacant eyes searching for spaces. Her face was made for—and of? the Saint asked himself—dreaming.'

The story gets stranger and stranger. The man states that his name in this dream is Big Bill Holbrook, but that he is really Andrew Faulds, a bank clerk, in bed and asleep in Glendale, California. The American equivalent of the upright citizen with furled umbrella, in the midst of one of his celebrated buccaneering dreams. As soon as he realises he is talking to the Saint, he says: 'What beautiful, wonderful luck ... The Robin Hood of Modern Crime, the twentieth century's brightest buccaneer, the devil with dames, the headache of cops and crooks alike. What a sixteen-cylinder dream this is.'

Before long, the Saint's log cabin gets a little crowded. Two minor crooks turn up, 'such types as B pictures had implanted upon the consciousness of the world'. Dawn herself appears, and Charteris's style becomes Haggard at the edges again. 'You are so beautiful,' says the Saint, 'that the world would bow down and worship you—if the world knew of your existence. Yet it's impossible that the world doesn't know. If one single person looked at you, the word would go out ...' He still doesn't credit the fact that he has stepped into one of his reader's dreams, even when the lily maid of Astolet starts calling him 'The Robin Hood of Modern Crime, the twentieth century's brightest buccaneer, the devil with dames' just as her boy friend had done.

What convinces him is when an enormously fat man, one Seldon Appopoulis, pops in, and holds him up at gunpoint. Appopoulis is definitely straight from an A picture, and one starring Humphrey Bogart at that.

'Mr Sidney Greenstreet, I presume?' Simon drawled.

The buttery chuckle sent a sea of flesh ebbing and flowing.

'A quick action, sir, and an efficient direction of action. I complement you, and am saddened that you must die.'

And the most extraordinary thing about this most extraordinary of all Saint stories is that the Saint *does* die.

The Saint felt a jar, and a flame roared inside his chest. Somehow he couldn't pull the trigger any more. The gun fell from his limp fingers. His incredulous eyes looked full in the mirror and saw a neat black hole over his heart, saw it begin to spread as his life's blood gushed out ...

Like a true myth hero, though, the Saint dies only to become alive again. He loses consciousness, and when he comes to the cabin is empty, and the wound has healed as completely as though it had never been. He rushes round to Glendale, California and looks up the bank clerk, Andrew Faulds—to find he had died the night before after a prolonged coma. Poor Andrew met a distressing end, he learns, in a high delirium during which 'he kept shouting about shooting someone, and talked about a Saint'.

Simon wonders 'what the psychic phenomena boys would do with this one. This, he thought, would certainly give them a shot in the aura'.

It should give the student of thriller-heroes a shot in the aura, too. What Leslie Charteris has done in this story—'Dawn', from *Saint Errant*, Hodder & Stoughton, 1949—is drawl a final, devastating 'Nuts, brother' to the forces of austerity, conformity and realism that have been shackling so many of the desperadoes, as if to a cellar wall, ever since 1939. He even cocks a friendly snook at the grey world of Dashiell Hammett, or at any rate at the Hollywood version of it.[1] The Saint, this story establishes with flamboyant relish, bears no resemblance to an ordinary crime-fiction hero. He is a myth figure from the magic thirties—many would say, *the* myth figure from the magic thirties. As such, he is fully licensed to be larger than life.... because if the magic thirties had any message at all worth passing on to future decades, it was the statement that each and every human being *is*, in the final analysis, mysteriously larger than the life he leads.

[1] In a sense, this story acknowledges that this sort of world has taken over from that of the desperadoes: Appopoulis is actually allowed to kill the Saint. But the Saint magically survives, and is around at the end when Appopoulis has vanished, which is an odd way of conceding *final* defeat.

CHAPTER EIGHTEEN

In which Blackshirt, with a mocking laugh, leaps clean across the generation gap

W E have observed, in the course of this study, a good many zig-zags by that contradictory old animal, the *Zeitgeist*. Now, though, it is beginning to be possible to discern some logic behind its gyrations and at least the hint of a recurrent pattern.

At the end of the First World War, the shaken public eschewed outright outlawry in favour of the safe and essentially patriotic Bulldog Drummond. But after five or six years, that lawless urge which is rarely wholly absent from the thriller reader's psyche began, cautiously, to surface, and in 1925 there arrived the perfect hero to embody it: one Richard Verrell, alias Blackshirt.

At the end of the Second World War, the shaken public eschewed outright outlawry, and more or less compelled its desperadoes to become safe, honest-living-earning crusaders. But after five or six years, that lawless urge which is rarely wholly absent from the thriller reader's psyche began, not so cautiously, to surface, and in 1950–2 there arrived the perfect hero to embody it: one Richard Verrell, alias Blackshirt.

The Verrell revival really began in 1950 itself, when Bruce Graeme's publishers decided to bring out a 25th anniversary edition of the original novel, *Blackshirt*. This was so successful that they followed it a year later with a new edition of *The Return of Blackshirt*, originally published in 1927.

In, I suspect, both these volumes, and certainly in the

1951 *Return of Blackshirt* (which I have in front of me as I write), there are some very slight revisions. Slight but not exactly insignificant. In the paragraphs which once stated that Richard Verrell was a young ex-hero of the First World War, it is now claimed that he is a young ex-hero of the *Second* World War. Blackshirt, in fact, is celebrating his silver jubilee in a highly original (and unquestionably enviable) fashion—by losing no less than a quarter of a century from his age. This, of course, puts the young Anthony Verrell of the wartime Son of Blackshirt series not merely out of business, but out of existence: but then he always had inhabited a queer hypothetical future, and could easily be written off as having never really been born at all. (One can imagine him fading slowly as he returns to the mysterious fourth dimensional world from which he came, his beloved pipe Agnes still clenched between his flashing RAF-type teeth.)

These updated Blackshirt adventures sold so well that the publishers began asking Bruce Graeme for new stories. Graeme, however, had wearied of Verrell as long ago as 1939, and the thought of re-imagining him as a young man of a second post-war era was more than somewhat daunting.

Thus it happened that the task of creating a nineteen-fifties Blackshirt passed to Bruce Graeme's son, Roderic. Roderic Graeme had begun his literary career when he was a second officer in the Merchant Navy. He had had some success with novels for teenagers—*Brandy Ahoy* and others—and had just given up the sea to study law. When his father suggested that he should take over the famous Blackshirt, he jumped at the chance.

The resultant situation is almost poetic in its symmetry. The fictitious son of Blackshirt has been faded out in favour of his father: the real-life creator of Blackshirt retires in favour of his son. Not that its symmetry is the only thing about the situation which is striking. I do not think there is another instance anywhere in literature of a son taking over a hero from his father, and re-styling him for his own generation. What adds an extra piquancy is the fact that Roderic Graeme was only twenty-five himself at the time (1951), which means that he was inheriting a hero who had been before the public for a year longer than he himself had been alive.

Verrell's first adventure under the new management was *Concerning Blackshirt*, published by Hutchinson in 1952. It is, as a matter of fact, a rather mild Verrell whom we meet. He is unquestionably of the fifties (one of his first fights is with a gang in zoot suits) but the most immediately obvious changes to the character are omissions rather than additions. For example, it is simply stated that Verrell 'had long ago earned sufficient by his writing to give up his other life—that of Blackshirt, the audacious cracksman. But the thrills of the hidden life were too great a temptation. And whenever the restless urge overcame him, he would go forth and satisfy his craving—and the more danger he encountered, the happier he was.'

The long explanations—you could almost say excuses —for Blackshirt's criminal tendencies (his Oliver Twist upbringing, and so on) do not appear. There is no mention, either, of his aristocratic birth, or of his spectacular reformation by the—

Ah, that's it, of course. That's the key difference. This is Richard Verrell as he was right in the first few pages of his first adventure, *a Richard Verrell who has never heard from his Lady of the Phone.*

One could build a towering pile of psycho-social implications on this simple fact. A quarter of a century earlier, the Lady of the Phone had been the means of changing Blackshirt from an amoral Raffles into (to repeat my own phrases from Chapter 4) an all but brand-new type of hero, a romantic, right-living Society Robin Hood. But in the nineteen fifties, romantic, right-living Society Robin Hoods were anything but a new type of hero. Roderic Graeme's generation (as I can say with some authority, as it happens to be my generation too) had been practically brought up on Toffs and Saints and Conquests. The way to intrigue *them* was clearly to reverse the whole process: to remove the Lady's influence and expunge her memory, returning Verrell to what might be called the square before Square One; making him, in other words, an audacious crook to whom the very idea of repentance was a load of old cod's wallop. (A precedent for blithely unrepentant criminals had been set, a year earlier, by Orson Welles's astonishing five-minute performance as Harry Lime in the Graham Greene–Carol Reed film, *The Third Man*. Neither Greene nor Reed had intended that the almost comically callous Lime should become a hero, but the public found something about him irresistible. Perhaps he fitted into the tail-of-the-forties 'couldn't-care-less' mood. More probably, it was a combination of those eternally formidable factors, daredevilry, impudence, and mocking laughter. Not since the Saint had any character so irrepressibly presented all three.)

The interesting thing about this counter-reformation operation on Blackshirt is that it could not have been attempted at any time between 1919 and, say, 1949. Generally speaking, to succeed in the twenties, a cracksman hero had had to be continually on the brink of reforming; to succeed in the thirties, he had had to have a reason for bitterness against Society—which had almost always turned out to be a romantically broken heart. And there had been no possibility of his succeeding in the War, or immediate post-War, years. The new Blackshirt returns us straight to the atmosphere of the pre-1914 era, suggesting, however curious it may seem, that in

241

certain respects the moral climate of the early 50s had a lightness not known since 1905.

Roderic Graeme wrote twenty Blackshirt novels altogether, between 1952 and 1969. One of my favourites is *The Amazing Mr Blackshirt*, which starts with Verrell attending an auction with the idea of pocketing a couple of precious pendants. Within a page, he has got rid of the auctioneer and is directing the bidding in his place.

Later in the same novel—which almost equals the early Conquests in pace—a gang of crooks attempts to frame Verrell by committing a burglary, and leaving his cigarette case (on which his name and address are inscribed) at the scene of their crime. They also purloin Verrell's car, and leave it in the vicinity, just to make the incrimination complete. Verrell, facing awkward police inquiries about the incident, realises that there is only one way to divert suspicion from himself, and that is to go into the red herring business wholesale. He sets about this in a grand manner directly reminiscent of Arsène Lupin at his liveliest. First, he steals a cigarette case and car from a respectable book critic, one Mr Quentin, who has incidentally attacked his last novel on unfair grounds. Second: he steals a £700 necklace from another address, leaving Quentin's case on the scene and car in the vicinity. Third: he steals a cigarette case and car from the home of Assistant Commissioner Simpson of Scotland Yard. Fourth: he breaks into still another house, waking the occupant by saying 'Boo' and then disappearing, leaving the Assistant Commissioner's cigarette case in the room, and the A.C.'s car (a baby Austin) parked outside.

Scotland Yard, faced with this welter of stolen and planted cigarette cases and cars, one of each involving its own Assistant Commissioner, is totally foxed. Then the man who has suffered from a 'Boo' in the night describes his visitor as having been a figure clad all in black,

242

and the whole police force sits back with an admiring sigh.

'Well, sir, that seems to be that!' Inspector Johns tells the A.C. 'Blackshirt having a little bit of fun. Just as though we hadn't enough to do. At any rate,' he adds, 'it means that Verrell is in the clear ...'

It is obvious that as far as perspicacity is concerned, Inspector Johns is the twin of Ganimard of the Sûreté. Or maybe his reincarnation.

There is one thing, though, which the new Blackshirt does *not* have in common with Arsène Lupin. Lupin, to the best of my recollection, was never beaten in a fight. Verrell frequently is, particularly when there is a lady of the opposite sex on the scene.

... He received a blow on his left shoulder which numbed the whole of that side. He had made the mistake of thinking of the woman present as a lady. She defied that description with the way in which she used her high-heeled shoe.

'Sock him one,' she screamed. Further destroying any illusions.

The man did as he was told. He charged with arms open, ready to crush, or to cosh, the half-immobilised Verrell.

He hit the wall with a satisfactory crunch as his intended victim performed an extempore flying spring-hip throw.

The woman screamed something and aimed another savage blow with her shoe.

Verrell, unable to bring himself to treat her as he had treated the two men, stepped back and fell over his first assailant, who was regaining his feet....

'Talk about the weaker sex,' he muttered disgustedly, as he experimentally wrapped his legs around the waist of the second man and squeezed.

The man yelped. Then all went blank.

The woman used a cosh she found on the floor,

brought it down on his head with a precision no mere male could ever hope to emulate.

(*The Amazing Mr Blackshirt*, John Long Ltd)

Poor old Richard Verrell. He may have magicked a quarter of a century off his age. He may have lost his class hang-ups, his guilt consciousness, his solemn reveries. He may have acquired an ability to perform extempore flying spring-hip throws. But he cannot lose his original fatal weakness. There is no hero in all the annals of crime fiction for whom a *femme* is *quite* so apt to be *fatale*, whether she is at the other end of a shoe, a cosh or a telephone.

The fifties were, taken by and large, a very good time for the desperadoes. There was even an addition to their number. In 1954, Frederick Muller launched a new series of hardback thrillers, aimed at the circulating libraries, which were still flourishing all over Britain. (It wasn't television itself which knocked those libraries out of business: it was the coming of ITV in 1955.) With this thriller series, Muller's launched a brand-new desperado: John Cassells' Ludovic Saxon, alias the Picaroon. (Not to be confused with Herman Landon's hero of the same name, published by Cassell in the thirties.)

The Picaroon doesn't really break new ground in heroes. He is an odd blend of just about everybody, from Bulldog Drummond onwards. His dialogue tends to be the purest Sapper at times. ('Go to bed, you old war-horse, you,' he says to his trusty ex-pugilist servant, McNab. 'The Dearly Beloved have tried their damnedest. The Unholy have turned their big guns on us. And here we are, fit and fighting. That, by God, is an omen. Good night: sleep well.'[1]) At other times, he drawls nonchalant witticisms like the Saint on an off-day. ('Turkish on this

[1] *Enter the Picaroon*—now published by John Long Ltd.

244

side—Virginian on that. The three in the middle are poisoned. I keep them for the Income Tax inspector.') Nevertheless, it is most refreshing to find a new boy joining the class after all these years, and, what is more, going on to graduate. The Picaroon is still triumphantly around here in the seventies, so he is unmistakably the stuff of which durable desperadoes are made. Perhaps it's his laugh which has done it. He has a 'low, rippling laugh which holds in its cadencies all the music of wood and hill'. In this and many similar passages, Ludovic Saxon seems to be waving clean across the centuries back to Robin Hood. And if he really should turn out to be the last of the desperadoes, that is surely not an unfitting thing for him to do.

A lot of things happened to the desperadoes and their creators during the fifties, most of them good. On 22 January 1953, John Creasey celebrated his twenty-first anniversary as an author by appearing for the first time on the Hodder & Stoughton lists. The book chosen to celebrate the occasion was the twenty-seventh Richard Rollison novel, *Call the Toff*. From then onwards, most of John Creasey's multifarious series began to be gathered together under the Hodder & Stoughton umbrella, and it was with them, two years later, that he launched his Commander Gideon in *Gideon's Day*, using for his purpose one last *nom de plume*, J. J. Marric—J. for John, J. for Jean (then his wife), MAR for his son Martin, and RIC for his other son, Richard.

Over in America, Leslie Charteris spent most of the fifties running his monthly *Saint Mystery Magazine*, for which he wrote one new short story every other month or so. Probably the most famous of these nineteen-fifties Saint stories was 'The Pearls of Peace', in which the Saint commits his meanest burglary, from the highest motives of all. (A poor blind man suffers from two delusions: that his ugly wife is a beautiful woman, and that a string

245

of beads he fondles is a pearl necklace which will enable him to afford to have an operation to restore his eyesight. His eyes are, in fact, too far gone to be restored. So the Saint stoops to stealing a rope of beads from a blind man, so that the latter can keep his illusions and his happiness. There is almost a Steinbeck tenderness in this story, and it is also a little reminiscent of Chaplin. Like Steinbeck, like Chaplin, Charteris was always on the side of dreamers.)

Back in England, Edwy Searles Brooks had now, at last, finished using up old Waldo the Wonder Man plots, and, through the fifties, gave Norman Conquest a succession of adventures which may not have quite matched the old ones in pace, but lacked absolutely nothing in gusto. In *Conquest in Command*, 1956, a millionaire villain mistakes 1066 for an unprincipled thug, and asks him to kidnap his grandson. That was an error, as Conquest makes crystal clear, in terms which still suggest Nipper of St Frank's addressing the Bounder of the Remove:

> 'Get it straight into your thick head that I'm not in the market for a kidnapping job,' continued Conquest, with icicles clinging to every word. 'I only came here to take a good look at you, face to face. I've seen you and you're just about what I expected. Your hard, unscrupulous nature is written all over your ugly face. In your rise to the top you have trampled on thousands, ruining good and decent people. So watch out, slug!'

A merry Blackshirt doing an Arsène Lupin all over the rooftops of the Metropolis. The brand-new Picaroon fighting a traditional Drummondesque war on the Ungodly. An emotional Saint being chivalrous to the blind and poor of Lower California. An unchanged Conquest wiping the smiles of slugs clean off their hard, unscrupulous faces.... Clearly, there was plenty of variety on the nineteen fifties thriller scene. To complete it,

246

Gerard Fairlie, the friend of Sapper and original of Bull-dog Drummond, who had taken over the Drummond stories on Sapper's death in 1935, even brought back Drummond's Black Gang—and resurrected Carl Peterson too. (*The Return of the Black Gang,* Hodder & Stoughton, 1954.)

The public, relaxing in the sunshine of their sudden freedom from austerity, and reacting strongly against both the primness of their post-war mood and the weariness of their 'couldn't-care-less' one, had a welcome for thriller heroes of every generation and every style, just so long as they were fun.

In 1953, they even had a welcome for a certain 'blunt instrument' of Her Majesty's Secret Service, although not much of one at first. The earliest Ian Fleming book, *Casino Royale,* sold rather badly for months. But between 1955 and 1958, the 007 novels suddenly exploded into the best-seller lists with the force of a thunderball, leaving every reader aware that he was in the presence of a new cult, a new myth, a new thriller world.

This little Indian Summer of the desperadoes had melted into the heyday of James Bond. And the implications of *that* development are the most fascinating to theorise about of all.

CHAPTER NINETEEN

In which we meet an unexpected relative

NOWADAYS, there are probably only four crime-fiction heroes whose names are known even to people who have never read a thriller in their lives: Sherlock Holmes, Raffles, the Saint and James Bond. Bond's importance is such that it will be quite impossible to tell the rest of the story of the thirties desperadoes without referring to him, and so it seems sensible to make a short unscheduled stop in Fleming territory. This takes nerve, I might mention: nowhere else in the thriller world are critics and theorists so thick on the ground, and with every step one is in serious danger of trampling on somebody's most fiercely cherished convictions.

Let me begin, then, by stating a cherished conviction of my own, which is that this whole business of thriller studying has a lot in common with astrology. The first step to understanding the nature and impact of a thriller hero is to analyse the influences around at, so to speak, the precise hour of his birth.

In 1953, when *Casino Royale* first appeared, Britain was still grey and shabby. Even major thoroughfares like Oxford Street and High Holborn were still a mess of uncleared bomb sites. Sweets had been still on the ration up to February of that year, and a lot of goods in the shops—branded goods particularly—were in short supply. Hardly anybody had television at the start of the year, but many people were hoping to get a set before the Coronation in June. When the set arrived, it took you perforce into the genteel world of Macdonald Hobley, Mary

Malcolm, Joan Gilbert, Sylvia Peters & Co. You could say that the BBC was on the same wavelength as the Anna Neagle films and, like her, projected the quality that rapidly became known as 'Gracious Living'. To live graciously became the almost universal conscious or sub-conscious aim and, naturally enough, it became linked with knowing the right things to buy. Half the advertisements in the papers seemed to feature Lady Barnett recommending some costly TV set. The other half were usually boosting chlorophyll products, and rarely failed to state that personal freshness through using X was a vital part of gracious living.

Branded goods were exciting because they represented freedom of choice after fifteen years of rationing and short supplies: the gracious living idea was captivating because it represented rebellion not only against austerity, but against post-war priggishness: and the feeling that simply by making the right choice of goods one could join the élite, the cognoscenti, the top people, was as heady as alcohol on an empty stomach.

All through the middle fifties, it was trendy to be a neo-snob. The Coronation had brought thunderous reminders (mostly from Richard Dimbleby) about our noble heritage. Churchill and a largely Etonian cabinet were now in power. Upper middle-class people now seemed to be making most of the news, and (certainly in the case of Roger Bannister and Chris Chataway) most of the running. The films and the West End stage—this was the era of *My Fair Lady*, *Salad Days*, *The Boy Friend*, *Funny Face*, *The Reluctant Debutante*, *Relative Values*, *High Society*—spotlit elegance as brightly, if not as warmly, as the thirties dream machine had done. The thirties sense of mystery, though, was almost completely lacking. The black light of mid-twentieth-century doubt was still full on: it had merely been disguised for the moment by a charming rose-coloured filter.

Throw all these developments against the world background of the first American H-Bomb tests, 1952; the British H-Bomb, achieved on a shoestring by the appropriately named Sir William Penney, around 1954; the continual Cold War crisis and the endless Churchill-instigated hopes of Parleying at the Summit (top people sorting out the world's troubles again) and you have the causes of a mood that is really the antithesis both of the 1945–51 Socialist dreams *and* the 1930s glorification of the Little Man. You have, in fact, a return to the old John Buchan concept of an elegant élite of 'in-the-know' people being the secret saviours of the world.

The difference is that it is no longer seriously implied that you have to be born into a good family to join these 'in-the-know' people. You have to be, simply, in the know.

James Bond, who functioned for his fans both as a thriller hero and a walking handbook on good living, was as right for this particular time as surely as the Saint had been right for 1931–2. Like the Saint, though, he had to battle to win a public. The Saint's difficulty had been his iconoclastic impudence, his indignant philosophy; in Bond's case, it was something rather different. The enemies of Bond—his critical enemies, not S.M.E.R.S.H. —accused the books of being snobbish, sex-ridden and sadistic.

Snobbish they certainly weren't. Fleming never makes the suggestion, so frequently found in Sapper, Dornford Yates & Co., that gentlemen and commoners are poles apart. (He may take an occasional crack at the suburban bourgeoisie, but they were fair game even to Leslie Charteris.) What he does suggest is that there is a big gulf between the cognoscenti and the ignorant, but that hardly matters, since he gives the impression that he is trying hard to initiate his readers into the ranks of the former. Talk to the average Bond fan, even today, and you will be regaled not by accounts of 007's adventures, but by awed descriptions of his personal effects. Your brain will be awash in a sea of objects—Rolex watches, Church shoes, Dunhill lighters, specially made cigarettes from Burlington Arcade, hand-made shirts and all the rest of it. I have known people—trendy admen, for the most part—who have spent a small fortune acquiring all the articles mentioned by Fleming. (All the obtainable ones, that is.) Fleming himself was exasperated by such excesses of zeal on the part of his readers. As far as he was concerned, the inclusion of actual names of shops and branded goods was mainly a technical trick to heighten verisimilitude, and there can be no doubt that the suspension of disbelief *is* enormously helped when Harrod's is called Harrod's instead of Harridge's.

The sex element in Bond is actually a fairly logical extension of 1940s trends. Fleming's heroines are pretty close relatives of the Saint's wartime girl friends and Peter Cheyney's dames, with the difference that in these post-*Forever Amber* days, it is no longer remotely necessary to keep the hero's knee off that bed.

As for sadism, that is the wrong word for Fleming altogether. What he does go in for in a big way is masochism. There never was a thriller writer who so luxuriated in descriptions of a hero in pain—or, more often, of him recovering consciousness after an unspeakably painful interlude.

In Fleming, even the romance can become masochistic. For an allegedly ruthless purveyor of sex and violence, Fleming allows his hero to talk a surprising amount about love and marriage, but no author is more keen on hitting the reader right in the solar plexus with a suddenly exploded dream of love in the final pages. Fiction may have banished the broken heart, but a distinctly battered and bleeding one has taken its place. *La plus ça change* ...

It has been remarked by some critics, in tones of

251

shocked surprise, that the popular thriller elements in Bond are highly derivative. Popular thriller elements—as we have seen throughout this study—usually are. In the hands of a genuine mythmaker, though, the hoariest ingredients can seem startlingly new, as no one has demonstrated more effectively than Fleming.

Actually, his tricks seem new largely because his *purposes* are new. When, for example, Norman Conquest —in some respects, as I have already suggested, a remote Bond ancestor—gets himself tied up in a cellar, Brooks's purpose is to demonstrate how neatly 1066 can turn the tables on his enemies. But when Bond gets himself in a parallel situation, his author's aim is often the reverse: it is to inflict on the reader four or five pages of sweaty vicarious suffering, and if a handy blade were to emerge from 007's wristwatch strap to slice through his ropes, it would spoil things completely. Bond is far from being one of crime fiction's most successful Houdinis, but he is, unquestionably, its most spectacular survivor.

Comparing Bond directly with a thirties desperado brings us, inevitably, to the key question. Has the thriller public begun slowly, fundamentally, irreversibly, to change? Virtually all the heroes we have been discussing represented, to a greater or lesser degree, a dream of personal individuality writ large. The Saint, Conquest, the Toff, Blackshirt, the Mixer, the Rat, Raffles—they were all, in the last analysis, their own men, and the thirties desperadoes were outright private citizens' St Georges. Bond, of course, appears to be very much the opposite of all that. He is under orders from M throughout; he has earned his '00' rating through carrying out impersonal killings on Departmental instructions; he is so far from being his own man that he cannot even choose his own gun. Does his immense success mean that the public has now lost its power, or its willingness, to identify with private-citizen heroes altogether? Has the personal St

George been slain by the combined dragons of neo-snobbery and the age of technocratic man?

I feel myself that this can be answered with a pretty emphatic 'no'. The real point about Bond's success is surely this. Popular thriller writing may not be, like politics, the Art of the Possible, but it *is* the Art of the Just Conceivable. And it was just not conceivable that in the age of the H-Bomb a private citizen could continue to perform what had once been the thriller hero's most popular function: that of periodically rescuing the world from disaster at the hands of arch-fiends. It is significant that none of the desperadoes had attempted anything much in the apocalyptic line since before the war. To tackle that sort of job a man had manifestly to be in a position where all the nation's technological resources could be wheeled in behind him; in other words, he had to be—superficially, at any rate—an agent, a paid operative, of the State.

This is not a situation that will be with us forever. I rather doubt, as a matter of fact, if it is with us today. Here in the seventies, H-bomb politics are half-forgotten, and communications technology is shrinking the world to the size of McLuhan's 'global village'. In a 'global village', the individual can operate on a global scale: real-life desperadoes, admittedly of a sickening kind, make world headlines just by hi-jacking jets. It could be argued that, although no one has noticed it as yet, the ball is bouncing back into the lone hero's court, and that the next great myth thrown up by crime fiction may not be a spy or a Yard man, but a private detective, or even a new-style desperado.

All such possibilities, though, are dependent on the supposition that the thriller public has never really changed its nature, never really mutated into something weird and new. We are back, then, to the question: was 007 an unprecedented monster, a robot of *realpolitik*, or was he basically a traditional, autonomous British thriller-hero, appearing, for reasons of credibility, in disguise?

If the latter, the disguise was certainly an exceptionally heavy one. There can be no doubting that it was Fleming's original intention to make Bond much more than superficially a paid operative. For much of *Casino Royale*, for example, the author seems to be gleefully rubbing his readers' noses in the fact that Bond is fundamentally an order-taker, a servant of the State.

But when it comes to the crunch—one of Fleming's juiciest 'romantic-masochistic' crunches, incidentally: the girl Bond loves has turned out to be a Communist agent, and has committed suicide through remorse—a very different James emerges.

> His fingernails dug into the palms of his hands and his body sweated with shame.
> Well, it was not too late. Here was a target for him, right to hand. He would take on SMERSH and hunt it down ...
> The business of espionage could be left to the white-collar boys. They could spy and catch the spies. He would go after the threat behind the spies, the threat that made them spy.
>
> (*Casino Royale*, Jonathan Cape)

Oh, yes? And what is M going to say about that?

It is quite obvious that suddenly, at this moment, M doesn't count. In those paragraphs, the whole secret service structure is swept into blurry, white-collared oblivion by its own blunt instrument. Bond, the romantic hero, stands alone against the menace that challenges the whole world of spies, and specifically excludes himself from the 'spy' category in the process.

But if he isn't a spy, and is capable of making major policy decisions without the slightest thought of M, and of

254

contemplating a lone-wolf battle against a fiendish organisation come what may, then what is he?

Quite obviously, not a *very* distant relative of the durable desperadoes.

CHAPTER TWENTY

In which two Desperadoes fall by the wayside, but three stroll nonchalantly on

THE *Zeitgeist*, having zigged sharply to the right during the Churchill–Chataway–Dimbleby days, proceeded, after Suez, to zag very spectacularly left: the period that cradled Bond was the very time on which, in 1956, Jimmy Porter so vociferously Looked Back in Anger.

The Gracious Living dream itself, though, did not by any means gurgle away down the kitchen sink. During the late fifties and early sixties, the most successful books, films and television series were usually the ones which conveyed an atmosphere of high living without seeming to condone the high life. Sometimes they did this by showing a working-class hero sourly conniving his way into affluent surroundings (*Room at the Top*); sometimes by retaining the class element, but totally sending it up (*The Avengers*); sometimes by off-setting the background elegance with a tough (the in-word was 'abrasive') businessman hero, firing junior executives between mouthfuls of lobster thermidor (*The Power Game*).

Now this game of presenting high-class elegance without snob connotations was distinctly old top hat to the desperadoes, who had been playing it non-stop since *c.* 1931, and had pioneered most of the tricks in the book. It isn't at all surprising that when the James Bond films began to appear, very early in the sixties, the character was modified for the screen by being brought significantly closer to the classical desperado. Sean Connery's Bond had a habit of lounging around, drawling nonchalant witticisms, which derived as much from Charteris & Co. as it did from Fleming. The Bond of the books was good at repartee when indulging in amorous dalliance with every kind of female from Miss Moneypenny up, but a very poor hand at answering back either at arch-fiends or at M. (In his scenes with the former, his role was either to suffer or to slaughter, which he normally did more or less silently.) The screen Bond didn't do much answering back, as such, either. He developed instead a brand of repartee that is best described as *esprit d'escalier*. He did not speak while fighting, but habitually delivered an appropriate epitaph over the victim's mangled corpse before leaving the room. (In one film, for example, before closing the door upon an assassin whom he had cooked to a crisp by plunging him into a bath in company with an electric fire, he drawls: 'Shocking. Simply shocking.')

It is interesting to compare this technique with the combat drollery (perhaps one should say drawlery) of the vintage Saint. His approach was always typified for me by the cover of the Hodder & Stoughton Yellow Jacket edition of *Getaway*, published in the early-to-middle thirties, which showed him hurling a hoodlum into a river and murmuring 'Saturday night is bath night, brother' while his victim was still elegantly in mid-flight. It is quite impossible to imagine the Saint saying that over a drowned corpse, but the lazy mockery is precisely the same as the Connery Bond's.

The Saint, of course, was very much present in person on the nineteen sixties scene. The immense success of Bond in the cinema coincided with a spectacularly long-running Saint series on television, starring Roger Moore. Moore may not have been everyone's idea of the Saint (I doubt if any actor could be), but he caught the rather difficult note of mischievous authority brilliantly. My only regret about the series was that Charteris's piratical iconoclasm was too rarely allowed to come through, even

257

in episodes based on Mark I Saint adventures. I may have missed the episodes concerned, but I somehow doubt if the TV Saint ever drawled things like 'Have some sense, old garbage man. You can't possibly murder me now. This episode still has forty minutes to run, or, allowing for the commercials, thirty-six.' It's curious, really. Thrillers with a send-up element were almost a hallmark of the nineteen sixties, and most people assumed that nothing like them had ever been done before. Yet hardly any writer, in any series, went anything like as far as Charteris himself in his Haydon heyday. Try to imagine Steed pausing in the act of shooting a scorpion to reel off some withering doggerel against Lord Thomson, or the Connery Bond writing a book with a coloured hero, and verbally slaughtering racialist readers over breakfast with Pussy Galore. That will give you some idea of how urbanely devastating the send-up thrillers of the sixties could have been if they had taken a leaf from just one 1930s Saint novel. (*The Holy Terror*, 1933.)

As it was, television produced an unreckless, but by no means wholly unrecognisable, Simon Templar; and much the same product (let's call him the Mark VI, or Assembly-line Saint) began to appear in the bookshops. Between 1967 and 1970, a string of Saint books came out—*The Saint on TV*, *The Saint Returns*, *The Saint and the Fiction Makers*, *The Saint and the People Importers*, *The Saint Abroad*—which had, to put it mildly, a somewhat mixed literary parentage. The first part of *The Saint on TV*, *The Death Game*, was typical. It originated from a story by John Kruse. Then it had been turned into a teleplay by Harry W. Junkin. Finally it had been subjected to a process described as 'novelisation' by Fleming Lee, under the editorial supervision of one Leslie Charteris. After all that, one expects to see 'Cigarettes by Abdullah' or even 'Haloes by Hartnell'.

More depressing still, these hotchpotch stories (and,

for that matter, reprints of earlier Saint novels) were prefaced, in paperback editions at any rate, with a secret-
service-file type description of the Saint, from which every
vestige of humour and humanity had been clinically
removed. You might have been reading about the latest
Gerry Andersen puppet hero instead of the most significant rascal of our time.

Age, 31. Height 6, ft 2 ins.
Weight: 175 lbs. Eyes: blue. Hair: black, brushed
straight back.
Complexion: tanned.
Special characteristics: Immaculately dressed,
always.
Luxurious tastes. Carries firearms.
Expert knife-thrower. Licensed pilot.
Speaks several languages fluently.

The 'Age, 31' bit is interesting. It means that the Great
Time Robbery has now reached astronomical propor-
tions. The last time I saw the above, it was on the cover
of *The Saint and the People Importers*, 1970, by which
year the Saint was actually seventy-one, if he was a day.
So he—or some front office blurb-computer—has filched
no less than forty years off the arch-fiend with the scythe.
Some of the best things about the assembly-line Saint
books were the forewords, in which the Charteris candour rises to almost majestic heights. The foreword to
The Saint on TV, for example, begins:

When, after many years of noble and lofty-minded
resistance, I finally broke down and sold the Saint to
the Philistines of television, I fear that I must have
added one more argument to the armoury of the cynics
who maintain that every man has his price; because
I certainly got mine.

259

Charteris goes on to defend his 'visible ghost writers' policy by citing the Barry Perowne Raffles and the Kingsley Amis Bond. (Amis had just announced that he was continuing 007's adventures, though *Colonel Sun* had not then appeared in print.) As soon as the creator of a popular hero is dead, Charteris argues, *ersatz* adventures are bound to appear by arrangement with the author's executors. By allowing this to happen in the case of his own hero while he is still alive, he is at least able to ensure that the resultant Saint is not altogether un-Saintly. The logic of this is irrefutable; it was clearly only reasonable that the best original episodes from the long TV series should wind up in hard covers; and it must be admitted that Fleming Lee, who undertook the donkey work of 'novelisation' throughout, did a rather thankless job as well as it could be done. But, for all that, the books are no fun for an aficianado of the Saint to read. Half of the time, you are trying to spot which bits are by Charteris. The other half, you're being irritated by bits that quite patently *aren't*.

I confess that, when I first planned this study, I intended to end this section with an exasperated and highly emotive sentence to the effect that, in the midst of the complex, glittering machinery of success, the real Saint had quietly vanished, without even pausing to give us a nonchalant wave of the hand.

I was making the cardinal mistake of underestimating the durability of a desperado.

The nineteen sixties are now themselves a part of the past, and in some ways, seem as remote as the nineteen thirties. The Saint has long disappeared from television screens (except in late-night repeat slots), and Roger Moore is currently under contract to be the new cinema Bond—further proof, incidentally, of how close the screen James has come in the public mind to the classic desperado.

And here, in this latter day of latter days, the indomitable Templar has suddenly popped up once again, reunited with his creator in *The Saint in Pursuit*, 1971.

The first thing Charteris does, on resuming full control, is to halt the Great Time Robbery, and hand back half the loot. The Saint is rung up by Hamilton of Washington, and discusses cases he investigated during World War II, which means that he must be verging on fifty, even in the terms of this particular story. ('Some milestones,' Charteris wryly, if belatedly, confesses, 'cannot be hidden from any student with a mastery of elementary arithmetic.') Nevertheless, the Saint remains singularly sprightly for his age, as one Curt Jaegar discovers when he tries to creep up behind him and propel him out of a wide-open window on the seventh floor of a luxury hotel. The Saint ducks, swerves and in the ensuing fight retaliates in the high old style to which his admirers have been long, long, long accustomed.

> The Saint baulked, braced himself, and freed a hand. He cocked back his fist and unleashed a short jab at Jaegar's nose. Jaegar staggered, letting go his grip on Simon, and launched a vicious kick.
>
> The Saint caught the flying foot in mid-air.
>
> 'Sorry to behave badly for a host,' he said, 'but I'll have to ask you to leave.'
>
> With both hands on Jaegar's ankle he whipped him round in a perfectly-timed swing that sent the other man not against the wall this time, but straight at the open window ...
>
> And suddenly there was only one man left in the room.
>
> (*The Saint in Pursuit*, Hodder & Stoughton)

As fine an example of Templar drawlery as you'll find anywhere in the Charteris cannon. And there's a point there which Roger Moore might like to note, now that he's switching heroes.

261

For all his fussing about whether a Martini should be shaken or stirred, Bond never did have such faultless *manners* as the Saint.

The Saint, then, at this moment of writing, is emphatically alive and well. But there has been a considerable thinning of the ranks of the desperadoes since 1965. Norman Conquest, who, as Waldo the Wonder Man, was the first of the durables to arrive, was also the first to go.

In December 1965, Edwy Searles Brooks died, very suddenly, at the age of 76. A last novel was already in the hands of his publishers called, half-prophetically, *Curtains for Conquest?* In the published book, which came out in 1966, the title has a question mark after it on the jacket and the title pages only. Through some odd oversight, on the cloth cover and at the top of each page of the story it appears, simply, as *Curtains for Conquest*, an omen direct and undisguised.

The story (Conquest beating a Communist villain called Zagora with the help of baby limpet bombs made 'in his own laboratory at Conquest Court') is not one of Brooks's best, and it must be admitted that the author's style is not exactly redolent of the nineteen sixties. You have to hurry rather fast past moments like this:

'It doesn't make sense,' said Williams, breathing hard. 'The entire security service couldn't find a trace of Loring—and yet Conquest does the trick off his own bat! What is he—a magician?'

'No,' said Joy softly. 'Just a he-man.'

(Curtains for Conquest? Collins)

It is very easy to make fun of Edwy Searles Brooks at times, not so easy to sum up the extraordinary phenomenon that he was. He was probably the second most prolific writer of our time, and he left behind him admirers in four separate categories. There is the enthusiastic cult which is busy collecting the 16,000,000 words of St Frank's stories he wrote in *The Nelson Lee Library*. There are the Sexton Blake fans who remember him for Waldo, the prototype Fleetway hell-for-leather desperado. There have been enough 1066 devotees to have kept Conquest novels (forty-nine titles in all) persistently on the shelves of public libraries for close on thirty-five years: I noticed a brand-new edition of *Leave It To Conquest* in my branch only yesterday. And there are the followers of another ex-*Thriller* character, Ironsides of the Yard, about whom Brooks wrote some forty-three further novels under the *nom de plume* Victor Gunn. (Not to be confused with the Raymond Burr TV Ironside series.)

For myself, I shall always remember Brooks best for the gale-force gusto of the initial Conquest adventures, which exploded on me in late childhood and gave me the idea—which I have never subsequently succeeded in getting out of my head—that first, last and foremost, a thriller should be fun.

Another desperado to drop out during the 1960s was Richard Verrell. In 1969, Roderic Graeme published his twentieth Blackshirt novel, *Blackshirt Stirs Things Up*. It sold well in Britain, but not too well overseas. Graeme decided regretfully that Verrell was unsuitable (perhaps too chivalrous?) for these rough, permissive times, and had reached the end of his long career. It is not necessarily, I gather, a final decision. If it were, it would mean that the title of most durable desperado is about to pass from Blackshirt (1923–69) to the Saint (1928–73), unless one counts Waldo-Conquest as one continuing character, in which case his is the longest run of all (1918–66).

Mention of Waldo and Conquest naturally raises the

question: what in the world had Monty Haydon been doing all these years since the closing of *The Thriller*?

W. Howard Baker, editor of the Sexton Blake Library during the later fifties and early sixties, has supplied me with some fascinating answers. Haydon, first as Controlling Editor and then as a Fleetway director, was behind the scenes all through Baker's spectacular endeavours to modernise Sexton Blake.

One day in 1957—a day which brought the biggest surprise to thriller fans since Conan Doyle announced the death of Sherlock Holmes—Blake became head of an entirely new organisation, Sexton Blake Investigations, ensconced in J. Walter Thompson-like offices in Berkeley Square. Instead of encountering the formidable Mrs Bardell, clients found themselves being welcomed by 'young, pretty, dark-haired, lively' Miss Marian Lang. Or, perhaps, if Marian was at lunch, they would be greeted by 'bespectacled but curvaceous' Louise Pringle, the office manager who worked next door to Blake's Chief Assistant (known as Tinker only to his very oldest friends).

And this wasn't the end of the surprises which Baker and Haydon had in store for readers of the new Sexton Blake Library. Next to Mr Carter's room was the office of 'a slim, beautiful young woman with deep, dazzling blue eyes' who 'hid beneath her ultra-femininity a capacity for rapid lethal action'—Sexton Blake's secretary, Paula Dane. In the main office, seated slightly south-south-west of a trendy creeping ivy plant, was Sexton Blake himself, minus his briar pipe, his dressing-gown and at least some of the inhibitions that had once made his name 'a synonym for austerity'.

Despite his glamorous entourage, the new Blake steadily lost ground against the heroes of the sex-and-blood paperbacks now flooding on to the bookstalls. Haydon retired in the early 1960s and the Sexton Blake Library folded

264

shortly afterwards, in 1963. It could have continued, but the Amalgamated Press had been taken over by the *Daily Mirror* group, and there was a new policy up top. Whereas the Amalgamated Press had always believed in running a large number of moderately profitable journals, the *Mirror* policy favoured weeding out all but the large money-spinners. Not since the thirties had Sexton Blake come into that category, and so he had to go.

Abortive as it proved, the modernisation attempt remains fascinating to the student of thrillers. It demonstrates that Monty Haydon was as ready to back *bravura* innovation in 1957 as he had been in 1932. Well, *almost* as ready. On one thing Haydon was very insistent: whatever happened, Blake had to remain recognisably Blake. He would have no truck with a Sexton Bond. If a story was shown him in which Blake was a little too aggressive or permissive to be in character, then he would politely suggest that the book be de-Blakenised, and submitted elsewhere. (Howard Baker's own well-known hero, Richard Quaintain, was originally a Haydon-reject Blake.)

As long as Blake behaved and expressed himself reasonably traditionally, though, almost anything was okay with Monty. On one occasion, he permitted Blake to have an old flame, and to recount the passionate episode in the first person. Sexton Blake's personal prose-style turned out to be almost reminiscent of Ruskin:

> 'There is a sadness which grows from the seeds of remembered happiness; there is a weariness which springs unrequited from the remembered fountains of youth; there is a nostalgia conjured from faraway places and moments which have long since ticked into the infinite fog ...'
> (*Come Dark, Come Evil* by Wilfred McNeilly. Sexton Blake Library No. 496, *c.* 1963)

Good old Sexton Blake. In this, his 80th anniversary

year, I am delighted to record that new adventures are still appearing, not only intermittently on TV, but in the Howard Baker Press's hardback Sexton Blake series. Quite definitely, the infinite fog hasn't got him yet.

From this sombre saga of downfalls and struggles for survival, it is a relief to turn to the triumphant advances of John Creasey.

By 1971, Creasey had sold a grand total of 80,000,000 books in 5,000 different editions in 28 languages, a high proportion of them on paperback counters. I have heard it said that every paperback with John Creasey's name on it is today a safe bet for a six-figure sale. This may be an exaggeration, but the proliferation of Creasey books, which still continues (taking hardbacks and paperbacks, new stories and reissues together, more than four hundred of his novels should be in print before the middle seventies) testifies to the fact that they don't exactly make a loss.[1]

There were two Creasey TV series during the nineteen sixties, one featuring Gideon, and the other the Baron. The less said about John Mannering's TV debut, the better. He was turned into a Texas cattle baron, and Lorna was replaced by an insipid girl assistant to enable him to have a different romance every week. In no Creasey TV series that I have seen has an attempt been made to isolate and capture the rather special Creasey atmosphere. It is a hard atmosphere to define, but let's have a go. Creasey has created more fictional worlds than any other crime writer, but one element is common to nearly all of them: a friendly, basically gentle hero anxiously sweating it out in a world where violence is fundamentally a mistake, a misunderstanding; where, for that matter, even anger is fundamentally a mistake and

[1] Creasey's world sales currently amount to some three and a half million books every year.

266

a misunderstanding. Creasey's heroes (and they have been this way since Palfrey, perhaps even since Craigie) are not merely troubled by crime and violence; they are under strain the moment they feel they are not getting along with their wives, friends or colleagues as well as they might. It is very curious that Creasey's greatest success should have coincided with an age of 'abrasive' thriller heroes. It suggests that there was a softer under-side to the sixties mood all the time—a wistful longing for a little more goodwill. (Wasn't it, after all, also the age of the Beatles, the Flower Children, and 'All You Need Is Love'?)

Creasey's personal philosophy is fully described in his book, *Good, God and Man* (Hodder & Stoughton, 1967). His central thesis, as I understand it, is that Jesus's com-mandment 'Love thy neighbour as thyself' has been dis-torted by the churches into 'Love thy neighbour but hate thyself', which is an impossibility. Self-love is natural to man, Creasey maintains, and nothing to be ashamed of. Indeed, it is a source of limitless power if only it is accompanied by a sense of human interdependence: a realisation that it is in one's own self-interest to harmonise with others.

It was his passionate hatred of disharmony that led Creasey to stand in by-election after by-election as an Independent candidate, pleading for an all-party alliance. He is leader today of a small, but highly organised and fast-growing movement called 'Evolution to Democracy' which argues, cogently, that Tweedledum and Tweedle-dee politics (and the parallel man-v.-management rows in industry) are a phoney farce, and an expensive one: they have cost Britain the respect of the world. And the same thinking is undoubtedly behind some startling de-velopments which have very recently occurred in the worlds of the Baron and the Toff.

For thirty-three years and forty-two books, the Baron's

arch-enemy had been Superintendent Bristow of Scotland Yard, arguably the real forerunner of Grice, West and Gideon. 'Arch-enemy' isn't quite the word: they had had a secret respect for each other ever since Mannering had saved Bristow's life at the end of *Meet the Baron*. Nevertheless, the feud between them had often been fierce.

Now, in *The Baron Goes A-Buying* (Hodder & Stoughton, 1971) all this is dramatically ended. Bristow retires from the Yard, and actually goes to work for Mannering in his Mayfair antique shop, Quinn's. It is an unprecedented event in desperado history—almost as astonishing as if Claud Eustace Teal had applied for a job as successor to Hoppy Uniatz. Bristow himself is fully conscious of its incongruity. Here he is nervously arriving at work on his first morning:

> Bristow turned into Hart Row slowly, at one minute after half-past nine. He felt as if all eyes were turned towards him, whereas probably no one recognised him. The sun was shining down the whole length of the passage, gilding the cobbles, and he was struck by the beauty of the buildings; the clean Georgian doorways on the one side, the old—age-old—buildings on the other ...
>
> Was this real? Or was it a long-drawn-out dream; an unreality caused by so much thinking, so much obsession, with this shop. Good God! He must have visited it a dozen times hoping to arrest, or at least hoping to charge, John Mannering. And here he was going to work here! ...
>
> Then he saw the Mogul sword, and stopped abruptly, staring as if it mesmerised him. Not many years ago, he had actually suspected Mannering of stealing the sword.
>
> He laughed, tension broken, and stretched out his hand for the brass doorknob of Quinn's.

The long war between the desperadoes and the police

isn't quite over, though. However keen one is on harmony, I doubt if it is possible to sustain a good Robin Hood series without a Sheriff of Nottingham in sight, still less with one deputising for Little John. Before long, Mannering is framed by a villain called the Black Knight, and is facing a murder charge. A nationwide manhunt is on for him, organised by a new inspector called Cooper, a distinctly awkward character who remains intractable despite all Bristow can do. Eventually, Mannering wins Cooper's respect by saving his life, just as he had once saved Bristow's—and the cycle seems to be beginning all over again. If the Baron keeps on like this, he'll finish up with a queue of ex-Yard men stretching out their hands for the brass doorknob of Quinn's.

Which brings us, finally, to the Hon. Richard Rollison, and to another completely unprecedented event in desperado history. In *Vote for the Toff* (Hodder & Stoughton, 1970) Rollison decides—or, rather, being Rollison, allows himself to be persuaded—that British politics needs some new blood. He consequently agrees to stand at a by-election as an Independent candidate.

The Conservative Party wants him, but the Toff will have none of that. 'I would be swamped by the party,' he states emphatically. 'I would be used as a glorious example of the upper classes' right to rule. Most of my relations would cheer themselves hoarse, nearly every friend would see me as the great betrayer.' He takes a leather-bound book from a shelf and shows his American girl friend Challis (who later, incidentally, starts living with him at his flat—a major concession to the Permissive Society) 'page after page of photographs.'

'There's Bill Ebbutt, East End born and raised, as brave and honest, as *good* a man as I know, and a doctrinaire Socialist all his life ... and Dicky Martin, Labour Councillor at Wapping for thirty-two years ...
269

They would wonder what had hit them ... That's what's wrong with this country, Challis, there are two sides and each has been taught to hate the other until they simply can't work together ... *Do you know what*?' Rollison actually shook Challis. 'I'd have been killed a dozen times if it hadn't been for Bill Ebbutt. And he would have had his skull cracked open and his throat cut as often if it weren't for me—or for the police or some of his own friends. When in heaven's name are we going to live together? When are we going to create a system that gets the best out of all, instead of the worst out of most?'

The degree of Creasey's personal involvement makes this an unusually intense Toff book. Before long, Jolly is weighing in with an in-depth analysis of the Toff himself.

'When you first went to the East End, sir, I always thought it was a kind of game—that you went out of your social background, your natural background, indeed, for the excitement and risks of the other. I—ah—was not particularly enthusiastic, sir. I believed ... that it would be short-lived, a matter of weeks or at the most months ...' He looked very directly at Rollison. 'But I soon realised that you were just as happy with Mr Ebbutt as you were with people of your own kind; that you liked people as people, not as representatives of a group or class ... And I was then, and I always have been, enormously impressed by the way you have worked with and befriended people from every possible background. You haven't simply thought it right, sir, you've *proved* it *to be* right ...'

This may seem an odd note on which to close the long history of the desperadoes. And yet somehow it's not an inappropriate one. To a large extent, the thirties desperadoes *were* born out of the class struggle—or, rather, out of the ordinary citizen's desire to rise vicariously

270

above it. And, if one reason has to be singled out to account for their durability, it should surely be the fact that they never really identified themselves with ruled or ruler, slave or system. Whether the *Zeitgeist* zig-zagged right or left, they adapted easily, and it disturbed them hardly at all: they were for the men and women in the middle, the people who saw themselves as *persons* and not class symbols. Which is why, although the desperadoes so effortlessly robbed Time, Time was never able to rob *them* of the smallest part of their fundamental essence. That speech of the Toff's was made in the seventies, but it could equally have been made in the sixties, or the fifties, or the forties, or the thirties. Indeed, it belongs to the thirties most of all, because its sentiments directly echo this century's most fragile and seemingly longest-forgotten dream: the dream of ordinary citizens revealing themselves as more than ordinary, and as *individuals*, putting the world to rights.

All these years on from his 1939 heyday, the durable desperado is still, at heart, what he always was. A Super Little Man.

CHAPTER TWENTY-ONE

In which the Toff shows off a topper, and the Saint goes to his destiny

THERE are, I suspect, plenty of other reasons for the durability of the desperadoes, but they go rather deeper, and even suggesting them will bring me into headlong collision with contemporary criticism. Not that any desperado fan should allow himself to be daunted by a little thing like that.

Although every desperado has, during his long career, received now and then some by no means unflattering notices, particularly in the provincial press, it must be acknowledged that the majority of critics have tended to dismiss the whole Gentleman Outlaw *genre* as childish rubbish, unworthy of serious attention.

The critical argument against the desperadoes (insofar as any critic has bothered to argue the matter at all) runs something like this. The only worthwhile function of literature, it is maintained, is to bring the reader into the closest possible contact with real life, real people, real situations. The sole touchstone by which a work of fiction should be judged *is* its closeness to reality, and by this test, the triumphantly, piratically larger-than-life desperado is disqualified from the start.

The contemporary critic has a favourite term for fiction of the desperado type. He calls it 'escapist', and the word is almost always used pejoratively. (Except by Kingsley Amis, who maintains that all literature is escapist, anyway.) The suggestion is that the reader of sensational thrillers is in fact addicted to a drug. He is taking refuge

272

in romantic daydreams, and will find the real world a darker, drabber, harder-to-cope-with place on his return.

Now most desperado fans are secretly half-persuaded by these arguments, and their defence is rather like that of a naughty schoolchild. ('I shall read what I want to, so there.') It rarely occurs to any of them that the whole attack is as specious, as question-begging, as the classic query about when one is going to stop beating one's wife.

What evidence is there that the *only* function of literature is to present real-life situations? Isn't *Alice in Wonderland* a work of literature? Isn't *A Christmas Carol, The Tempest, A Midsummer Night's Dream*? Hasn't the stage of literature down the centuries been crowded with Falstaffs and Quixotes and Micawbers, or, more to the point, d'Artagnans and Rassendylls and Cyranos, all of whom succeeded precisely *because* they were outrageously, gloriously larger than life? Coming directly to crime fiction criticism, what sort of logic is it which grants that Holmes and Father Brown & Co. were valid creations a short half-century ago, but denies validity to any character who is similarly beyond conventional credibility today?

In any case, what *is* this strange, puritanical obsession with fictional realism that has come upon us all? Go, go, go, said T. S. Eliot's bird: human kind cannot bear very much reality. Why should it suddenly be regarded as so desirable to force one's readers to rub their noses in it all the time?

There is a rather more important question than this. *Is* it, in fact, desirable?

Some years ago, an interesting experiment with sleeping subjects was conducted in the United States to determine the importance of dreams. I can describe what happened only from memories of newspaper accounts, so I can't guarantee the complete accuracy of details. But the main facts, as I gathered them, were these. It is now possible to detect when a sleeping subject is dreaming because, in at any rate the most vivid dreams, the eyeballs beneath the closed eyelids of the sleeper move from side to side, as though he were actually seeing his fantasies. The subjects in this experiment were asked to go to sleep, with an electronic detector device attached to their eyelids. Over several nights, 50% of these subjects—let's call them subjects A—were wakened whenever this vivid dreaming began, but were otherwise allowed to sleep in peace. The others—Subjects B—were given the opposite treatment: they were allowed to stay asleep during the comparatively short periods when the device showed they were dreaming.

It was found that Subjects B—the ones whose sleep had been decimated, but who had had their full share of dreams—were able to cope quite successfully with events when they woke; but Subjects A—the ones who had been allowed a full night's sleep, but no recordable dreaming[1] —very rapidly began to suffer from hallucinations and mental confusion.

I do not know what the experimenters themselves made of this, but to me it suggests the following rather shattering possibility. It isn't from sleep, it is *from our dreams* that we awake refreshed. In other words, it is only through our nightly encounters with the myths and mysteries of the theatre of the subconscious, half-forgotten by the morning though they seem to be, that our minds retain their rational balance, their power to face up to reality at all. If that is the case, it throws a new light on the whole operation of the human psyche, and one could go on to argue that perhaps all of us, whether waking or

[1] It is now considered doubtful if there is any such thing as totally dreamless sleep. In that case, what Subjects A had actually been deprived of was their most important dream experiences— the ones with the highest emotive, or most significantly mythical, content.

sleeping, depend far more on our myths for sustenance than is generally supposed.

There was a fascinating documentary on the Navajo Indians on television recently. When a Navajo is suffering from a severe depression—usually after living away from the reservation in a big American city—psychoanalysis is of very little use. Psychiatrists have found that the only way to treat him is to hand him over to his own medicine men, who effect a cure through a nine-day ceremony, in which the patient joins with the whole community in re-enacting a traditional hero-myth.

It may be a far cry from that distraught Navajo Indian to an English thriller-fan, cheering himself up on the bus with a Saint story before going to a painful interview with his bank manager, but the basic principle of both operations is surely the same. Neither the Indian nor the thriller-fan is in flight from reality. On the contrary, each is busily reviving his psyche, re-charging his batteries through contact with the hero-myths of his race, and both will subsequently be able to cope with reality *more easily* as a result.

The critics, of course, would deny this, at any rate in the thriller-fan's case. Their claim is that he would get off the bus a blurry-minded fantasist, whereas I see him strolling into the bank with such a Saintly swagger that he is granted an overdraft on sight. I am romanticising, of course. But if he feels in the slightest degree more confident, if he manages to give his side of the interview a fraction more lightness and style, then surely my point is made: the point that a myth is the complete opposite of a psychological escape-hatch. Valid myths endure for decade after decade, generation after generation, precisely because of the power they have, especially during troubled times, to *facilitate* the facing of reality.

I am not suggesting, of course, that everyone who reads a desperado book necessarily goes around trying to emulate a desperado. It would be a distinctly livelier world if he did. But anyone who has ever fallen deeply under the spell of the desperadoes, especially in childhood, carries at the back of his mind a vague ideal of piratical nonchalance. He is forever suspicious of pomposity, subservience and solemnity, and quite powerfully fortified against despair. Even on his darkest days, he can never entirely silence a mischievous voice drawling that life is a mysterious adventure; that, for all we know, there may be a chuckle instead of a tear at the heart of things; that there's always a way out of the cellar, even if the water's rising past one's neck. Illogical though such feelings may be on some occasions, they are undeniably handy things to have in an age of facile pessimism.

Not that pessimism may remain a major characteristic of the age much longer. I have tended to write about the thirties as though its moods were so remote from us as to be beyond recall. But, in one respect at least, the nineteen seventies are getting closer to the thirties all the time. The essentially mysterious nature of reality is being rediscovered at such a rate that by the end of this decade, perhaps even by half-way through it, a quasi-metaphysical outlook such as the thirties had will once again be the norm. The universe which science is now revealing—pockmarked by black holes in which a second stretches to eternity, riding above a superspace in which even Einstein's laws are void, and containing (according to one major authority) unmistakable hints that man may after all have a special place in a Grand Design —makes it impossible for life to be seen as anything *but* a mysterious adventure.

It is a universe which will boggle the minds of us all— but I suspect that it will dismay only people who have been weakened by acute myth starvation.

Myth starvation.

From that, no *aficianado* of the durable desperadoes can fairly claim to have suffered. The sheer scale of the writing achievement represented by the chronicling of their adventures is staggering. To date there have been fifty-four Toff novels, forty-four Barons, forty-nine Conquests, forty-four Saints (including the five that were merely supervised by Charteris) and at least thirty-two Blackshirts—some twelve by Bruce and twenty by Roderic Graeme. I make that two hundred and twenty-three books about these five heroes alone.

From this vast bank of storytelling, I propose to rifle just a handful of trinkets more—a short farewell extract from each of the series, selected to sum up, as far as possible, the essence of author and desperado, mythmaker and myth.

In the case of the Blackshirt stories, two extracts are called for, since we have two mythmakers at work on one myth.

It is fascinating to see how close Roderic Graeme's Verrell comes to his father's at times. Here is the original Blackshirt making a typically stylish escape from guards and bloodhounds in the vicinity of a village fête, back in the middle twenties:

> He lifted his voice so that the echo of it travelled through the trees to where the guards were keyed up expectantly.
> 'Tally-ho! Tally-ho! Catch me—if you can!' he called ...
> He came within vision of the limelights. The guards saw him. With a bellow of anger, they braced themselves ...
> He was nearly to them, a yard more and he would be in their grasp; but the next moment, to the amazement of the pack which followed and the guards who waited, Blackshirt rose into the air, clinging to the end of an eight-foot pole.

High into the air he vaulted, over the heads of the men, over the tall wire fence, and then he landed safely just on the fringe of the light.

With a wave of the hand he started off, and the next moment there was no sign of him, for he was lost in the dark. As the mocking echo of Blackshirt's laughter floated back to the guests of the fête, there was a hilarious roar of amusement from the younger members as they realised that Blackshirt had won again.

(The Return of Blackshirt, 1927)

And now here, some thirty years later, is Roderic Graeme's Blackshirt making a not dissimilar exit:

They rushed to the third floor—the top floor ... Ahead of them, a door opened. They dashed into the room.

On the window ledge a man was standing. He turned.

'Adieu, Superintendent.' His light tone of voice gave no hint of the tension within him.

The other charged forward.

Blackshirt suddenly disappeared. Threw himself out of the window.

'What ... ?'

They ran to the window, looked out. It was incredible.

Blackshirt was plummeting towards the ground in a long arc. The guards at the gate stared fascinated. Then the arc swept upwards.

Bishop realised what was happening. Gave a cry of despair. He was helpless.

Blackshirt was at the end of a long pendulum of rope. One end was made fast to the high branch of an immense coniferous tree standing forty yards away from the house. He was at the free end. It carried him up and over the fence. He let go, landed, rolled over, stood up.

He turned towards the house and waved. Then vanished.
(*The Amazing Mr Blackshlrt*, c. 1957, John Long)

Stylish 'Adieu, Superintendents' and carefree acrobatics were seldom in the Baron's line—not in later years, at any rate. Being a Creasey hero, he was rarely free from anxiety about the other characters in the case. Here he is, in a cottage surrounded by police who are advancing from all sides. He stumbles up into the attic:

There was a window, small but big enough for him to squeeze through, giving him hope that there was still a chance of getting out on to the roof and dropping down to safety.

The alternative was to open the door when the knocking began, to tell them the truth and hope the police would believe him. Surely no one in their senses would seriously believe that *he* had murdered Ausliss!

But whether they did or not, the police would have to hold him, and he would be able to do nothing more to help Joanna. He had a mental picture of Joanna, pale and still, and of Dr Ignatzi, deeply worried because he believed that someone had poisoned the girl.

The choice was already made; he had to try to get away. If he failed and were caught, then he could tell the truth; there would be almost as much hope of being believed then as now.

Wedging the two pictures inside his jacket, he edged towards the window.
(*The Baron and the Missing Old Masters*, 1968,
Hodder & Stoughton)

For a hero totally uninhibited by anxieties or anything else, you really can't do better than Norman Conquest. There is no one in fiction—except possibly Lupin—who so firmly believed that stone walls do not a prison make.

The door closed with a thud, and they heard the
279

heavy key grating in the lock. In that moment, Joy ran forward and threw herself in Norman's arms.

'I'm frightened!' she whispered.

'Silly! What about?'

'This—this place!' she said, with a shiver. 'It's a real *prison*, Norman. Even you, with all your tricks and ingenuity, won't be able to find a way out!'

He laughed.

'Chin up, young Pixie,' he said softly. 'I'm just beginning to enjoy myself.'

'But what are they going to do?'

'Ass! You should ask—what am *I* going to do,' he said cheerfully. 'One window, I see ...' He walked across to it. 'A pretty hefty bar, this, although it's deeply rusted. The shutter, beyond, is a new fixture. Well, well! Things could be a lot worse.'

She was comforted by his coolness and the sparkle of impish mischief in his eyes. It was the old fighting light which she knew so well.

'But what's going to happen?' she said breathlessly.

'You'll see, funny face—and you won't have to wait long,' he replied, hugging her. 'In a very short time the fun will begin in earnest.'

(*Conquest in Command*, 1956, Collins)

These last-minute reprises give me an opportunity to put myself right with Toff fans, who will be wondering how on earth I could have written so much about the Hon. Richard Rollison without once mentioning his celebrated Trophy Wall. Planned, executed and regularly dusted by Jolly, this mural Black Museum contains souvenirs of almost every Toff case, from

... a poison phial to a pencil-pistol, from a bloodstained dagger once used to stab to a lipsticked silk stocking once used to strangle. A preserved scorpion and the feather from the neck of a dead chicken; a torn glove; and the faded score of an old song-sheet. Closest to the ceiling was a top hat, two bullet holes through

the shiny nap of the crown told a story: that hat, worn during one escapade nearly twenty-four years ago had first earned Richard Rollison his soubriquet—the Toff.
(*Stars for the Toff*, 1968, Hodder & Stoughton)

I don't think Creasey ever chronicled that top-hat escapade. Presumably it happened in the boisterous old Monty Haydon times, the period when Rollison's soubriquet was only breathed in the murky saloon bars of the East End 'where the scum of the earth got drunk'. It's a good job, when you come to think of it, that the Toff let a few decades roll by before he started canvassing the area for votes.

It is from the vintage *Thriller*, real birthplace of the thirties Gentleman Outlaw, that I have picked my final quotation—the one that, as nearly as possible, 'says it all'. It even has Monty Haydon himself onstage, in the person of Monty Hayward. Though his role is strictly that of observer—an admirer, you might say, of a wondrous protégé.

Monty watched him releasing the smoke again through his lips and nostrils with a slow widening of that new-born Saintly smile. The tanned rakish contours of that lean face, cleared now from their coating of dust and dirt, were more reckless than he had ever seen them before. The black hair was brushed back in one smooth swashbuckling sweep. No one else in the world could have been so steady nerved and at ease, so trim and immaculate after the rough handling of his clothes, so alive with the laughing promise of danger, so carefree and debonair in every way. The Saint was going to his destiny.
(*Getaway*, 1932, Hodder & Stoughton)

I wonder if Leslie Charteris, when he wrote that forty years ago, had the remotest idea how extensive the Saint's destiny would be. Or how many other desperadoes would prove durable enough to share it with him.

281

Select Bibliography

Books actually quoted in the text are marked with an asterisk.

* *The Amateur Cracksman* by E. W. Hornung (1899)
* *The Black Mask* by E. W. Hornung (1901)
  (Both shortly to be republished by Chatto & Windus under the title *Raffles, the Amateur Cracksman*)
* *Snobbery With Violence* by Colin Watson (Eyre & Spottiswoode, 1971)

Boys Will Be Boys by E. S. Turner (Michael Joseph, 1948)
*The Confessions of Arsène Lupin, translated by Joachim Neograschal, with an introduction by Michael Gilbert (Hodder & Stoughton, 1964)

The Murder Book by Tage la Corr and Harold Mogensen, translated by Roy Duffell (Allen & Unwin, 1971)
* *The Sacred Sphere* (author unknown) from *Union Jack*, 29 November 1913. Amalgamated Press (now IPC Magazines Ltd
* *The Innocence of Father Brown* by G. K. Chesterton (Cassell, 1911)
* *The Four Just Men* by Edgar Wallace, original competition edition (The Tallis Press, 1905)
*Bulldog Drummond by Sapper (Hodder & Stoughton, 1919)
*The Black Gang by Sapper (Hodder & Stoughton, 1922)
* *Blackshirt* by Bruce Graeme (T. Fisher Unwin, 1925; now published by John Long)
* *The Barring Out at St Frank's* by Edwy Searles Brooks (Howard Baker Press Ltd, 1972. Originally published by the Amalgamated Press Ltd)
* *Angel Pavement* by J. B. Priestley (William Heinemann, 1930)
* *The Mixer* by Edgar Wallace (John Long, 1927)
* *The Brigand* by Edgar Wallace (Hodder & Stoughton, 1927)

* *Edgar Wallace* by Margaret Lane (Hamish Hamilton)
* *The Triumph of the Rat* by Denise Robins, from the Gainsborough film of the same name, sub-titled by Roland Pertwee (Philip Allan, 1927)
* *The Saint and Leslie Charteris* by W. O. G. Lofts and D. J. Adley (Hutchinson Library Services, 1972)
* *X Esquire* by Leslie Charteris (Ward Lock, 1927)
* *The White Rider* by Leslie Charteris (Ward Lock, 1928)
* *Meet the Tiger* by Leslie Charteris (Ward Lock, 1928)
* *The Bandit* by Leslie Charteris (Ward Lock, 1930)
* *Getaway* (The Saint's Getaway) by Leslie Charteris (Hodder & Stoughton, 1932)
* *The Holy Terror* (The Saint vs. Scotland Yard) by Leslie Charteris (Hodder & Stoughton, 1932)
* *Seven Times Seven* by John Creasey (Melrose, 1932)
* *The Death Miser* by John Creasey (Melrose, 1932)
* *Introducing the Toff* by John Creasey (John Long, 1938)
* *Meet the Baron* by Creasey as Anthony Morton (Harrap, 1935) (Both *Introducing the Toff* and *Meet the Baron* are now in library editions as Lythway reprints)
* *Mr Mortimer Gets the Jitters* by E. S. Brooks as Berkeley Gray (Collins, 1937)
* *Miss Dynamite* by E. S. Brooks as Berkeley Gray (Collins, 1939)
* *The Misfortunes of Mr Teal* (The Saint in London) by Leslie Charteris (Hodder & Stoughton, 1934)
* *Here Comes the Toff* by John Creasey (John Long, 1940—now a Lythway reprint)
* *Trent of the Lone Hand* by Wyndham Martyn (Herbert Jenkins, undated)
* *The Ten Black Pearls* by Cecil Freeman Gregg (Methuen, 1935)
* *The Return of Blackshirt* by Bruce Graeme (T. Fisher Unwin, 1927. Ernest Benn, 1951. Subsequently, Blackshirt became a John Long series)
* *Son of Blackshirt* by Bruce Graeme (Hutchinson, 1941)
* *Lord Blackshirt* by Bruce Graeme (Hutchinson, 1942)
* *Six Feet of Dynamite* by E. S. Brooks as Berkeley Gray (Collins, 1942)

* *The Conquest Touch* by E. S. Brooks as Berkeley Gray (Collins, 1948)
* *The Saint in Miami* by Leslie Charteris (Hodder & Stoughton, 1942)
* *The Saint Steps In* by Leslie Charteris (Hodder & Stoughton, 1944)
* *The Saint on Guard* by Leslie Charteris (Hodder & Stoughton, 1945)
* *The First Saint Omnibus* by Leslie Charteris (Hodder & Stoughton, 1939)
* *The Second Saint Omnibus* by Leslie Charteris (Hodder & Stoughton, 1952)
The Baron Comes Back by John Creasey as Anthony Morton (1943)
* *The Toff Goes to Market* by John Creasey as Anthony Morton (John Long, 1942—now a Lythway reprint)
* *The Toff on Ice* by John Creasey (John Long, 1946)
The Saint Sees It Through by Leslie Charteris (Hodder & Stoughton, 1947)
* *Call for the Saint* by Leslie Charteris (Hodder & Stoughton, 1948)
* *Saint Errant* by Leslie Charteris (Hodder & Stoughton, 1949)
* *Concerning Blackshirt* by Roderic Graeme (Hutchinson, 1952)
* *The Amazing Mr Blackshirt* by Roderic Graeme (John Long, *c.* 1957)
* *Enter the Picaroon* by John Cassells (Muller, 1954. The Picaroon books are now a John Long series.)
Señor Saint by Leslie Charteris (Hodder & Stoughton, 1959) containing *The Pearls of Peace*
* *Casino Royale* by Ian Fleming (Jonathan Cape, 1953)
* *The Saint on TV* by Leslie Charteris and others (Hodder & Stoughton, 1967)
* *The Saint in Pursuit* by Leslie Charteris (Hodder & Stoughton, 1971)
* *Curtains for Conquest?* by E. S. Brooks as Berkeley Gray (Collins, 1966)

Good, God and Man by John Creasey (Hodder & Stoughton, 1968)

* *The Baron Goes A-Buying* by John Creasey (Hodder & Stoughton, 1971)
* *Vote for the Toff* by John Creasey (Hodder & Stoughton, 1971)
* *The Baron and the Missing Old Masters* by John Creasey (Hodder & Stoughton, 1968)
* *Conquest in Command* by E. S. Brooks as Berkeley Gray (Collins, 1956)
* *Stars for the Toff* (the 50th Toff book) by John Creasey (Hodder & Stoughton, 1968)

Index

The principal references are printed in bold type

286

Saint clubs, 232
St Franks, 84-6, 166
Saint Mystery Magazine, 245
Sanders, George, 176, 210, 211, 214
Sapper (H. C. McNeile), **58-67**, 69, 72, 82, 101, 126-8, 153, 186, 250
Saxon, Ludovic (the Picaroon), 244-5, 246
Shadow, the, 15, 181
Smith, Anthony (the Mixer), 92-95, 100 n, 104, 129 n, 221, 252
Spider, the, 15, 181
Standish, Tiger, 181

Teal, Inspector, 120, 130-1, 179, 209, 211 n, 268
Templar, Simon (the Saint), 13, 19, 22, 24, 94, 102, 103, 104, **112**, **115-32**, **144-5**, 149, 151, 162-5, 168, **176-9**, 186-7, 199, 201, 205, **206-14**, 221, **232-7**, 245-6, 251-2, 257, **262-3**, 275, **281**
thirties desperadoes, lists of, 181, 183
Thriller, The, 90, 118, 149, 153, 162, 185; writers, 150
Toff, the, *see* Rollison, Hon. Richard
Trent, Anthony, 181-2

Uniatz, Hoppy, 178-9, 209, 233, 268
Union Jack, 22, 43-4, 87, 90, 99, 118, 204
Usborne, Richard, 58

Vance, Louis Joseph, 15, 183
Verrell, Anthony (Son of Blackshirt), 193-7, 199, 239
Verrell, Richard (Blackshirt), 13, 24, **73-81**, 82, 96, 106, **191-7 passim**, 231, **238-44**, 246, 252, 263, **277-9**

Waldo the Wonder Man, **87-91**, 99, 118, 164, **204-5**, 262-3
Wallace, Edgar, 22, 53-7, 67, **69-71**, 83, 92-5, 100, 101, 129 and n, 186
Watson, Colin, 32, 58
Wheatley, Dennis, 135-6, 137, 154, 216
Williams, Inspector, 200, 203-4, 262
Wodehouse, P. G., 20, 61
Wu Ling, Prince, 44-50, 118

X Esquire, *see* Mannering, Terry

Yates, Dornford, 15, 22, 67-8, 69, 250
Yellow Jackets (Hodder & Stoughton), 67, 116
Yvonne, Mlle, 22, 44-50, 89, 118

288